The Art of Showing Up

"Miller has penned a fresh, wise, practical, modern guide for figuring out how to be true to yourself while also meaningfully connected to others. An important contribution to the larger, complicated project of solving loneliness."–**PRIYA PARKER,** author of *The Art of Gathering*

"Rachel's advice is smart, straightforward, and empathetic. *The Art of Showing Up* offers a road map to becoming a better friend and happier person. Read this book!"–**ALISON GREEN,** author of *Ask a Manager*

"This is an incredibly practical book full of easy yet meaningful ways to develop more friendship and love in your life. Through steps that anyone can do, Rachel helps us find the support that we all crave in our lives and leaves us feeling ever more hopeful!"
–**SHASTA NELSON,** author of *Frientimacy*

"Rachel Wilkerson Miller has given us a toolbox for strengthening our relationships with one another and with ourselves. This book is the resource that twenty-, thirty-, and forty-somethings were missing–and that we didn't know we absolutely needed."
–**CAROLINE MOSS,** coauthor of *Hey Ladies!* and
host of *Gee Thanks, Just Bought It*

ALSO BY RACHEL WILKERSON MILLER

Dot Journaling—A Practical Guide

The Art of Showing Up

How to Be There for Yourself and Your People

Rachel Wilkerson Miller

THE EXPERIMENT
NEW YORK

The Experiment, LLC | 220 East 23rd Street, Suite 600 | New York, NY 10010-4658
theexperimentpublishing.com

This book contains the opinions and ideas of its author. It is intended to provide helpful and informative material on the subjects addressed in the book. It is sold with the understanding that the author and publisher are not engaged in rendering medical, health, or any other kind of personal professional services in the book. The author and publisher specifically disclaim all responsibility for any liability, loss, or risk—personal or otherwise—that is incurred as a consequence, directly or indirectly, of the use and application of any of the contents of this book.

THE EXPERIMENT and its colophon are registered trademarks of The Experiment, LLC. Many of the designations used by manufacturers and sellers to distinguish their products are claimed as trademarks. Where those designations appear in this book and The Experiment was aware of a trademark claim, the designations have been capitalized.

The Experiment's books are available at special discounts when purchased in bulk for premiums and sales promotions as well as for fund-raising or educational use. For details, contact us at info@theexperimentpublishing.com.

Library of Congress Cataloging-in-Publication Data

Names: Miller, Rachel Wilkerson, author.
Title: The art of showing up : how to be there for yourself and your people
  / Rachel Wilkerson Miller.
Description: New York : The Experiment, 2020. | Includes bibliographical
  references.
Identifiers: LCCN 2020000618 (print) | LCCN 2020000619 (ebook) | ISBN
  9781615196616 (paperback) | ISBN 9781615196623 (ebook)
Subjects: LCSH: Friendship. | Interpersonal relations--Social aspects.
Classification: LCC BF575.F66 M55 2020 (print) | LCC BF575.F66 (ebook) |
  DDC 158.2--dc23
LC record available at https://lccn.loc.gov/2020000618
LC ebook record available at https://lccn.loc.gov/2020000619

ISBN 978-1-61519-661-6
Ebook ISBN 978-1-61519-662-3

Cover and text design by Beth Bugler
Author photograph by Elena Mudd

Manufactured in the United States of America

First printing April 2020
10 9 8 7 6 5 4

Contents

Hello!

howing up is what turns the people you know into *your people*. It's at the core of creating and maintaining strong, meaningful bonds with friends, family, coworkers, and internet pals. Showing up is the act of bearing witness to people's joy, pain, and true selves; validating their experiences; easing their load; and communicating that they are not alone in this life. It's a concept that I experience on such a deep-rooted emotional level, I sometimes struggle to describe it. I know it when I see it, and I'm betting you do, too.

The thing about showing up is that it's not exactly *easy*. It doesn't just happen; it takes intentionality, effort, and practice. And truly showing up for others requires you to do something that can be even harder—to show up for yourself first. That means really getting to know yourself, taking care of your physical and mental health, being kind to yourself, and setting boundaries. Showing up for yourself will allow you to be a better and more present friend or partner; will prevent resentment, one-sided relationships, and burnout; and will help you figure out exactly what showing up for others should look like in practice. Showing up for yourself isn't about feeling happiness, exactly; it's about feeling grounded and content and believing that you are enough.

*

Some people might resist the idea that showing up is something that can be taught or learned; they believe it's common sense or that it just comes naturally. To which I say: If showing up is so easy, then *why are so many people so bad at it?*

And we are, in fact, kind of bad at it! Think about the last time somebody made a really thoughtless comment to you or someone you know. Or the last time you said, "I'm fine" (or "It's fine") when things were . . . extremely not fine. Or the last time you didn't get nearly enough sleep! It happens all the time. And I get it. Showing up isn't an innate skill, nor is it part of most formal education. Which is why this book exists.

Here's the thing: There are real, very bad consequences to not showing up for ourselves and each other. According to Robert D. Putnam in *Bowling Alone: The Collapse and Revival of American Community,* social capital— connections among individuals and the sense of reciprocity and trustworthiness that arises from these social networks—plays a huge role in virtually every aspect of our lives: our personal safety, children's welfare, economic prosperity, *democracy.* By all accounts, poor social capital is extremely bad for our health and longevity.

So, how are we doing in that regard? Well, a 2018 Pew Research Center Survey found that one in ten adults in the US report feeling lonely or isolated "all or most of the time."[1] (That's a lot of people and a lot of the time.) Suicide rates have increased in nearly every state since 1999. And according to one survey, 70 percent of teens list mental health as a "major problem" among people their age in their community.[2] In a lot of ways, technology is what makes showing up possible—we can easily search for articles about mental health, send a text to check in, or read a series of tweets that tell us what to say to someone who is struggling. But the realities of modern life are also what make showing up more difficult, and more necessary. Because what's the alternative here, y'all? Keep doing the bare minimum to stay alive, and never cross over to thriving? Maintain friendships that aren't serving us and never make any new friends? Continue saying "I'm fine" when we are definitely not fine? Stand back and let the world burn?

Showing up is an alternative to living that faux "I'm fine" life. If you never feel like you're doing enough (while also somehow constantly feeling like you're doing too much), it's time to sit down and do the work of figuring out what, exactly, "enough" means to you. That's where this book comes in. It offers a set of principles for taking care—a sort of code of behavior for treating yourself and other people well. Of course, you might not always be able to make it happen (or get your desired outcome), but it's helpful to have a starting point. *Not* having anything resembling a baseline makes it difficult to stay the course, to deviate intentionally, and to realize when you've lost your way. When you're feeling adrift, showing up—for yourself, for your people, for everyone—can be your North Star.

Your People

I'll use the terms *your people, friends, loved ones,* and *nearest and dearest* interchangeably throughout the book, but *your people* is my go-to. I like *your people* because it's not quite as limiting as "friends" can be. *Your people* can expand to include your coworkers, acquaintances, family members, and whoever else you want it to—it's basically anyone you care about and have a connection with.

What Is Showing Up?

My definition of showing up follows a similar but sliiiiightly different trajectory as that of the University of Michigan's Compassion Lab.[3] They define "compassion" as noticing, feeling, and responding; I think of showing up as noticing, processing, naming, and responding.

1. *Noticing* is perceiving behavior, words, or circumstances that communicate a need. And the need doesn't have to be negative; it could be a need to celebrate or connect.

2. *Processing* is using the knowledge you already have—about yourself, about the other person, about certain behaviors, etc.—to analyze what you've just noticed.

3. *Naming* is identifying the "what's really going on here"—the deeper need, the bigger behavior, the narrative of what actually happened— and recognizing its legitimacy and worthiness. Naming can be sort of small (e.g., "What is being described sounds really effing annoying") or pretty significant (e.g., "What is being described sounds incredibly abusive"). Naming is *powerful*—it's validating, and is how our experiences begin to take shape and make sense to us.

4. *Responding* is reacting in a way that makes the receiver (which, remember, might mean you!) feel seen, supported, and more whole. (And by the way, in practice, responding might *be* naming the behavior.)

What It Takes to Show Up

Showing up for yourself and others is rooted in nine core values: curiosity, intelligence, intuition, compassion, generosity, creativity, self-awareness, confidence, and a willingness to be vulnerable.

Curiosity: Curiosity leads to *noticing,* and is at the heart of intelligence, our next core value.

Intelligence: Regularly learning and remembering new information about different situations and life experiences will give you a big well to draw from when you or a friend is going through something significant.

Intuition: When it comes to showing up, it's not enough to be book smart; you also have to be emotionally intelligent, able to sense and feel what others need or want.

Compassion: Showing up is impossible without the ability to feel sorry for another's sorrow or misfortune.

Generosity: Generosity allows us to give time, money, and energy to others without hesitation and to believe that others really are doing their best.

Creativity: So often, the conventional wisdom for how to help a friend in need isn't that helpful or particularly practical. Creativity allows us to figure out how to show up for people in a way that makes sense in modern life, while still honoring the truths about struggle, grief, and loss that have remained constant for hundreds of years.

Self-awareness: Without a working knowledge of your own personality, character, and feelings, you can't figure out what you need or fully grasp the way your actions affect other people (for better or worse).

Confidence: It's often hard to wrap your head around the idea that *you* could possibly make someone (especially someone you're not super close with!) feel *good*. But of *course* all of us are capable of having a positive impact on other people's lives. Confidence in your intentions, decisions, and abilities is what will help you push through your feelings of inadequacy when you're faced with an opportunity to show up.

Vulnerability: Showing up for yourself requires acknowledging your own needs . . . but so often, we'd prefer to pretend we don't have those! Meanwhile, showing up for others requires taking a risk. You have to set aside your fear of looking foolish or failing.

Who Am I?

I'm someone who cares deeply about making the world a kinder, healthier, lovelier, and more pleasant place to be! I'm a professional service journalist, which means I write articles that teach people how to live better. But it's not just my day job; it's my hobby, my passion, my life's work. I spend a *lot* of time thinking a lot about the ways in which we can be good to ourselves and each other.

I've also experienced a not insignificant amount of trauma in my life. My dad left the family when I was four, and died when I was thirteen. My (now-ex) husband abandoned me without warning, turning my life upside down for three years. These experiences shaped my identity and my worldview, and gave me a clear sense of the transformative power of showing up.

I think of myself as pretty good at showing up for myself and others. That said, I'm by no means perfect. (I typed and deleted the sentence about being good at showing up more times than I can count!) A lot of the advice in this book is based on situations I've gotten *wrong* or wish I'd handled differently. I say this not to justify thoughtless behavior—mine or your own—but to remind you that showing up is *hard.* It takes time and practice. I don't always get it right, and neither will you.

About This Book

This book is divided into two parts: Part I is all about showing up for yourself, and Part II is all about showing up for others. They are in this order for a reason—because showing up for others builds on the concepts we cover in Part I, and because you *can't show up for others if you aren't showing up for yourself first.* You just can't! So if you're tempted to skip the first part and go straight to the "fun stuff" where you show up for your friends, it might be worth thinking about why, exactly, you think taking care of yourself and your own needs is optional. Maybe you really do have showing up for yourself figured out and you don't need my help. Great! Good for you! But if thinking about your own needs, setting boundaries, or being truly kind to yourself makes you uncomfortable (or you think you don't have time for that), reading Part I is *exactly* what you should do first.

This book is meant to be a reference that you can pick up time and again, when you are struggling, feeling a little lost or discouraged, or experiencing something new (like, say, the first divorce in your friend group) and are unsure how to handle it. It's for everyone who has ever said or thought, "I feel bad and I don't know what to do." Whether you're already good at showing up or you know that you have a long way to go in this regard, this book is for you.

Not everything covered in this book will apply to every person or relationship or situation; you should treat everything* you're about to read as a gentle suggestion, not a hard-and-fast rule. Showing up is about **knowing your audience.** If you have a strong negative reaction to something, or know you or your BFF or coworker or *whoever* would hate a particular recommendation, that's OK! If you can't do something I'm suggesting—for whatever reason—that's cool! Like, I don't know your life!!! Feel free to tweak my suggestions to better fit your circumstances or to just ignore me entirely! It's fine! Everything is gonna be fine!!!

---

* Except my take on wearing a helmet in Chapter 3.

Part I

Showing Up for Yourself

Chapter 1
Getting to Know Yourself

elf-knowledge is at the core of showing up—because you can't possibly take care of yourself if you don't actually know what your needs are. Once you figure out who you are (and who you are not), it becomes *much* easier to understand what you want to do (and not do), and to recognize the types of people you want in your life (and those you don't). There's not much space for generosity, confidence, or vulnerability when you're constantly worried about whether you have enough and *are* enough.

Knowing yourself is also at the heart of showing up for other people. At a basic level, if you aren't self-aware, it's impossible to recognize how you're making other people feel. But it goes even deeper than that: The more you unpack your own motivations and patterns, and name and honor your own needs, the easier it becomes to do the same for others—to understand why they are behaving a certain way, to view their needs as legitimate, to withhold judgment when they are struggling, to be kind and compassionate, and to respond in a way that makes them feel seen. When you are firmly rooted, you can fully stand up for others.

So, what does knowing yourself even mean?

- Being able to name the main qualities that make you *you*
- Having a clear sense of your core values and your priorities
- Knowing what you like and don't like
- Identifying what makes you feel comfortable and uncomfortable
- Acknowledging what you are willing and unwilling to do
- Being aware of how you're likely to react (or *are* reacting) in a given situation

Seems easy enough, right? But it's not exactly, or at least, it's not easy for everyone. If you've gone through life believing one story about yourself—either a story you invented, or one others wrote about you—it can be hard to suddenly stop and ask yourself if it's actually true. Figuring out that truth can, at times, be an uncomfortable process. But it can also be enlightening and therapeutic and fun.

As you read this chapter (and, really, this whole book), try to resist any urge you have to immediately overhaul your life based on your newly acquired self-knowledge. I know how hard this can be—intense self-examination can make you want to burn down your entire life ASAP. (But, like, in a good way? Sort of?) But I feel pretty strongly about holding tight for a moment, because it's important to get comfortable with the first three steps of the showing-up process—noticing, naming, and processing—and just sit in that place for a sec before you move on to the fourth step: responding. (This is *extra* important if you tend to love big goals; are very all or nothing; or have, on more than one occasion, gotten extremely excited about a "magic" solution that you swore was going to change your whole life and then . . . did not do that.) Listen, I love a grandiose resolution and the ensuing shame spiral once it fails as much as the next gal . . . but the goal here isn't a big makeover montage; it's *acceptance*.

When I say acceptance, I mean bearing witness to what is true about yourself and your life—even the messy, painful, embarrassing parts—so you can respond to *that* reality. Acceptance is about being brave enough to look at who you are and not turning away or immediately looking for a fix when you don't like what you see. It's not about *settling;* after all, you may still want to make significant changes that will ultimately make your life better. It's about *grace*—offering yourself compassion and mercy, even if you're not totally convinced you deserve it.

If you don't know yourself, you can't accept yourself . . . and if you don't accept yourself and your own limitations, you can't truly show up for yourself or anyone else.

So, let's begin.

During this getting-to-know-yourself process, consider starting a journal expressly devoted to, well, you, and to the things about you that seem unchanging, significant, and close to your heart. That could include answers to some of the questions in this chapter; compliments or kind words you want to remember; prayers, meditations, or mantras that move you; things you like about yourself; and your go-to self-care ideas. Think of it as an encyclopedia of you, a little scrapbook of the soul. It's a simple way to document what's in your heart and to stay grounded when the world around you feels out of control. When you're feeling lost or overwhelmed, you can return to this notebook and remember that you are still here, and you are enough.

Your Values

If you're not a fancy private school or a bland corporate website, you might find the idea of listing your core values to be a bit formal. But I'm going to encourage you to do it anyway! Our values are incredibly important to who we are; they inform our priorities and decisions, guide our behaviors, and shape our relationships. And yet, I'm pretty sure most of us could rattle off a few years' worth of inane celebrity gossip faster than we could name our personal values, probably because most of us just don't think about our values all that much. Sure, they are in our brains, vaguely, up there *somewhere*.

But making decisions without a working knowledge of your own values is a bit of a fool's errand! As I write this, it's 10:00 AM and I've already had to make a lot of choices. I had to decide whether to hit snooze, what to have for breakfast, what clothes to wear, whether and how to respond to several text messages, if I should have more coffee, whether I should check my email, and whether to do the crossword, open Twitter, pick up the novel I've been reading, or just start working. And that's not counting any of the decisions I made about the work itself!

Sure, some of these choices might feel fairly low-stakes, but even the smallest ones have an effect on my mood, my energy, my relationships, my health, and my livelihood—and are rooted in my values in *some* way. So many of our decisions are related to how we'll spend our most valuable resources: our time, money, and energy. (More about these later! See page 36.)

Here are some of the everyday decisions that are typically tied to your values.

- How you get to school/work
- The foods you eat
- The clothes you buy and wear
- Who you spend time with (friends, family, coworkers)
- How much time you spend with them
- How much time you spend on your phone and what specifically you're doing on it

And it's not like you can simply opt out of the values–decisions connection; if your choices aren't rooted in *your* values, it just means that someone else's values will dictate what you do.

So take a little time (either right now or, say, in the next couple of days) to think about your values, with the goal of identifying five to ten that you feel represent you. If you're not sure what your values are, here is a short list of values that may or may not resonate with you to use as a jumping-off point. (And if none of these seems to be quite right, a quick Google search will turn up lists with hundreds of highly specific and very inspiring ideas.)

Acceptance	Faith	Knowledge
Achievement	Fame	Obedience
Adventure	Family	Open-mindedness
Advocacy	Financial security	Popularity
Confidence	Friendships	Positivity
Community	Hard work	Power
Compassion	Health	Resilience
Dependability	Honesty	Self-control
Environmentalism	Humor/fun	Self-expression
Fairness	Independence	Tradition

If you're wondering, mine are curiosity, intelligence, generosity, sincerity, service, dignity, practicality, discipline, loyalty, and justice.

Once you've made a list of the values that seem to really define you, spend a little time thinking about each one. What personal experiences made you value this quality or principle? How do these values currently manifest in your life? Do you feel like you're currently embodying that value? Why or why not?

Also! Don't overlook the values that you *used* to care about a lot but no longer do, or any values that you had a strong negative reaction to as you read this list; these can be quite helpful as you're getting to know yourself. What made the value so important to you at another point in your life? What changed? How do you feel about this shift? Do you miss that value, or are you glad it's no longer on your list?

You could also pick a few of the values you don't identify with at all and think about the reasons someone else might have chosen those. How might those values benefit them, and the world? Whenever I spend time really considering the options I didn't choose in a given situation—and thinking more about the motivation of the people who did—I feel better equipped to show up for others, even if we couldn't be more different.

Your Preferences

PSA: Your likes and dislikes can change over time—and you are *allowed* to change your mind! It's easy to believe your likes and dislikes as something that are established when you're a child or a teen. You pick a favorite color at five years old and that's it, you're done—purple forever! And that's often how our families treat our likes and dislikes, right? You briefly express an interest in, say, narwhals when you're in sixth grade and now, more than a decade later, your older relatives are still clipping articles that reference narwhals out of the local newspaper and mailing them to you.

It can be difficult to revisit our likes, because the idea that they might have changed is, well . . . scary. It can make you feel like your entire identity is somehow invalid or a sham. But it's really worthwhile to regularly pause and consider what you like. I also know most people won't just do that unless they are explicitly asked about their preferences by some curious individual. So . . . I'm asking you! *I'm* the curious individual!

Below is a list of categories; for each one, write down three things you like and three things you don't. (And yes, I think you should actually write/type/record them in some way.) Your answers can be broad (for example, you can say "sweets" are a favorite food) or specific (e.g., **likes:** candy bars, strawberry ice cream, brownies; **dislikes:** chocolate ice cream, birthday cake frosting, whipped cream). There are no real rules as long as the exercise is serving you in some way.

The reason I recommend identifying things you *don't* like is because a) it can be a huge relief to admit that you dislike something, and b) it allows you to work backward and figure out what you *do* like. For example, if you dislike the beach, your process from there might look something like this . . .

"I dislike the beach because I hate wearing a bathing suit."
I like my body to be mostly covered when I'm in public.
I like spaces that aren't very crowded.
I like being in the shade.

"I dislike the beach because I hate the amount of gear I need to enjoy myself."
I like activities that require minimal gear/equipment.
I like activities that are inexpensive.
I like activities I can walk to.

And remember: It's OK if you used to like something but now actually don't. It's also OK if you one day decide you like something you originally put on your "dislike" list.

Cool? Cool. Here's the list.

Colors	Smells	Sports (to play or to
Weather	Music (songs, artists,	watch)
Animals	bands, genres,	Games/puzzles
Clothing	eras)	Outdoor activities
Design styles	Movies	Indoor activities
Art	TV shows	Vices/guilty
Foods	Books (specific	pleasures
Drinks	titles, authors,	Qualities in other
Restaurants	genres)	people
Flavors	Cities	

Once you're done, take a look at your list. How many of the items from the "like" side do you get to experience on a daily or weekly basis? How many things from the "dislike" side are you still putting up with? Is there anything you can do to shift that ratio a bit? It could be as simple as telling your coworkers, "I don't like eating at this restaurant for lunch every day; I'm going to grab something else," or as earth-shattering as telling your great-aunt that you no longer care about narwhals.

Breaking the Ice with . . . Yourself

Icebreaker questions aren't just for getting to know your coworkers during corporate retreats; they can also help you get to know yourself better. Here are some of my favorites for self-reflection.

What was the last thing that pleasantly surprised you?

When was the last time you really wanted to scream?

What is the exact level of famous you'd want to be?

What was a trip or vacation you took that lasted too long?

What's something about yourself that you hope will never change?

What is the best compliment you've ever received?

What is your favorite birthday memory?

What are you a natural at?

Your Comfort

Now let's take this a step further and talk about what makes you feel *content* and *comfortable* and what makes you feel *off* or *uncomfortable*. The goal is to determine what arrangements or qualities allow you to experience satisfaction, relief, encouragement, and enjoyment in a given day or situation.

When you have a clear sense of what *specifically* makes you feel good (or bad), you can improve your self-awareness, recognize your true needs, set boundaries, and effectively respond to problems (big and small). But so many of us have been trained *not* to take our personal preferences and comfort seriously or to advocate for our basic needs. Sure, you can't always optimize your life for max comfort—we do, after all, live in a society—but it's still important to know what your preferences *are*. Without that baseline, you can't possibly know how and when you're deviating from it.

The following questions are designed to help you figure out what makes you feel most satisfied in your environment, your everyday life, and your interactions with other people. But! Don't worry if you can't answer them all! Don't feel like you *have* to! (It's also OK to have different answers within different contexts!) If you feel overwhelmed, remember that this is a gentle conversation between you and yourself, and your answers are just for you. By the time you're done, you will have a working list of your preferences.

YOUR EVERYDAY LIFE

- How much do routines matter to you?
- Do you prefer familiarity or trying lots of new things?
- Are you a morning person or a night person?
- When during the day do you feel mentally sharp?
- When do you feel most creative?
- When do you feel most social?
- When do you most want to be alone?
- Are you spontaneous or do you like to make plans far in advance?
- What are (at least) three things that energize you?
- What are (at least) three things that exhaust you?
- What are three everyday-ish activities or parts of daily your routine that you just *love* and feel good about?
- What is your ideal evening activity/nightly routine if you hope to get a good night's sleep?
- What are three everyday-ish activities that you hate doing or dread?
- When you're going about your day, do you like having background noise? What kind?
- What activities do you like doing alone?
- What activities do you prefer to do with other people?
- How much does your physical appearance matter to you? What effect does your appearance have on your mood? When do you feel most attractive? Least attractive?

YOUR ENVIRONMENT

- Do you prefer being indoors or outdoors? When do you crave being outside? What makes you want to be inside more?

- How much does tidiness matter to you? What about cleanliness? Does the answer change if you're talking about home versus work versus public spaces versus other people's spaces?

- What is your preferred mode of transportation?

- How do you define a "crowd"? Think of a situation in your life where the crowd level felt good and right. What about an instance when a crowd felt stressful or scary?

- What's your comfort level with sounds/noises? For example, are you comfortable in a space with loud music playing? Is there a type of noise or sound that you just can't stand?

- What, if anything, is likely to make you feel physically unwell?

- What everyday activities do you prefer to do IRL? Which do you prefer to do virtually or through an app?

- How comfortable are you with technology? What technology do you rely on? What do you wish you relied on less?

FEELINGS, EMOTIONS, AND RELATING TO OTHERS

- Do you enjoy chatting with strangers and/or new people?

- Do you like physical touch? Are you a hugger?

- How comfortable are you talking about feelings (your own and other people's)?

- What topics do you consider too private to discuss with casual friends? What about close friends?

- How modest would you say you are?

- Do you consider yourself a serious person?

- What kinds of jokes/humor/pranks do you like? What kinds piss you off?

- How sentimental are you? What holidays, anniversaries, or events do you care about the most?

- How comfortable are you with uncertainty?

- Do you consider yourself a chill person? How important is it to you to be seen as "chill"?

- Do you prefer to always have a plan? And do you like to be the person who makes said plan, or would you rather someone else do it?

- What kinds of rules do you care about or respect the most? What kinds of rules do you shamelessly flout?

- How do you respond to other people's expectations?

- What are three things that *really* stress you out?

- How do you respond to stress in general?

- What are your preferred methods of communication? (Note: This can be different depending on who you're talking to, but try to figure out *your* ideal.)

- What does your ideal friend hangout look like?

- What does your ideal average evening with a romantic partner look like?

Once you finish this exercise, you should have a better sense of what helps you thrive and what makes you feel kind of terrible. Are you regularly able to experience comfort and satisfaction? If not, you don't need to overhaul your life; instead, try to sit with this knowledge and put some thought into what got you to this point.

The Four Levels of Mental Energy

I often turn to Gretchen Rubin's four levels of mental energy to help me figure out what I want and need and should be doing with myself in a given moment. Here's how she defines the four levels.

Level 1: Contemplative Energy–planning, deciding, creating, inhibiting (holding yourself back from saying, doing, or thinking something), setting priorities, making transitions

Level 2: Engagement Energy–talking to other people; reading or observing, using critical thinking

Level 3: Audience Energy–passively watching or listening

Level 4: Habit Energy–mindlessly executing a habitual behavior

Realizing that I can't tackle Level 1 activities (at least not successfully) when I'm at a Level 3 was a light-bulb moment for me. Of course, I don't always have a choice, but even just naming the level I'm currently at makes me feel better–more in control, more realistic, and more capable.

I Endorse: Personality Tests

We're currently living in a golden age of personality tests. (One 2018 article in *The New Yorker* said there are more than *two thousand* personality tests available on the market right now.)[4] But humans were into the idea of assigning labels to people's behavior well before the first viral BuzzFeed quiz. Early forms of astrology existed in ancient cultures,[5] and Hippocrates believed that human behaviors and moods were based on our *humors* (our bodily fluids) and identified nine human temperaments. Love them or hate them, personality tests aren't exactly *new*.

So, do personality tests "work"? I mean, it depends how you define "work." I'll be honest: I'm not terribly concerned with whether personality tests have been peer-reviewed (they . . . have not). It's not that I'm anti-science; I just think that this question misses the point.

I view personality tests as a tool that helps us understand ourselves and each other a little bit better. And if that's their purpose, then yes, I'd say they do work. (Or, at least, they *can*.) Taking personality tests over the years has genuinely made me more self-aware, because reading the different results has helped me name my qualities (good and bad), my needs, and my preferences, and made me realize that some of ways I act or react in certain situations aren't actually universal. It's so easy to tell yourself everyone does something until it's called out as something that's unique to you (or to a somewhat limited group of people).

Of course, no personality test is completely accurate, and many of them are frustratingly black-and-white. But in general, they provide a helpful jumping-off point for self-examination. You might read about "your" personality type and think, *That's not me at all,* and have tons of examples to prove it. Or you may know, *That* used *to be me, but I didn't like that about myself, so I worked really hard to change it.* Or you might think, *I* wish *that were me.* And that's all *really* helpful information to have!

Personality tests also give us a shorthand way of communicating who we are and what we want. Think about it: after taking a personality test, what do you *immediately* want to do? Share your results with a friend, and then get them to take the test, too. And those conversations are valuable! I've found that the best way to get something out of a personality test is to discuss the results with someone you're really close to—that person who can say, "Actually . . . you *do* kind of do that," when you're insisting you don't. Personality tests create a safe space for naming and sharing needs. And they give us a shared vocabulary that allows us to be better at showing up for each other. Once I'm familiar with my friends' love languages, for example, I can demonstrate that I care about them way more effectively. Even just having terms like "introvert" and "extrovert" in the public consciousness makes it a little easier for us to be good to each other.

Personality tests to try:
Enneagram
16 Personalities
The 5 Love Languages
The Four Tendencies

I like personality tests because they take what can be a very vulnerable experience—self-examination—and make it more fun. Let's face it: it's *way* less painful to be gently dragged by a personality test than by a person who actually knows you.

Your Emotions

I regret to inform you that we now have to talk about our feelings! (Trust me, I'd *much* rather talk about personality tests.) Like our values, our feelings play a major role in our everyday choices. Being able to perceive and name your emotions is critical to self-awareness and identifying what you need—so, two major aspects of showing up.

According to clinical psychologist David Walton, "Being able to give the emotions you experience a name is not some touchy-feely idea about sensitivity. Naming it involves consciously thinking about what is happening and choosing how to react. If you can find words to describe how you feel at the time, and (even better) what's causing it, you will automatically become more sensitive and aware."[6] When you can name your emotions and connect them to your behavior, you can avoid the behaviors and habits that you know haven't, *uh,* always worked out so well for you (or for *anyone*).

For example, if you feel *angry* about something, your next move might be quite different than if you actually feel *irritated, sad, scared,* or *hurt.* Some feelings call for a conversation; others call for a trip around the block to cool off and let it go. Naming your feelings will also give you a better sense of how strong a feeling is. There's a big difference between *furious* and *cranky,* and it's better to identify what specifically you're experiencing instead of just going with "I DON'T KNOW, I JUST FEEL ANGRY!!!!" and then blowing up accordingly.

If you need to get better at naming your emotions, the Center for Nonviolent Communication's website has a fantastic list of feelings to describe what's going on with you in a given moment, which might help you strengthen your emotional vocabulary. But really, naming your emotions begins with checking in with yourself regularly. Walton says, "Real awareness asks you to turn a switch, focusing on 'What's going on inside me at this moment?'"

Your Needs

Once you've identified an emotion or feeling, it's important to stop and ask yourself what underlying need is causing it. It's the part of the showing-up process when you go from "I feel angry that so few people have responded to my birthday party invite" to "I feel anxious about my birthday party because I want it to be special. I want to be celebrated by my friends. I'm feeling lonely and I need companionship. I need affirmation that my friends actually care about me. I just want to feel like I belong here, and that people accept me."

Admitting you need something is a vulnerable act, which is why it can be so difficult. The word *needy* isn't typically used as a compliment; being called needy (or simply *feeling* needy) can be a blow to our pride, our sense of identity, and our belief in how we "should" be. But you simply can't take care of yourself if you don't know what your needs are, so these days, I try to make a habit of naming my needs regularly—especially when I'm feeling very strong emotions, or reacting in a way that I'm not proud of.

Once you figure out your underlying need, you can move forward in a way that truly honors your need. And that path forward won't necessarily look like confronting other people or sharing your needs with them; sometimes, it'll simply mean you need to respond to *yourself* in a different way. Here is a list of common needs[7] that might come in handy if you find yourself feeling A Way but can't quite put your finger on why.

Acceptance	Ease	Security
Affection	Empathy	Self-expression
Appreciation	Freedom	Space
Beauty	Humor	Stability
Belonging	Inclusion	Support
Choice	Independence	To know and be
Closeness	Intimacy	known
Communication	Joy	To see and be seen
Community	Love	To understand and
Companionship	Mourning	be understood
Compassion	Nurturing	Trust
Consideration	Order	Warmth
Consistency	Respect	
Cooperation	Safety	

Also consider these physical needs (which we'll talk about more in Chapter 3).

Food	Movement	Sex and/or touch
Water	Fresh air	Quiet
Sleep/rest	Physical or	To use the bathroom
Cleanliness	mental space	

Naming your needs can be uncomfortable at first, especially if you've been telling yourself for years that you don't (or shouldn't) have needs, or that your needs don't matter. If you're struggling with this part, it can feel "safer" to begin by reflecting on past needs instead of attempting to name your current ones. So reread the list above and try to identify three to five needs you experienced in the past two weeks. How did the needs present themselves? What emotions did you feel? Did you address the need in any way? Did you share the need with anyone else? What happened?

HOW TO COMMUNICATE YOUR NEEDS TO OTHERS

Once you've identified a need, the next step might be communicating it to someone else. If this is something you really struggle with, I suggest starting very small. Don't jump in with the big asks; practice sharing needs that are relatively low-stakes, and do it when things are going pretty well for you overall. My approach? Begin by communicating your needs to strangers when they ask or offer.

In practice, this might look like . . .

- telling your dentist "That actually really hurts" when they ask "Is this OK?" during a procedure

- saying "Yes, that would be great" when you're freezing in a cab and the driver offers to turn the A/C down

- responding honestly when a masseuse asks you "Is that too much pressure?"

Next, you can move on to communicating your needs to people you know when they ask or offer, and to strangers when they don't ask or offer. That might look like . . .

- replying to a coworker who asks if their music is bothering you with, "Actually, it's a bit distracting; would you mind turning it down a little?"

- asking your cab driver if they could please turn the heat up when your teeth are chattering

- flagging down a flight attendant and requesting a second in-flight snack.

Over time, you'll start to realize that most of these requests are fine! Even if you don't get what you want, the act of asking probably won't lead to a SWAT team descending on you and arresting you for daring to say you'd like an additional snack. So from *here,* you can start communicating your needs to people you know when they don't ask or offer. That could mean . . .

- telling your friends "I need to stop for a bathroom break" during a long and tiresome road trip

- saying to a friend "Can we do happy hour this week in a place that makes it possible for me to sit and hear?"

- asking your coworker "Would it be OK with you if I closed the blinds? The glare is making it impossible for me to see my computer screen right now."

- shouting "BAD TOUCH!" when your mother-in-law starts stroking your hair. (Just kidding, kind of.)

I promise: Telling people what you need really does get easier! I say this as someone who is now fairly good at sharing needs like the ones above (and who is decent at sharing bigger needs) but *who didn't used to be this way.* I'm not naturally fearless; I just *practice.* I became confident in asking for what I need the old-fashioned way: one terrified-but-ultimately-fine request at a time.

Your Boundaries

Taking care of something means protecting it, and strong, well-considered boundaries—which therapist Andrea Bonior defines as "principles that you establish in order to keep yourself feeling safe and comfortable, emotionally and physically"[8]—will allow you to protect yourself from all of the negativity waiting just outside the gates: draining conversations, useless apps, toxic people. Similar to values, boundaries are something we all *have* (yes, even the people whom you look at and think "Wow, they have zero boundaries") but can't always easily *name.* Which isn't good—because if you can't name them, it's going to be harder to confidently enforce them. If you want to show up for yourself, it's important to put real thought into the boundaries you hold dear.

To get started, consider the following list of general areas in which you're allowed* to set and enforce boundaries. You don't have to limit yourself to one boundary for each of these items; you can (and likely will!) have different boundaries with different people or types of relationships, and those boundaries can change. You also don't have to set or enforce particularly strict boundaries for all of these items; I certainly don't! This list is meant to show you what a boundary *can* be, so it'll click when someone is crossing the line . . . *or* when someone is attempting to set a boundary *with you* but doesn't have quite the right language (or the courage) to communicate that it is, in fact, a boundary.

YOUR BODY

- Your physical space (how close people stand to you)
- Your meatsack (You don't have to engage with comments or questions about your weight, height, hair, race, sex, genitals, etc.)
- Details about your health (basic bodily functions, menstruation, ailments, disabilities, medications, etc.)
- What you will and will not ingest (food, drinks, alcohol, tobacco, drugs)
- Who is allowed to *view* your body (you are allowed to not want your mom and your friends to look at your titties or your ass or your nudes)
- Who is allowed to touch your body in a non-sexual way (think: hugging, handshakes, and general touchy-feelery)
- Sexual contact: You get to decide who you will and won't touch bits with and what sexual acts you're comfortable with; you're also extremely allowed to change your mind about these at any point
- Your physical safety: You can insist on wearing a helmet, using condoms or dental dams, having access to a seat belt, not being around weapons, and not getting in a car when the driver has been drinking or doing drugs

---

* If you're under the age of eighteen or a young adult living at home with your parents, you might not have access to all of these boundaries, at least from a technical, legal POV.

YOUR HOME AND BELONGINGS

- Who you'll allow in your home and/or your room
- What illegal or risky behaviors you'll allow in your home or in a shared living space
- Items you will or will not loan to other people (and who is allowed to borrow your things without asking first)
- Who is allowed to rifle through your stuff (including your phone and computer)
- Any password/account information

YOUR MONEY

Your money is . . . your money! Here are some categories where you might encounter particularly annoying expectations/attitudes, or where people may hassle you about what you will or won't spend.

- Gifts (who you'll buy gifts for, how much you'll spend, etc.)
- Loans (who you'll give them to, how much you'll give, how quickly you expect to be repaid)
- Friend activities (concerts, dinners, bachelor/ette parties, travel, etc.)
- Friends' business ventures and charitable causes
- Rent and/or transportation
- Food and drink (meals out, how you split the bill, etc.)
- Alcohol and drugs
- Clothes
- Makeup, skincare, and hair
- Entertainment
- Travel
- Health/fitness
- Charitable giving

You can also set boundaries more broadly around your finances; you can choose not to share your income, your partner's income, your parents' income, or anything else.

YOUR TIME
You get to decide how much time you're willing/able/choosing to spend on . . .

- work
- romantic partners
- dating
- family
- friend activities
- friends in general
- attending religious services
- hobbies, activities, and general leisure
- the internet/your phone.

YOUR ENERGY AND ATTENTION

- How much energy you reserve for yourself
- When/how you choose to be alone
- How much attention you give romantic partners, friends, and family
- How "on call" and available you are to others
- Favors you're willing to do
- How comfortable you are hearing private details of other people's lives
- The types of conversations and language you're willing to bear witness to
- The amount of airtime you give certain topics of conversation, especially when said topics are being argued in bad faith
- The type of media you consume, including content that is scary, violent, sexual, or offensive

- How much energy you spend educating other people about topics specific to your identity or lived experiences

- How you allow people to talk to you and treat you—for example, you're allowed to refuse to be yelled at, or to exit a conversation where a person is belittling you

- How willing you are to change your behavior, interests, or habits

YOUR PRIVACY

You aren't obligated to share details about your life with other people, including your friends/family/parents/coworkers/strangers on the internet! That includes . . .

- details about your childhood, your grades, your marriage, your job, your health, your reproductive plans (or lack thereof), your family, your sexuality, your gender identity, your sexual history, your salary; you are especially allowed not to share this information when being honest would compromise your safety

- details about other people's lives (e.g., the fact that your partner is in therapy, or that your sibling is going through a tough time)

- your phone number; you really, really, really don't have to give it to every person who asks for it (but if you're doing that because it feels safer than the alternative, I get it)

- your private messages, including your mail, emails, DMs, and texts

- your digital accounts—you get to decide who is allowed to friend/ follow you, and what you share on apps and social media; you can also request that people don't share details about your life, photos of you, photos of your children, photos of a private event, or tag your location

- who is allowed to view/track your location via GPS

- who is allowed to see your body—again, it's perfectly fine to say that no one except your partner, your OB/GYN, and your god is allowed to look at your bits!

Of course, just because you set a boundary doesn't mean it will be respected. And there will certainly be instances where enforcing a boundary could stand in the way of achieving greater intimacy, or prevent someone from being able to really show up for you. It's also wise to remember that boundaries are both cultural and personal, and someone who is crossing your line isn't necessarily a terrible person. (To be clear: They might be a terrible person! Just not *necessarily,* in every case.) In their family, friend group, or workplace, what they are doing could be *completely* normal, and they might not mind at all if they were on the receiving end of said behavior.

That said, it's still necessary and important to communicate your boundaries. And if your boundaries turn out to be something of a deal breaker, that's fine, too! If a new pal wants a friend who is, say, comfortable with talking about sex in explicit detail, and you're just never going to be that friend, that's really OK.

You can clue people in to your boundaries before a line gets crossed the same way you'd share *any* preference or opinion: Mention it when the relevant topic comes up, keep your tone confident and fairly light/neutral, and try to avoid shaming people who might feel different. (Much of that will come through in your tone, but you can add "I know not everyone shares this belief" or "I know I'm in the minority on this, but it's just something I feel strongly about" to any of the phrases below.) If you want a little inspiration, here are some ideas to get you started.

💬 **What to say**

"[Thing] makes me so uncomfortable."

"I'm really not a fan of [thing]."

"I'm a fairly private person" or "I'm fairly private when it comes to X."

"Oh yeah, that's not for me" or "That's not something I'd ever be OK with doing."

"I find it hard to do X with people I just met" or "I prefer not to do X with people I don't know very well."

"I don't really like to talk about X."

"I'm a big believer in [not discussing my marriage with friends/having a set amount of alone time every week]."

"I take [family time/studying/sex/saving money] really seriously" or "X is really important to me."

"I've noticed you ask me about X a lot, and I'd prefer you didn't."

"I never joke about X" or "I don't think jokes about X are funny."

"Oh, I'm not a [hugger/very touchy person]!" or "Oh, I can't stand having people touch my hair."

If someone explicitly asks "Is this OK?" or "Do you like this?"

"Oh, no thank you!" or "I'd prefer not, actually" or "That actually makes me feel a bit [squeamish/stressed/etc.] and I'd love to [change the subject/sit this one out]."

Some of these statements will also work if the person has already crossed the line and you're trying to gently readjust. But if/when it's past that point, you'll probably need to have a more serious conversation, which we'll cover in Chapter 10. And, of course, you should notice when folks are making similar statements *to you*—because they are communicating their boundaries, and it's on you to adjust accordingly.

Alanis Morissette's Four Boundaries

In an article for SELF, Alanis Morissette shared her idea of four essential boundaries, which she has also passed along to her children: "You can't tell me what I'm thinking, you can't tell me what I'm feeling, you can't fucking touch my body/you can't do anything with my body, and don't touch my stuff."

That's pretty much the stuff that matters, you know?

Chapter 2
Making Space

howing up for yourself isn't possible if you don't make space for yourself—space to notice and respond; space to flourish and thrive; space that you can fill with the habits, activities, and people that truly make you feel good. But space is not always easy to come by. There's a growing expectation that we will always be on, reachable, in communication with dozens of our closest friends (virtually or IRL). No wonder we're all exhausted.

Making space begins with making choices. If you don't decide how you want to live your life, other people will decide for you. Making space means you have to say no sometimes—no to your beloved friends, to your coworkers, to the things you "want" (but don't *really* want), to the things you genuinely want (but not right this second), to your notifications and goddamn phone. You can't be your happiest, most authentic self if you regularly abdicate this responsibility. I know this can be difficult, but I've found that it's considerably easier when you are able to do it intentionally and wholeheartedly, confident in who you are and secure in the knowledge that your decision is the best one you could make in this moment. Or, to put it another way, if you know what, exactly, you're saying *yes* to instead.

Your TME

If you're reading this book, there's a good chance that you're someone who is always doing a lot—trying to excel at work, at home, and with friends; attempting to read/watch/ listen to whatever new thing smart people say you should check out; and basically earn A's in all aspects of life. But everything we do costs us time, money, or energy (also known as TME). Your TME is your most valuable resource, and if you want to better show up for yourself, it's helpful to think about how you're spending it—and how you'd *like* to be spending it.

The exercises from the previous chapter should have given you a better sense of what your values, tastes, and preferences are; now it's time to look at where your TME is going so you can nail down your *priorities*. Because, unfortunately, your TME is in limited supply. Most of us don't want to admit this, but the reality is that no one—not even the wealthiest, most extroverted, most on-top-of-their-shit individual—is able to do all the things they dream about doing. Like, you cannot finish a book a week, have a hobby, cook delicious homemade meals, exercise, watch every Instagram story, listen to every popular podcast, read every interesting article that is published every day, excel at work or school (or both), get enough sleep, and maintain a *huge* network of close friends. That said, you'll be able to do a lot (if not all!) of the things that *truly* nourish you once you start giving less attention to the activities and people you don't actually care about. As Laura Vanderkam writes in *168 Hours: You Have More Time Than You Think,* "When you focus on what you do best, on what brings you the most satisfaction, there is plenty of space for everything."

THE AUDIT

To get a clear sense of where your TME is going, first do a time and energy audit. (For the moment, let's leave money out of this—tracking money will make this exercise too overwhelming!) There are a couple different ways you can approach your audit.

	Monday	Tuesday	Wednesday
6:00 AM	Woke up, scrolled on phone		
6:30 AM	On phone; replied to text from overight		
7:00 AM	Shower		
7:30 AM	Tried on four different outfits		
8:00 AM	On phone (texts, emails, IG, FB)		
8:30 AM	Breakfast, phone		

Your personal time sheet

Start with a blank weekly calendar that is broken down by the day, and then by the half hour or quarter hour. (Spreadsheets work well for this, but you can also use graph paper, a journal, or a calendar app.) For the next week or so, use it to record how you spend your time. Try to update it every sixty minutes, if possible, but if it's not, just do it as often as you can, doing your best to remember all of the "small" activities that can actually fill a lot of time. While you're at it, rate your energy during each time slot on a scale of 1 to 5, with 1 being the lowest and 5 being the highest. You can rate your physical energy (PE), your emotional energy (EE), and/or your mental energy (ME), *or* you can just rate your overall energy. Do whatever feels right for you; all that matters is that you understand the entries when you're done. If you can do this for a full week, great! If not, that's also fine.

I'm not going to lie: Doing a personal time sheet can be *hard*. It's not fun to write down all the ways you "waste" time or to admit that your energy is low whenever you hang out with certain people. Remember to be gentle with yourself. The goal is simply to get a better understanding of how you're spending your time and energy, so aim to observe without judgment, and try not to rush to any conclusions or start making changes to your routine as you go.

Once you've finished your audit, spend some time going through your data. Where is the bulk of your time and energy going? What patterns do you notice? How much time are you spending on self-care? How much time are you spending on or with other people versus yourself? How much time are you spending on bullshit (by your own definition)? What do you feel good about? What, if anything, do you feel sad or anxious about or wish were different?

Your ideal schedule

As an alternative to your personal time sheet—or immediately following it—here's a similar but slightly different approach: Fill out a blank weekly calendar (broken down by the day and then by the quarter hour) with your *ideal* schedule. I don't mean "ideal" in the sense of having unlimited wealth and no responsibilities; I mean ideal for you right now. What do you *want* to be doing?

This can also be a difficult exercise! *We're not meant to play God,* you'll think as you realize just how many fifteen-minute increments there are in a single day. If this isn't for you, consider trying this idea from *Emotional Agility* by Susan David that I really love: "Answer a single question, in writing, each night before bed: 'As I look back on today, what did I do that was actually worth my time?'"

If you're feeling guilty or embarrassed about how you've been spending your time, it might be helpful to consider the difference between excuses and reasons. In her book *Unf*ck Your Habitat,* Rachel Hoffman defines the two: "Excuses are things that people use to justify not doing something because *they don't* want *to do it.* Reasons are how people explain not doing something because *they aren't* able *to do it.* See the difference? Saying you don't want to wash the dishes because they're just going to get dirty again later is an excuse. Saying that you can't stand up for more than a few consecutive minutes to wash dishes because you're having a pain flare-up is a reason."

Once you've finished your time and energy audit, you can put everything we've covered so far together: Who are you? What do you value? What do you need and want? What does your life *really* look like? What do you *realistically* have time and energy for? How are you *actually* spending your days? And going forward, what will you *prioritize?*

Do Less

During and after your audit, there's a good chance you'll discover that you're spending time and energy on activities or relationships that aren't making you feel good, and that you can easily dump. But you might also feel like you *still* don't have enough time to do everything you want to do. And I get that! I love *doing,* and the idea of cutting anything out is extremely hard for me. "What do you mean, 'You don't have to make custom koozies for everyone attending the party this weekend'?" I'll say dismissively, cranky because I've been DIYing decorations for three days straight and have forgotten to eat. When I have really strong feelings about something, it's easy for me to forget that just because I *can* do something doesn't mean I *should.* I've finally begun to see the power and practicality in just doing a little bit less more often.

It started when I was constantly stressed about work. So much of that stress was rooted in my attempts to always do more. I'd gotten it in my head that the only way to do something was perfectly, and I applied that to everything. And I was just tired. I felt like my brain was on fire all the time. So I stopped doing so much (which is exactly as easy and as difficult as it sounds). And it felt *great?!*

Doing less manifests in a few core ways in my life. From a time management perspective, it means "You literally do not have time to do all of these things." Like, of *course* you can't do everything! No one can! But for some reason, we all assume everyone else is doing everything—maintaining strong friendships, going on romantic dates with their partner, working out every day, *not* crying in the office bathroom, wearing the right bra size—which is why, I suspect, we so often feel like we're fucking up and failing at life. But it's a huge relief to be honest with yourself and others about what you can do. And by "do," I don't mean "do if everything goes perfectly and I am a slightly better version of myself." I mean "do most days, being the person I am with the life I have." There are 168 hours in a week, but we aren't robots! We can only realistically do so much in that time. While I genuinely believe that evaluating how you're currently spending your time and energy will make it possible to do *more* of the things that matter most to you, I don't think any of us will ever be able to do *everything* we'd like to do. I certainly can't!

Doing less means not always trying to do The Absolute Most. It's recognizing that sometimes, you don't have to go to three stores to get your friend the perfect "OMG, so *them!!!*" birthday card in existence—because any birthday card you choose will do. It's planning to make guacamole for your next potluck, and then taking a look at your schedule for the next few days and remembering that—if I may quote Ina Garten here—*store-bought is fine*.

Doing less means no longer saying yes to every request because you know that's what someone else wants to hear you say—or because that is what *you* want to hear yourself say. It's telling the truth about what you're capable of doing, and being OK with that.

Doing less means being willing to do a less-than-perfect job at something that kind of doesn't matter. We all know the old adage that perfect is the enemy of good. But how many of us believe that this advice only applies to *other* people, and that we personally have to do everything perfectly? (Guilty!!!) But it's actually fine to not be the best at something, to not give 100 percent to *everything*. It's *especially* OK if the task at hand doesn't matter to you (or to anyone *but* you). As a high-achiever who always wants to do more and make things a little better, it's been hard to get to a point where I can admit this. But the truth is, since I've started letting good enough be good enough, the world hasn't ended. I doubt anyone has even *noticed.* And I truly believe that will be the case for you, too.

Doing less means just letting some shit go. (Are you having a heart attack reading this yet? I'm so sorry.) If you're the type of person who loves to solve problems and is driven by an urge to *fix,* it can be incredibly difficult to leave things messy or imperfect or unfinished or uncertain or un-googled. (Again, I'm dragging myself here.) But sometimes you can't, or don't need to, or the amount of work required to fix the problem is more than you actually have.

It can be hard to admit that you don't have unlimited TME, especially if you've spent years telling yourself a story about the power of self-control. But what's the alternative? Letting yourself and other people down because you overpromised and now can't deliver? Running yourself into the ground? Feeling constant low-level guilt that makes it impossible to enjoy what you're *actually* doing? I mean, sure, you *could* do that. But what if you just . . . did less?

What if you didn't have to offer the best and most thorough answer (or any answer!!!) to every question that arises in your orbit? What if you just let your coworker who is wilding out over something inconsequential go off and didn't make correcting them your problem? Take it from me, a lifelong answerer and corrector: The world would not end.

Once you start doing less, you begin to realize that it almost always gives you *more* of what you actually want: more time, more space, more focus, more genuine enjoyment, and a higher likelihood of achieving your goals. But don't do it for that reason; do it because it'll make you feel better.

"Do less" is what I say to remind myself that I have *limits* and I also have *agency*—and that even if I'm not perfect, I'll still be OK.

How to Be Alone

A lot of the struggle to honor your own boundaries (and to respect other people's) is rooted in a fear of being alone—of not having friends, a partner, a family, anyone. *I don't want to ask for help because I'm worried people will judge me and leave me. I don't want to be my true authentic self because I'm worried no one will love me. I don't want to say no because I'm worried I'll stop being invited.* All of this is completely understandable! The need for company and attention and a social network is a very real, very *human* need, and there's no reason to be ashamed of wanting it.

It's impossible to honor your own needs if you're constantly worried that everyone you care about is going to leave you. Being OK with being alone is critical to showing up for yourself, and to living an authentic, fulfilling life. So if you're *deeply* uncomfortable being alone—whether that means going to a movie by yourself, or being single—to the point where it's dictating your decisions or interfering with your relationships, you might want to first spend some time working on accepting yourself.

To be good at being alone, you have to like your own company and have confidence that being alone sometimes (or a lot of the time!) isn't some huge character flaw or moral failing. But also: Being more comfortable being alone—like everything else!—is something you can get better at with practice.

Some definitions: Going forward, I'll use "solo" to refer to being in a public space without any sort of companion (e.g., running errands by yourself, but with plenty of strangers around). I'll use "being alone" to refer to being truly physically alone (so, say, being alone in your home). And I'll use a definition of "solitude" (and solitary) that comes from authors Raymond Kethledge and Michael Erwin: "a subjective state of mind in which the mind, isolated from input from other minds, works through a problem on its own." Solitude can happen when you're alone *or* solo as long as you're not receiving *any* inputs (so: not listening to music, not watching TV, not texting or scrolling through your phone, etc.).

If you think you could stand to get better at being solo, alone, and/or solitary, here are some ways to practice.

Reduce the number of inputs you're receiving when you're not alone.
Being a *little* more solitary when you're with other people is a great place to start. It's not exactly the same as being alone with your thoughts, but it's a step in that direction. First, consider shutting off other sources of entertainment or background noises when you're with people. (For example, try not listening to the radio if you're in the car with your partner, or turn off the TV once your roommate arrives home and you start debriefing on the day.) Next, try minimizing inputs when you're solo. That might look like turning off your music when you're working out at the gym or putting your phone in airplane mode while you run errands.

Find little ways to go out into the world solo more often.
Being solo can be intimidating, so start small until you build up your tolerance! Look for activities that aren't too commitment heavy, meaning you can exit at any point. (Sitting at a coffee shop alone is easier than sitting at a bar alone, which is easier than eating at a nice restaurant alone.) You could also be solo in places where people likely won't notice you or the fact that you're alone—and/or where you'll likely never see these people again. So, instead of going to a restaurant alone (where you might feel like other diners keep looking at you), you could go to a movie alone (where everyone is watching the screen) or go to a bar alone when you're traveling to a different city. And take note of all the people who are solo when you're out in the world; you'll likely start to notice that there are a lot of them, and it's totally *fine*.

Try meditative *activities* that aren't actually meditation.
Meditation is a great way to practice being solitary. But it's intimidating! Here's what finally got me over the hump: I tried activities that gave me a taste of what meditation might feel like but that didn't ask me to go all in. For me, this looked like puzzles, embroidery, and calligraphy, but it could also be building model trains, woodworking, knitting, or baking bread. Think:

activities that are repetitive and a bit mindless but still feel stimulating and energizing. If you need to, you can let yourself have one passive input when you start (so, say, listening to music or a podcast), and build up to doing it without any inputs at all.

Reduce your inputs when you're alone.

I'm comfortable being solo and alone, but I'll admit that it gets much harder when I don't have my phone on me. Meditation helped, but so did just doing it more often. One habit that had a major positive impact: putting my phone in airplane mode and reading a book for an hour every Saturday. That meant no longer pausing to Google a word I didn't recognize, seeing that I had an Instagram notification, opening Instagram, reading and responding to a few DMs, scrolling for twenty minutes, and then forgetting about the word and the book entirely. I thought it would be hard but it actually felt *great.* I always felt calm and relaxed afterward, and I never once missed anything important.

Try shutting the world out for a few hours by putting your phone on Do Not Disturb and/or airplane mode during solo and alone activities like cooking, running errands, commuting, and getting ready in the morning; you might be surprised by how refreshed and content you feel.

Try reducing your *outputs* while you're solo and/or alone.

A lot of the conversation around social media use is framed around *consuming* content and overlooks the *creation* part, which is a shame. Because even if you're not an influencer, there's a good chance you're still *generating* content—so, posting photos, updating your status, texting your people, and documenting your day or your activities . . . *or* responding to others' photos, statuses, texts, and documentation. And that's a problem! First, the moment you begin to document something, the less present you are. And the more you create, the more you invite *responses,* which traps you in a cycle of liking and responding even more. Constant output is super distracting, saps valuable energy, and ensures that you're never (or rarely) *really* alone.

A lot of people take breaks from consuming social media, but it's also worth taking a hiatus from *creating* it. Because if you're constantly texting and posting and messaging, you're not *quite* alone with your thoughts, observations, and experiences. When I'm struggling with this, I've found it's helpful to ask myself why I feel such a strong urge to share in the first place, and what, exactly, I'm seeking (or avoiding) in that moment.

How to Say No to an Invite When Your Reason Is "I Just Don't Want To"

There are few social interactions more panic-inducing than the moment a kind, friendly person invites you to do an activity or attend an event that you really don't care to do or attend, but you also don't have a "good" reason to say no. *You* know the reason is just ". . . nah," but you are *also* a kind and friendly person, so you aren't going to just *say* that. You have manners! And empathy! And—now, apparently—an obligation to get up and go roller skating next Saturday with a bunch of strangers, even though you deeply don't want to!

Of course, there are times you should genuinely consider the invite, especially if the person is a close friend who is inviting you to something that means a lot to them. Sometimes, having friends means doing things that aren't exactly your idea of a good time. You should definitely give your friend's improv show or housewarming party real consideration before you reflexively refuse. But in the instances when it's not a super close friend and/or the invite is relatively unremarkable (like, say, to see a movie you're not interested in or to go out to dinner on a weeknight at a restaurant that's across town and too pricey for your taste)—when you can *technically* go but you just don't want to—it's OK to decline. Really!

Saying no to hangout requests is a gateway to setting boundaries in general. Realizing you have the right and the ability to say "No, thanks" or "I'm not into that" without the world coming to an end is life-changing. Do it a few times and you'll begin to see that a cornucopia of possibility and freedom awaits! If, on the other hand, you can't tell a total stranger "Oh, no thank you, I'd rather not" when they try to offer you a perfume sample at the mall or get you to sign their petition in the park, you're probably not going to be comfortable telling a friend it's time to change the subject when their "I hate my boss" monologue enters its third hour. It's a good idea to practice saying no to the small(ish) asks when they present themselves; over time, the bigger requests will begin to feel less daunting.

Saying no also gives you a chance to learn more about the people in your life and how they treat you. Here's the thing: Anyone who refuses to take no for an answer with regard to the seemingly small requests probably isn't great at respecting boundaries in general—which is helpful information to have! Because boundaries are about *way* more than just roller skating on a Saturday; they can also be about your bodily autonomy, your money, your belongings, and your privacy. And you might find that a person who reacts very badly to "Oh, thank you for the invite, but I'm actually not a big fan of roller skating" has problems taking no for an answer when it comes to the bigger stuff. If your people are guilt-tripping you, pressuring you to do something, or otherwise not "letting" you say no, that's a Them Problem, not a You Problem. The people who are worthy of your TME will take care to communicate that they respect your needs and preferences, even if they feel disappointed by your "no" in the moment.

Refusing an invitation early on also allows you to avoid the scenario in which you dread the event for weeks and ultimately cancel at the last minute. We can all agree that dreading an event for weeks is a bummer (and *way* more emotionally draining than just saying no in the first place!), and being canceled on at the last minute is truly frustrating. Also frustrating: hanging out with a person who doesn't actually want to be there! If my options, as the inviter, are "be momentarily disappointed before finding a buddy who *will* enjoy the activity I'm proposing" and "spend *my* valuable TME hanging out with someone who doesn't want to be here, and secretly— or not-so-secretly—resents me for it," I'm going to choose the former every time! Agreeing to do something you *really* don't want to do isn't necessarily kind; it can actually be pretty selfish.

Speaking of selfish, when I'm feeling guilty about the idea of saying no in these situations, I find it's helpful to think about whether saying my no is *really* going to break this person's heart, or if I just think my presence is way more important than it really is. It can be easy to tell yourself your attendance is a huge deal, or that this event means soooo much to this other person . . . only to say no and have them shrug and invite someone else without giving it a second thought. Of course, sometimes they do care if you say yes! But even if they're disappointed, they will likely understand and get over it—which is a fine outcome! Taking medium-sized care of yourself is more important than avoiding low-key disappointing your friend. So before you grudgingly agree to go, step back and ask yourself if you're overvaluing how much your attendance matters.

Declining an invitation can feel stressful or guilt inducing in the moment, but it doesn't have to be that way! It just takes practice. The more you do it, the more you'll realize that most people can actually handle it, and that it won't negatively affect your relationships. If you need help formulating a response for these situations, below are some scripts based on conversations I've had in my own life to get you started. As always, you can/should tweak these so they feel right for the request and the relationship.

Regardless of what you say, aim for a warm but relatively neutral and matter-of-fact tone. And keep it *short.* There's also no need to beg for forgiveness, get into your personal reasons, or present an eight-part defense as though you're in a *Law & Order* rerun. Treat saying no as normal (because it *is* normal).

What to say

If it's date-specific, and you'd prefer to be doing Not This on the day/time in question:

> "Oh, thank you so much for thinking of me! Unfortunately I won't be able to make it, but thank you for the invitation!"

> "Oh, that sounds lovely, but I won't be able to make it. But have a great time!"

If you're probably never going to be up for doing an activity at the suggested day/time:

> "Oh, that concert sounds really fun, but I can't really do big outings on weeknights! But have a great time!"

> "Ah, that sounds lovely, but I have a rule that I don't make plans on Sundays—it's my day [to decompress and not talk to anyone/catch up with my parents/do all my chores]. But thank you for thinking of me!"

> "Oh, that sounds like a blast, but I'm pretty committed to my 10:00 PM sleep schedule on weeknights these days. But thank you for the invite!"

If you're *never* going to be up for this activity:

> "Roller skating isn't really my thing, so I'm going to sit this one out!"

> "Thank you for thinking of me, but [music festivals/the beach/ amusement parks] aren't really my speed!"

You can also add something like:

> "But I'd love to see you and catch up soon! How about [some alternative programming that you both enjoy]?"

If it's . . . everything:

> "Ah, I'd love to [see you/catch up/hang out], but I haven't been able to get much time for myself lately and I promised myself I'd just hunker down and have a quiet weekend!"

> "I don't really have the bandwidth for much socializing right now, but I would love to [do something else][at some date in the future when you'd be up for it]."

> "I don't have much room for extracurriculars these days, but I would love to [do something else][at some date in the future when you'd be up for it]."

"Ah, that sounds [lovely/fun/amazing], but I haven't been sleeping well lately and promised myself I'd stop going to so many [happy hours/pool parties/roller-skating networking events] so I can establish a more consistent schedule."

"I know I haven't been able to come the last few times you've invited me, but it's not because I don't want to! [My schedule is just busy] [I'm feeling broke][I can't really do things on weeknights][In general, roller skating isn't really my jam][I've been pretty depressed, honestly, so socializing is a bit of a struggle right now]. But I hope the stars will align soon and I'll be able to attend!"

This last one is a good option when you've declined a couple of invites from the same person and are concerned that they'll think you're canceling because you just don't want to hang out with them. In my experience, it's way better to be honest and clear about why you're declining invitations, especially if they're from close friends who would probably love to know a) how you're doing, and b) that it's not about them.

If you need a moment to compose yourself before you respond:

"Let me check my calendar and get back to you!"

(And then actually get back to them quickly—don't wait for them to follow up!)

In general, it's a bad idea to fabricate a reason when declining an invite. Here's why: If you tell a lie that you can't attend on that particular date (when it's really about the activity itself), the person might respond by asking you to do this activity on a different day, which will put you in an awkward position. Or they might assume you actually *love* roller skating and want to be on the invite list for all future local roller skating events. This outcome isn't good for *anyone!*

Alternatively, if they somehow find out you didn't actually have "real" plans (or the plans you claimed to have) that day, or they later discover that you do, in fact, like roller skating, they might actually feel worse—because they'll assume it was personal. (Which may or may not be true! But even if it *is* about them, you're probably not trying to *communicate* that.)

When you're simply honest about the reason you can't make it, you communicate important information: *I do, in fact, like you. But I don't, in fact, like roller skating or weeknight hangouts.* The honest response tells them that you trust them enough to be authentic and open with them, and that you care about them enough to build a relationship where you feel seen and known.

But also: Refusing an invitation is not that deep! It's literally fine.

Let People Decline Your Invitations

If we want to be allowed to say no, we have to be willing to extend that option to others. So remember: If someone declines your invitation, it's really, really OK. It doesn't necessarily mean they don't like you or that they don't want to be your friend. If someone only ever declines your invitations and you start to suspect they don't really want to be friends, that's another matter. But it also might mean they don't want to be your friend! Which is disappointing and stings, but is also fine–because you don't actually want to be friends with people who don't want to be friends with you or who don't share any of your interests.

If you're feeling bummed about a "no, thank you," remind yourself that declining an invite can leave a person feeling vulnerable and requires courage–even from relatively assertive people. I've also found it helpful to view a "no" not as a slight, but as a *favor*–because, again, there is nothing worse than knowing someone was dreading spending time with you or regretted investing their TME in something you wanted to do. They're also doing you the favor of saying no now instead of saying yes and then flaking on you. And they're giving you permission to say no to them someday.

So, if someone says, "I can't make it," let that be good enough. Trust that they have their reasons, respect their willingness to protect their TME, and move on. If someone says, "I don't like roller skating," believe that they simply don't like roller skating. If someone says they are too busy, don't judge them for spending the evening "doing nothing" instead. (Making the choice to do nothing, when you are otherwise busy, is a big deal!) If someone says they can't afford to join you for dinner, don't mentally catalogue all of the expensive shoes they own and the amount of five-dollar lattes you've seen them consume this week. Know that a "no" simply means "This is not how I want to spend my TME at this moment," and that even if it feels a little bad, it's OK.

How to Say No to Being a Bridesmaid

This situation is fairly common and *so* stressful, and a lot of people genuinely don't realize they *can* say no. But being a bridesmaid is a huge commitment, even when your best friend or sibling is getting married. Being in the bridal party, like being somebody's best friend, is neither 100 percent responsibility nor 100 percent honor; it's a little of both. And stepping into the role when your heart isn't in it leads to unmet expectations, resentment, frustration, and hurt feelings for everyone involved.

The script below may or may not work for you, but I hope it will at least help you craft your own. Ultimately, it's important to be honest, firm, kind, and *extremely* gentle, and to give the person space to be upset with you.

INTRO
"I am so honored that you asked me to be one of your bridesmaids, but I'm going to have to decline."

REASON
If your reason is time, money, or energy: "I know that being a bridesmaid [even for a friend who is chill and doesn't expect a ton from their bridesmaids, like you!] requires a fair amount of time and money, and I'm stretched so thin right now because of [grad school/work/my newborn]."

If your reason is you aren't super close and there's no way you're buying a dress you'll never wear again/flying to Mexico (which is still a TME reason): "I know that being a bridesmaid is a big commitment and I don't feel like I'm up for the task [right now/this year]."

CONTRITION

"You deserve bridesmaids who are all-in and can really show up for you every step of the way, and I know I can't do that right now. I care about you and [Partner] a lot, so this isn't a decision I'm making lightly. I totally understand if you're disappointed or upset with me for saying no."

IN CONCLUSION

If you'll still attend the wedding: "I'll still be there on your wedding day [weeping during your vows][embarrassing myself on the dance floor][making your grandpa behave himself]."

You could also say, "I'd love to show up for you in other ways that day, if there is another role you need filled, or you just need a warm body to guard the gift table," (if that is, in fact, something you are up for doing).

If you won't be attending the wedding: "I am so excited for you and [Partner] and I'm so sorry I can't be there with you on the big day."

Canceling Plans

Canceling plans sits at the intersection of showing up for yourself and showing up for other people. From the perspective of showing up for yourself, skipping a social event can be a much-needed self-care move. When you know in your heart that you don't have it in you to socialize, and are confident that doing it anyway is going to make you feel terrible, it can be a *huge* relief to let yourself opt out. And so often, canceling is perfectly fine, and the other person won't mind or think much of it. (They might even be relieved!) Sometimes, canceling plans is the best way to be a good friend—after all, you can't fully show up for other people if you're not taking care of yourself, and regularly attending hangouts when you aren't up for it isn't good for *anyone*.

On the other hand, sometimes "showing up" for others means literally showing up for them, and, well, it can be frustrating to be on the receiving end of a cancelation, particularly if you're the one who arranged your schedule around the plans, were really looking forward to this get-together, or are dealing with a person who regularly flakes. Canceled plans can be inconsiderate and disrespectful, especially if you're dealing with a repeat offender.

That said, sometimes you just need to bail. You're coming down with a cold or you're emotionally drained or you have to work late—whatever. It happens! If you're a people pleaser who is trying to get better at prioritizing self-care, here are some questions to ask yourself the next time you're struggling to decide whether or not to cancel.

How are you feeling right now? What's making you want to cancel?

It's easy to think, *Uggghhh, I don't want to goooooooooo,* without really knowing why. Start by taking inventory of your feelings and try to figure out what, specifically, you need in this moment. Getting to the root of your desire to cancel can help you determine whether canceling will actually solve your problem—and whether being social will do more harm or good.

How will you feel during and after the get-together?

Will you be able to be truly present—that is, fully focused on your friend, with your phone off and put away? Or will you feel stressed, impatient, and/

or distracted? Will you feel happy and energized the next day . . . or will you resent the friend for inviting you in the first place, or for the time and money you spent on the outing? Be honest about whether you're going to be able to give your friend your best (or best-*ish*) self in this moment. If you're going to be there *physically* but will be on another planet emotionally and mentally, that's a strong sign you should cancel or reschedule.

If you bail, how will you feel?

Take a minute to consider how you'll feel during and after canceling. If you opt out, will you *actually* relax/study/rest/do chores with that time, or will you just feel guilty and futz around on Instagram instead? Will you spend *more* time and energy trying to make it up to the person later than you would if you just went? If your goal is to make a decision confidently and fully own your choice, it can be super helpful to think about it from different angles.

Is there anything you wish you'd done differently early on?

Perhaps when you were making these plans, you told yourself you'd feel more enthusiastic about roller skating or amateur improv or music festivals by the time the big day rolled around . . . but now that day is tomorrow and wow, yeah, you still hate all of those things and *really* want to cancel. Which I get! I used to find myself in that position regularly! That's why I'm such a big believer in saying no to invitations when you're asked. If you determine that you should have just declined at the outset, or spoken up about your needs and preferences sooner, consider making a deal with yourself: You can opt out this time, but the next time a similar invitation comes your way, you *have* to be honest and say no up front—even if it's hard, and even if you don't have a "good" reason. You owe it to yourself and to your friends to do that work.

Is this more of a Them Problem than a You Problem?

If you're inclined to cancel because you feel terrible every time you hang out with this person or these people, that's very good information to have! In that case, don't *just* consider canceling; consider whether this relationship is actually serving you and worth your time in the first place. (If it's not, you may find the friend breakup tips in Chapter 10 helpful.)

You OK, buddy?

If you're regularly canceling plans (or just seriously considering it) because you feel tired, overwhelmed, or just not up for it, do yourself—and your pals—a solid and consider whether something deeper is going on. Losing interest in socializing and being perpetually exhausted can be a sign of mental or physical health issues, so it might be wise to start keeping track of these instances in a journal or an app. Or just take a look at your calendar for the past few months and do some self-reflection! If you find that you're canceling more plans than you're keeping, or you feel drained all the time, it might be time to talk to a health care provider or therapist.

HOW TO CANCEL PLANS GRACIOUSLY

If you do decide to cancel, it's not the end of the world. Seriously! Sure, your friend might be bummed out—but it's helpful to recognize that this is the natural and correct response from them, even if you definitely made the right choice for yourself in this moment. You're not wrong to cancel, and they're not wrong to be kind of disappointed. That said, putting a little thought into *how* you cancel is what will keep canceled plans from turning into five-alarm friendship fire. Here are some tips to keep in mind.

Think about whether you can adjust the plans in any way.

More often than not, our friends just want to see *us* and don't care about going to a fancy restaurant or doing a cool activity. So think about what you *would* be up for doing, and consider offering that as an alternative to your pal instead of outright bailing. You might say something like:

> "Hey, friend, I'm completely exhausted and broke right now, and am honestly feeling very stressed about our plans for tomorrow night. I really want to catch up with you, though—would you be up for coming to my place and letting me cook you dinner instead of us going all the way to New Jersey? And we could still plan to go to Medieval Times next month, once I've finished this big project and my bonus paycheck has hit."

Even if they say they'd rather just cancel, most people will *really* appreciate the fact that you asked them to be a part of the decision-making process. It communicates that you genuinely care about them but still know how to set boundaries and honor your own needs.

Own the titles of Captain Rescheduling *and* Chief Next Hangout Officer.

If at all possible, reschedule in the same conversation so the friend knows you are still genuinely interested in hanging out with them. If they don't confirm or they don't seem very interested, follow up within a week to try to plan something new.

Be as honest as possible about why you're canceling.

Y'all: Don't say your car broke down if you're actually hungover as hell. A lot of the time people can tell when you're bullshitting them, and an obvious fib can do more damage than the reality you feel a tad embarrassed about. Remember that being honest is an act of vulnerability, and that vulnerability can actually *strengthen* a friendship.

Be considerate.

Acknowledge that canceling, especially at the last minute, can cost your friend time, money, and energy. That might mean Venmoing them for, say, the cost of their ticket, or the cancellation fee they're now on the hook for. If it was a group gathering where you were responsible for bringing something (wine, dessert, etc.), offer to drop it off anyway or send it with another friend, if that's feasible. And always make this part of your initial cancellation message. (So: "I'm so sorry to have to do this, but I'm not going to be able to make it to our mani-pedi appointment tomorrow. The salon's website says we'll be charged a twenty-dollar fee, which I will obviously pay.")

Own what you should have done differently.

Most of us just want to feel like the person at fault for our minor inconvenience or disappointment is taking the situation seriously, and showing that you've done some self-reflection can really help communicate that. You might want to say something like, "I've realized that when I'm this busy with work, I'm probably never going to be able to make weeknight hangouts happen, but I didn't want to admit that when you invited me, and I apologize for that."

Make sure your tone/apology is appropriate for the nature of the event. There's a huge difference between asking to reschedule a coffee date with a coworker pal and telling your best friend you won't be coming to their wedding next week. If you're overly apologetic for a fairly minor cancellation (e.g., "I'm the absolute WORST. Do you totally hate me? Can you ever forgive me?"), you run the risk of making your buddy feel like *they* need to comfort *you*. But being really casual and nonchalant about a significant cancellation isn't a good look either. If you're tempted to overcompensate (or be rather dismissive), it might be because you're actually feeling vulnerable or uncomfortable about your choice. While that's totally normal, it's a good idea to take a moment to center yourself and really own your decision, which will allow you to operate from a sincere, confident, and emotionally honest place when you do ultimately cancel.

Dealing with Boundary Violations

Hopefully by now you are getting more comfortable with the idea of telling people no or asking for what you need. But communicating a boundary violation—even one that's seemingly small and straightforward, like telling someone to stop asking for your Netflix password—can feel particularly fraught. You not only have to be vulnerable, you're also criticizing another person for something that can feel close to who they are instead of just being about their behavior. And because it all seems so personal, you might feel the need to be extra sure that you're "allowed" to say something at all. But of *course* you're allowed to say something! And, in fact, you often should!

If you're hesitant to speak up because you're not sure whether something really *did* cross the line, that's totally understandable! We don't always "just know" that something isn't cool with us, and the boundaries that are considered obvious or normal (from a legal, cultural, and psychological perspective) are constantly changing. That said, there *are* established norms when it comes to boundaries, and if you're ever unsure about whether something "counts" as bad, it can be helpful to turn to experts to help you see what is healthy and unhealthy; appropriate and inappropriate; abusive or safe or "normal."

Or you can just talk to other people you trust! Of course, this method isn't foolproof—you may discover that your loved ones have *extremely* outdated definitions of consent, for example—but it's a good place to start. Sometimes you have to share an experience out loud or see it written down to realize how messed up it is.

Once you're sure that someone *has* crossed a boundary, it's time to communicate that their behavior is not acceptable. Feel free to dial these suggestions down to extremely gentle, or way up to "Seriously, fuck off."

💬 What to say

"That's actually really not OK with me at all."

"Yeah, I'm not cool with that, to be honest."

"I'm really not comfortable [doing this thing], and I need you to let it go."

"I find that question pretty inappropriate actually."

"That's a really private topic, and it's not something I want to talk about with you." (Note: It can feel incredibly rude to say "with you" to someone, but it's important, particularly if the person is assuming you have a closer relationship than you want to have, or if they are going to immediately start whining that you do want to talk about it—with other people.)

"I think we have pretty different comfort levels with regard to this, but my stance is X, it's not going to change, and I'd really like for us to drop this forever and move on."

"This is a no-go for me, and I really need you to accept that."

"I really don't [like that/want to discuss this with you]. Please stop."

"I know this is something you [expect me to do/really want/think all friends should share] but I just don't feel the same way, and I'd really like you to stop asking me about it or trying to convince me to see it your way."

"I feel pretty strongly about this and you're not going to change my mind. I'd like to change the subject now, please!"

"I've told you several times that I'm not OK with you [doing this thing]. The fact that you keep pushing me on this is really weird and extremely not OK, and it needs to stop."

"What you're doing is gross and probably illegal, and it needs to never happen ever again."

"I'm reaching my limit on how much of this I'm willing to put up with."

"I've told you how I feel about this; why do you keep pushing it?"

And if appropriate, you can communicate the consequences that will occur if the person doesn't respect your boundary. That might sound something like . . .

"If you keep pushing this, I'm going to call it a night and head home."

"I know X is important to you, but I feel very different about it, and if you continue to pressure me, it's ultimately going to get in the way of our having a close relationship."

"I can't be friends with someone who doesn't respect this boundary."

"If you can't hear me on this, I think we are going to have a pretty serious problem."

"I have to be honest: If you keep doing this, I'm going to stop [talking to you/hanging out with you/attending your parties/being a member of this group]."

"I want to have a relationship with you, but you're not respecting a boundary that's important to me, and I really need that to change or I'm not going to come around anymore."

Finally, remember that being misaligned about boundaries might be a deal breaker—and that doesn't necessarily mean that either of you are doing anything wrong. It just means this friendship isn't meant to be, or isn't meant to progress past a certain point—which is fine!

Your Phone

Like many people, I spend a fair amount of time looking at various screens. And while I don't believe our phones are the root of all evil, I acknowledge that when it comes to showing up for myself (and others), my phone regularly gets in the way. As Cal Newport writes in *Digital Minimalism,* "Increasingly, [our phones] dictate how we behave and how we feel, and somehow coerce us to use them more than we think is healthy, often at the expense of other activities we find more valuable."[9]

Now, you may be thinking, *But I use my phone to talk to my friends, which is a form of self-care.* Which is true! That's why I'm not advocating for renouncing all technology and moving to the woods.

The overall evidence on using the internet to foster social connections is mixed. But there are some things we do know and that are worth real consideration. First, interacting with people mainly through your phone and social media means you have less time to spend connecting with people in real life, and that real life connection is still pretty important from a cognitive and psychological perspective (even if it doesn't necessarily *feel* different or important to you). Further, communicating digitally can easily overwhelm our brains in a way that in-person interaction just doesn't. And the less we socialize in the real world, the harder it becomes to reenter the meatspace again.

Track Your IRL Conversations

Author Celeste Headlee says that while she was writing her book *We Need to Talk,* she kept a pen-and-paper running tally of every face-to-face interaction she had each day. "Before this exercise, I estimated that I probably had three or four substantive conversations a day," she writes. "But after tracking them carefully, it turned out that most days I was having perhaps one or two, sometimes none. It felt like more because I was communicating with people all day. But I was rarely talking to them." I don't even need to make a list to know this is true for me too. (And not just when I'm in a foxhole writing a book.) And it was far more pronounced when I was living alone, not dating anyone. If you are convinced you're getting plenty of IRL interaction, it might be helpful to start tracking this and see what you learn.

What's more, staying in touch with people might actually be overrated. One of the most compelling articles I came across when researching this topic was an interview in *The New York Times* with Dr. Robin Dunbar, a professor of evolutionary psychology at Oxford. Dunbar told the *Times* that social media apps allow us "to maintain relationships that would otherwise decay."[10] While most of us tend to think of this as a good thing, it's actually not. Some of these relationships actually should decay—that's necessary for us to have the time and space to establish and nurture new ones.

Even if you feel your phone usage is healthy overall, it's likely that your phone (and social media apps more specifically) cost real time and energy that could have been used to show up for yourself or someone else. Think about how many times you've told yourself you're going to do something that will make you feel good—take a shower, email a friend, make dinner, go to bed—and have spent that time doing something far less valuable on your phone instead.

That isn't to say that mindless scrolling is always bad; sometimes, self-care looks like shutting your brain off for a little while. This is why it's helpful to get really clear on exactly how and why you're using your apps—so you can then decide if they should be a priority or not. It's also worth exploring if you're using the app for your core purpose most of the time or if you're starting out with good intentions (say, connecting with your long-distance siblings) but quickly devolving into something that *isn't* so good (looking at your high school frenemy's baby photos and talking shit about them to your other friends).

To unpack this more, start by making a list of the social apps you use the most. Think: Facebook, Instagram, Twitter, Snapchat, TikTok, YouTube, and whatever app hasn't been invented yet but will be our latest obsession by the time this book goes to press. (By the way, I'm going to cover messaging—texting, Facebook Messenger, WhatsApp, Slack, Google Hangouts, etc.—on page 66, but you can definitely include messaging apps in the following exercises if you want to!)

Go through each app on your list and write down the *core* reasons you are using each one. It might be things like . . .

- to see what my friends have been up to
- to connect with people like me
- to get creative inspiration
- to catch up on important news
- to find new, interesting things to read.

Once you've done that, identify any ways in which your current app usage isn't helping achieve that goal and/or is bringing about other negative consequences in your life. Then brainstorm other ways you might fill that same need, but via a more direct (read: app-free) route. Even if the alternatives seem like they might be impossible, write them down anyway. So, your list might look something like this . . .

Facebook

Core reason I use this app: To see what my friends have been up to
Problem: The people whose updates I actually care about are getting lost in all the noise.

Alternatives: I could call my close friends, email them, or video chat with them regularly. I could also unfriend and unfollow about 90 percent of the people whose posts I'm currently seeing.

Instagram

Core reason I use this app: To get creative inspiration

Problem: I'm distracted by Stories, memes, influencer #sponcon, and DMs with pals, and I'm spending more time consuming inspiration (and garbage) than I am actually producing anything.

Alternatives: I could seek out creative inspiration in the real world—going to museums, reading books, attending talks, etc.—and set aside phone-free time each week to actually produce something.

Twitter

Core reason I use this app: To catch up on important news; to find interesting things to read

Problem: I have to wade through a sea of clickbait, drama, Nazi propaganda, and memes that make me feel old.

Alternatives: I could read the a news website at a set time each day, read the physical paper, or watch the morning and evening news. I could sign up for newsletters, go directly to my favorite users' profiles to get their recommendations, or visit my favorite websites to see what's new.

Any app

Core reason I use this app: To zone out

Problem: I'm zoning out for too long or too often, and I feel guilty because I'm not getting to do the other things I care about and want to do.

Alternatives: I could recognize that we all need to zone out every once in a while and not be so hard on myself. I could also set time limits around my zone-out times, make that the reward for doing other things, or experiment with other forms of zoning out that feel healthier or more contained.

Of course, some of these alternatives might seem impossible—for example, calling a friend or writing them an email takes time, which you may not feel like you have. But perhaps you *would* have the time if you weren't spending so much time scrolling through inane bullshit on your apps under the guise of connecting with friends. Instead of spending an hour a day on Facebook, you could have twenty-minute phone calls with two or three different friends—which will *definitely* feel more meaningful.

Consider, at the very least, setting boundaries around your app usage. Here are some that I've found personally helpful that you might want to try.

- Don't check your phone in bed in the morning. Try keeping your phone on Do Not Disturb (or airplane mode) overnight and don't open any apps or respond to any texts until you're out of bed and mostly ready for work.

- Hide apps so they aren't on your home screen. I now have to swipe through several screens to open Twitter, Instagram, and Facebook, and I've been shocked by how much my app usage has decreased. Turns out, I was opening these mostly out of habit; I didn't miss them once I couldn't see them.

- Delete social media apps from your phone and force yourself to use the desktop version instead.

- Replace your go-to "I'm bored" social media app on your home screen with an e-reader app.

- Turn off all notifications except phone calls (and *maybe* messaging). That means no alerts for coupons, internet quizzes, @-mentions, *anything*.

- Turn off all notification *sounds*. You can make your main texting sound "none" but give VIPs (like your mom) their own personal text tones, so you can respond to their messages quickly. Then you can keep your phone's volume on (so you won't miss actual calls) but your phone won't be whizzing and banging every twenty seconds when the group chat starts popping off.

- Treat your phone like a landline and only use it in a certain spot in a certain room.

- Set boundaries around where/when/how you'll check apps—and when you won't. (For example, I don't look at Twitter on Sunday mornings because Sunday morning Twitter is truly the worst, and starting my day there is a recipe for Sunday Scaries.)

- Get your news fix from podcasts, television, or physical newspapers (basically, any form of media that doesn't encourage you to read comments or click other links).

- Take a thirty-day break from one of your apps (or all of them) and see how you feel at the end of it. You might find you don't miss it.

Texting/Messaging

I have to be honest: I *love* messaging—texting, Slack, all of it. It's convenient and fun and allows me to stay in touch with people, particularly long-distance friends.

That said, I also recognize the ways it has been a problem in my life. It's terrible for my wrists, neck, back, and eyes. Knowing I can stop what I'm doing at pretty much any moment to text a friend makes me far less present in my daily life. In many cases, it's simply made me *too* available—to people I really shouldn't be *that* available to. By the time I realize this, it's too late. I'm trapped in a cycle where I feel like I have to respond, and quickly—because I've given the impression that I will—and that if I don't, they'll be disappointed. As my friend Gyan once put it, "Replying to people feels like a full-time job."

Messaging isn't all bad; in fact, a lot of it is great! I genuinely treasure the conversations I have with friends via text. But I can't deny the fact that having several side conversations during the day—some of which were part of my job, but many of which were not—had a negative effect on my creative output and how I felt overall. It's shockingly easy to expend a *lot* of mental and creative energy on this steady drip-drip-drip of words all day, which can leave you feeling quite drained, even though you're not actually *producing* anything.

Messaging made it harder for me to do the things I actually wanted to do (read, engage in hobbies, not accidentally step into traffic); felt like a huge obligation; and was skewing my ratio of showing up for others versus showing up for myself too far toward other people. And every time I'd pick up my phone to respond to a message, I'd inevitably waste more time looking at other dumb apps I didn't actually care about.

So I *finally* set boundaries around messaging. It turned out that *most* people didn't really care if I responded to a message in five minutes or five hours. And I realized that the people who hassled me about it were less interested in talking to *me* and more interested in having a responsive, friend-shaped receptacle where they could unleash their every thought whenever they felt like it. And that felt really shitty, and not like a friendship at all.

If messaging is stressing you out or interfering with your goals and your life, it's time to establish new boundaries and reclaim your attention. Here are some questions to think about as you examine your current messaging habits and consider how you ended up here.

- How often are you the one starting text conversations? Do you notice any patterns about when you typically start them or the mood you tend to be in?

- What is the substance of the conversations? Is it personal and meaningful? Mostly memes and "haha cool"s?

- How balanced are the conversations? Is one person contributing a lot more from either a quantity or a quality standpoint?

- Did you fall into this habit at a different time in your life (e.g., when you were still in school, when you had a boring job you hated, before you got a hobby, when you were depressed or lonely)?

- When do you feel like these conversations energize you? When do they leave you feeling negative or drained?

- Do you often find yourself sending the same exact messages to a bunch of different friends? Do you ever feel like your friends are doing that to you?

- What need is frequent messaging meeting in your life? Is it rooted in boredom, a desire for intimacy, a lack of IRL connections, a desire to write/speak on topics that matter to you, etc.?

- Does messaging allow you to avoid something else in your life (e.g., your job, your partner, your family, or making new friends)?

- How might you feel if you changed something about your current messaging habits?

- Is there another form of communication or a communication schedule that would ultimately serve the same needs but wouldn't leave you feeling as icky?

- Once you have a better understanding of how you've gotten to this point, you can start to think about what role you'd like messaging to play in your life going forward, and how to communicate that to your people.

- With most people in your life, it'll likely be fairly easy to reset the conversational cadence. You can just respond slower and see what happens (it'll likely be *fine*), or give yourself set times each day (or week) where you'll be more *on*. In this case, the real work will be letting go of the idea that you have to be super responsive 24/7.

- When it comes to the people who have come to expect immediate replies from you, or who get upset if they don't hear from you within thirty minutes, you may need to have a conversation to reset your boundaries.

💬 What to say

"I've realized that I need to be more focused during the day, which means I can't keep up with our normal messaging anymore."

"I love our chats, but I'm so busy right now, I can't deny that the frequency is keeping me from getting [work/studying/other obligations] done."

"I love talking to you but I've realized that [being on my phone so much/texting with friends all day/chatting up until bedtime] is really interfering with my [productivity/big life goals/sleep schedule]."

You could also add:

"Trust me, I'd much rather be chatting with you all the time, but I recognize that I need to suck it up and do this." And then: "So I'm going to [turn off messaging notifications entirely/delete FB Messenger from my phone/be completely unavailable during the day]."

And if—*if!!!!!!*—you want to, you can say something like:

> "But I love talking to you and would love to catch up [once a week on a Skype call/via phone while commuting home/at our regularly scheduled coffee date]."

Try not to overthink it or bend over backward apologizing; what you're asking for here is reasonable, and you don't need to justify your decision or argue about whether this is fair. They might be disappointed, but no relationship guarantees any of us the right to another person's attention and energy whenever we feel like chatting.

Then—and this is huge—you have to *actually do it*. This part can be hard, particularly if the person continues to message you as if nothing has changed. (In my experience, a lot of people will do just that, often framing it as, "I know you're offline so I'm just leaving this here for you to read later.") It's not just about asking them to change their behavior or adjust their expectations; it's about training *yourself* to be OK with unread messages and those little red notification bubbles and the idea of disappointing people. If you *don't* hold firm, you're teaching them that your boundaries don't actually matter.

Remember that texting is a relatively modern invention, and so is the expectation of constant availability. As Andrea Bonior says of ye olden days before smartphones, "People simply had no expectation that if they had a thought while they were driving across a bridge, they'd be able to share it with their friend Shirley right that very second."[11]

Finally, consider that if you have to do *this* much work to enforce boundaries around messaging, or spend a ton of time and energy brainstorming creative solutions to appease a person who wants to message you constantly, it might be a sign of a bigger problem with the relationship. Constant availability isn't a given in friendships, particularly as people get older, and as partners, children, and other priorities begin to take precedence. (And even with a romantic partner or a child or parent, you're still allowed to say, "This is too much.") In my experience, people who aren't great with respecting my boundaries and needs when it comes to communication aren't great at respecting my boundaries *in general*. So should you find yourself in this situation, or if this advice *really* resonated with you, be sure to take an honest look at the relationship as a whole.

Monotasking

Since we're talking about how to have more time and energy, I'll share one of the biggest ways I practice showing up for myself: by monotasking.

First, some definitions: Monotasking is focusing on a single task for a set period of time. The opposite of monotasking is what experts call *switch-tasking*. Switch-tasking is moving between cognitively demanding tasks, like checking your email, updating a spreadsheet, responding to IMs, and shopping online. And it doesn't just happen at work. You could switch-task by toggling between Instagram, Facebook, Twitter, and texting, or by going from folding laundry to responding to a DM to changing the channel on the TV to Googling the answer to a *Jeopardy!* question. Meanwhile, *background-tasking* is doing something like listening to a podcast while you clean your bathroom, and isn't quite as big a deal. (It *does* matter when it comes to solitude, though—see page 42.)

Like a lot of people, I used to switch-task pretty much nonstop. I dabbled in monotasking for a bit, but I didn't *really* prioritize it across all areas of my life until I read the management book *The Mind of the Leader,* in which the authors write that switch-tasking makes us "masters of everything that is irrelevant."[12] YIKES. But also . . . true? Experts agree that switch-tasking simply doesn't work. When your attention is divided across tasks and tabs and devices and conversations, you end up feeling less whole. It left me feeling drained and scattered, and the scientific evidence and my own lived experience told me that I wasn't actually getting shit done this way.

Even when you know switch-tasking is bad, it's still so damn appealing. For starters, humans are basically hardwired to do it. In the moment, all of those pings and tasks can make us feel important and special and *popular*. And not being available to everyone all the time can leave us feeling *guilty*. I don't know about you, but I *like* being responsive; it makes me feel like a good, attentive friend. But the reality is, I'm not showing up for the people I'm with, the person who is pinging me, *or* myself when I'm switch-tasking. So I gave it up.

Monotasking takes practice; if you're used to switch-tasking, focusing on a single task will feel kind of stressful at first. I started small: I stopped texting while I walked. Then I put my phone in Do Not Disturb mode while cooking and focused entirely on the food. I started going offline during the day at work. Unsurprisingly, I got so much done this way—tasks that I thought would take me forty-five minutes only took me twenty. And I just *felt* better.

Do I stick with monotasking all the time? I do not. It's hard! But monotasking is now something I think of like exercising or eating healthy: a habit I need to stick with most of the time as a way of showing up.

Stop Hurting Your Own Feelings

To hurt your own feelings is to engage in completely optional behaviors that you know make you feel bad. And the *optional* part really is key. This isn't about the situations in which you can't avoid terrible or annoying or abusive people; it's about the situations when you know the "block" and "mute" and "unfollow" and "log off" buttons exist, and you're simply refusing to use them.

Hurting your own feelings *very* often happens online. The posts, photos, videos, and comments in our everyday feeds can fuel rage, hopelessness, fear, or all of the above. Our apps fuel *envy,* which is often behind the feelings of anxiety, inferiority, unease, irritation, and anger that follow a 30-minute jaunt through Facebook, Instagram, and/or Twitter. (Hell, I'll even acknowledge the existence of LinkedIn for this one! Job envy is real!)

Not hurting your own feelings online means knocking off the social media behaviors that you know make you feel bad or are simply a waste of time. Think: looking at your ex's photos; looking at your ex's new partner's photos; looking at photos of your ex's new partner's *family and friends;* posting selfies just to see who likes/responds; following an Instagram influencer or colleague whose posts make you feel bad; and following anyone you think is extremely ignorant or who you wish would shut the fuck up and log off. Like, I *get it* but also: *You* shut the fuck up and log off!!!

Not hurting your own feelings means making the choice to stop spending valuable time and energy pissing yourself off. Because whether it's happening in the real world (like at work) or on social media, continuing to pay close attention to people who have hurt you or who you don't like or whose life updates leave you feeling A Way does cost you. For example, every time you see their posts or hear mention of them, you're going to think about all the reasons they suck (or feel like *you* suck), and those negative feelings are going to take up space in your brain and your day, even if you're not *directly* interacting with them. And who is that hurting? Hint: not them!!!!

If you've already decided that someone upsets you, you don't need more evidence. And if you continue to look for more proof of this person's shittiness (or their "unearned" success) so you can nurture your grievances, you'll find yourself trapped in a negative feedback loop that . . . does what exactly? Maybe you feel powerful or self-righteous for a moment, but that feeling never *really* lasts. So not hurting your own feelings is saying, "This person upsets me for [insert reason]. There is no new information I could possibly glean from following them/interacting with them and then stewing over or yelling about the most recent thing they did." When you know, unequivocally, that someone sucks, all the additional evidence does is make you feel worse.

In other instances, hurting your own feelings might look like testing other people and waiting for them to disappoint you—so you can then be angry about it. It's asking to be included in a work meeting you *know* you aren't going to be included in. It's trying to date people who are definitely unavailable. It's refusing to share what you want or need, and then lashing out when you don't get it. Not hurting your own feelings means replacing those behaviors with ones that make you feel affirmed and whole, like you're making meaningful progress toward the life you want to live, or that you're simply good enough as you are.

We hurt our own feelings for the same reason we pick at scabs—because even though it isn't exactly *positive* behavior, it provides a rush that can, in the moment, feel . . . well, not *good,* but something sort of *like* good. Hurting your own feelings can make you feel like you're solving a problem (even though you're not) and allows you to believe for the moment that you're in control. After a breakup, it's a way to continue giving the person attention even though you aren't really allowed to give them attention anymore. And when we're feeling sad or disappointed or worried or vulnerable, it's so much easier to assign blame to other people—or to simply distract ourselves—than it is to name all of our negative and uncomfortable feelings, to simply sit with them, or to admit we're powerless to change the situation.

Making space is ultimately about protecting yourself—your time, and also your heart—and not hurting your own feelings is a way to remind yourself that you have some agency. Like, there are enough cruel people in the world who are more than happy to hurt us; we really don't need to do that work for them.

Chapter 3
Showing Up for Your Body

The human body—the ol' meatsack!!!—is beautiful and sacred and special . . . but also messy and annoying and the site of trauma and pain for a lot of people. It's often just a *hassle*.* And I have some bad news: You do, in fact, have to feed yourself (annoying), exercise (rude), sleep (fine), pee (who has the time?????), and regurlarly wash your body and your hair (kill me).

When it comes to showing up for yourself, you can't overlook the importance of your corporeal form. Think about it: It can be hard enough to get through a day even when you *are* meeting your basic needs. When you have a need that isn't being met, it's nearly impossible to think of much else. But even though you probably know that you should get eight hours of sleep every night and eat a vegetable once in a while, a lot of us *aren't* doing this stuff or are struggling to do it consistently. Perhaps it's because these tasks *are* so basic that it's easy to treat them as something that just happens automatically and doesn't require us to pay attention or make choices. And because

---

* Am I going to start every part of this chapter by telling you how much I hate doing said thing? I'm not *not!!!*

these needs aren't exactly sexy or fun or *new,* we tell ourselves that they must not *really* matter that much.

But they do matter! I actually don't believe it's possible to show up for yourself or others long-term if you're not taking care of yourself in the most basic, low-level ways. So let's talk about how you can better show up for your body—taking care of it so that you feel solid and fortified, able to move through the world comfortably and handle all of the other shit you need to do, and the (fun, sexy!) stuff you *want* to do.

I'm not a fan of "so easy, everyone can do it!!!" language because it overlooks the lived realities of a *lot* of marginalized folks as well as people with disabilities and/or health conditions. I know there will be instances in the next few chapters where my suggestions (or the scientific evidence!) simply might not be possible or make sense for you. Even if you can't do anything about your circumstances right now (or for the foreseeable future or ever), it's still worth knowing what a baseline level of self-care *could* look like if and when you're ready. I hope this chapter will make it easier for you to recognize when you're deviating from that baseline and help you determine what (if any!) smaller things you can do to feel a little better until you *do* eventually have more resources. But I also recognize that some aspects of our lives are unchanging. Ultimately, I hope that you will be kind to yourself, and remember that not showing up for yourself isn't a personal failing; it's a natural consequence of the outrageous cultural expectations and deeply broken system we're all operating within.

Going to the Doctor

I didn't have a regular doctor for several years in my twenties and I know I'm not the only one. Moving around repeatedly and/or changing insurance carriers every year and/or not having insurance for long stretches of time is so common—which is a shame, because going to the doctor regularly is one of the most important things you can do to show up for your body.

If you don't have any providers at the moment but know that you *could* (because you have insurance, money for co-pays, transportation, etc.), it's absolutely worth investing the time and energy to find a doctor/dentist/ optometrist sooner rather than later. It's just so much easier to research in-network doctors and get an appointment when you are feeling well, and the fact that your need isn't particularly urgent means you can take the time to find someone whom you actually like and trust.

Once you have a doctor, you should *actually go to said doctor.* There are few things I find more frustrating than a friend with health insurance, an understanding boss, a good PTO policy, and all the privilege in the world who won't go to a doctor when they are sick or have some other ailment. And, look, I get it: Going to the doctor is a hassle! If I have a sore throat, cough, runny nose, intense headache, swollen sinuses, and am tired as hell, I'd *much* rather complain about it to anyone who will listen than pick up the phone (THE!! PHONE!!), make an appointment, drag my ass across town to my doctor's office, miss ninety minutes of work, drag my ass *back* across town to a pharmacy, and wait in line at said pharmacy, all to treat an infection that I (being not a doctor and all!!!) am *positive* will go away on its own in a few days.

But I will still do all of the above because when I refuse to go to the doctor—again, as an insured, able-bodied person who has paid sick days—I'm not just hurting myself; I'm hurting other people. At a really basic level, I'm potentially contagious. (Fun fact: A single sneeze can fill *an entire room!*) But "toughing out" a sinus infection (or *whatever*) makes me less present, less fun to be around, and less able to show up for others. And that's *before* it develops into full-on bronchitis. So if you are lucky enough to be able to go to a doctor, please actually go!

Find Yourself a Therapist

As my colleague Anna Borges has written,[13] instead of asking, "Do I need therapy?" a better question is "How might I *benefit* from therapy?" Therapy isn't just for people dealing with trauma or serious mental health issues; you can also talk to a therapist about dating woes, setting boundaries with friends, tension with your parents or siblings, job stress, low-level anxiety or sadness, and pretty much anything else that's a source of difficulty in your life. And just because you go to therapy once, you aren't locked into going forever; it can absolutely be a shorter-term deal.

If you care about being emotionally intelligent, feeling your best, and having good relationships, therapy can be a great addition to your showing-up routine.

Food

I enjoy food and I like eating, but I find the process of feeding myself three vaguely healthy meals a day rather tiring. Meal planning, grocery shopping, going to pick up a salad for lunch, chopping vegetables, cooking, doing dishes . . . it's all just *work,* and it's not work I personally enjoy. It takes TME, and I resent that. But there's no getting around the reality that we all do, in fact, have to eat! So finding a handful of moderately nutritious, somewhat cheap, and relatively easy-to-prepare things to eat can be a gamechanger, and is *absolutely* worth your while.

Like all things self-care, feeding yourself starts with knowing yourself. The definition of "healthy" or "unhealthy" eating is incredibly personal, and I'm not here to define it for you. But I do think it's worth defining for yourself, especially if nourishing yourself is a source of stress or something you feel like you're struggling with. If things are going well for you overall at the moment, it's a great time to think about this topic—because when you eventually hit a rough patch, feeding yourself can get a lot more difficult.

To begin, spend some time really considering your preferences and priorities with regard to food. Below is a list of questions to ask yourself—answer on a scale of a lot, a little, or IDGAF.

HOW MUCH DO I CARE ABOUT . . .

- keeping my grocery bill under a certain amount
- keeping my total food budget under a certain amount
- trying new recipes
- making sure I'm eating enough every day
- learning to cook
- using cooking/baking as a hobby
- food as function versus food as art
- packing my lunch (or breakfast, or dinner)
- eating in a way that minimizes environmental impact
- eating more/less of certain food groups (protein, fruits/veggies, etc.)
- eating certain kinds of food (fresh, local, organic, canned, frozen, shelf-stable, etc.)
- spending less than thirty minutes (or an hour) cooking each day
- spending less than a certain amount of time grocery shopping each week
- going to a particular grocery store
- eating in restaurants less and/or ordering takeout less often
- making X amount of homemade meals per week
- stocking up on healthy snacks so I don't get hangry
- meal prepping X amount of times per week
- basically just avoiding getting hangry at all costs.

Once you've finished this exercise, you can begin to define your approach to nourishing yourself. This step isn't about meal planning (though you can certainly do that later) or creating food rules; it's about establishing a lightweight philosophy that can guide your daily and weekly decisions so you feel less stress overall.

For example, if you decide that eating five servings of fresh vegetables is a super-high priority—higher than, say, saving money on groceries, or cooking meals for yourself—then you can buy your fourteen-dollar organic kale salad every day and not feel so guilty about it. If you want to eat lots of vegetables and prepare home cooked meals but neither is a high enough priority for you to invest a lot of time or money in (or you simply don't *have* the time/money), you might decide to stock up on microwave-in-the-bag frozen broccoli. The idea is to simply come up with an approach that you feel confident is the best plan for you right now (but that you can change whenever).

It's important that your approach to nourishing yourself reflects the *current* you—not some idealized version of you who goes to the farmers market every weekend, always leaves work at 5:30 (instead of 7:15), and/or is actually just Ina Garten. So put some thought into your present reality: how you *actually* feel before, during, and after time spent cooking/preparing/procuring food; the role food plays in your social life; how much motivation you have outside of work/school/other obligations; what other circumstances (life, health, etc.) play a role in what and how you eat; what's working well for you at the moment; and what your biggest barriers to nourishing yourself are (if there are any). Once you better understand your current circumstances you can take better care of the version of yourself you are right now.

Finally, remember that eating "healthy" can just be . . . eating. It doesn't require buying three new cookbooks, scouring Pinterest for hours, going paleo, or making something from scratch every single day. It can be as simple as eating rice and beans; scrambled eggs; tuna casserole; chicken nuggets with green beans; Greek yogurt with granola and (frozen/thawed) fruit; toast and tea; or a simple quesadilla.

Water

Even though I roll my eyes every time a celebrity claims that drinking lots of water is the secret to being (normatively) beautiful or having flawless skin (instead of admitting that the secret is a combination of good genes and lots of money), I can acknowledge that water is, you know, *good*. And I can also acknowledge that on the days when I don't drink enough water, I often get a headache and feel tired, hungry, and generally *blah*.

The reason I'm mentioning the wildly clichéd tip of drinking water is because it's a relatively easy way to show up for yourself. When you're busy or overwhelmed or sad, drinking water (or tea or seltzer) is likely the lowest-hanging fruit on your self-care tree. And I've found that doing one small, good thing for myself often motivates me to do other things, or at least makes me feel less bad about the ways in which I'm still neglecting my body. If you can't do anything else for yourself, at least try to drink some water.

Go Pee

My friends and I are divided on the topic of peeing. Some of them enjoy it; they see it as a moment of true privacy and relief. Meanwhile, I hate it; I think it's a waste of time and I feel that I have better things to do. (How many books would I have written by now if I didn't have to go pee?! A LOT.) But even though I think it's annoying, I know that peeing is an extremely necessary form of self-care; it's truly impossible to be present or relax or feel your best if all you can think about is your bladder.

Now, you might be thinking, *Why is she even including this? We all have to go pee at some point; it's not like it's optional.* And that's true! But I've noticed that a *lot* of people (and women in particular) tend to treat peeing as something that can be delayed or ignored in the interest of making other people more comfortable.

Last summer, I was on a flight from New York to San Francisco. It's a long flight, so it's not unusual to need to use the restroom while in the air. I was sitting in an aisle seat; next to me was an older man who spent most of the trip dozing off; a woman around my age was in the window seat. A few hours into the flight, she got my attention and whispered to me, "Do you think it's OK if I ask him to move so I can go to the bathroom?" I told her yes, so she nudged him, and he obliged, and we all moved on.

It turned out that the woman and I were headed to the same destination: a weekend summer camp for adult women, where asking for what you want in life was a central theme. During one group discussion, the woman from the plane told everyone that she had *nearly wet her pants* on her flight to camp because she didn't feel like she had the right to wake up her seatmate and ask him to move. It stuck in my mind because it's such a clear example of the small ways in which we are uncomfortable showing up for ourselves.

This story ended fine(ish????). But it doesn't always! Consider this story my friend Hana recently told me:

In college, I made ends meet by teaching Photoshop workshops to freshmen. I was teaching the basics on a regular schedule of two classes per night, Monday through Thursday. I usually had enough time in between sessions to run to the bathroom and grab a coffee, but sometimes an overeager photog-minor would stick around asking questions and I'd oblige. On one such night, I'd spent all of the time between classes by teaching someone about the tolerance setting on the magic wand tool, so I launched into my next class without taking a break.

About halfway through the lesson, it became apparent that my need to piss was approaching the red zone. In my short life, I'd never seen a teacher excuse themselves from an ongoing class to use the restroom, so in my mind it was a tire iron to the shins of my credibility as a Photoshop workshop teacher to do so. Instead, I decided that I would have to let a little off the top to hold me over until the end of the session. I figured that if I maintained an air of confident authority I could pull basically anything off. So mid-lesson—behind a podium, but before God and my students—I let 'er rip. Instead of simply releasing the bare minimum required to save my kidneys from exploding, the whole situation exited my body and onto the linoleum floor of the computer lab. I was wearing a skirt so I was able to avoid any obvious stains, and the puddle stayed concealed behind the particle-board podium. But yes: I openly pissed myself in class that day because it felt like "too much of a disruption" to stop for the two minutes it would have taken to run down the hall to the bathroom. Once the class ended, I bolted for paper towels and cleaned it up thoroughly, but I felt a secret pride that I'd managed to pull it off *and* pass as someone who hadn't pissed her skirt, shoes, and classroom. As if I'd risen to the call of duty and done what was needed. In reality, I pissed myself because the alternative was exhibiting what I saw as signs of weakness.

Guys? *Guys.*

I know the concept of ~listening to your body~ can feel sort of squishy at times, but peeing can be a *great* place to start. It's such a basic part of being comfortable and is a fairly uncontrollable human need that you really don't need to apologize for or feel embarrassed about. "I don't have to go *that* badly; I can wait until I get home/get to the next destination" is not an ideal way to live your life. My friend group now abides by the rule "pee at the function." Peeing at the function requires you to check in with your body and then actually listen to what it's telling you. So go pee! (Even if you just went!!)

Sleep

I have occasionally been described as "horny for a good night's sleep," which . . . accurate. I don't *love* sleeping, but I *respect* it. Getting enough quality sleep is the foundation of my physical and mental health; when I'm running low on sleep, it's so much harder for me to cook and eat healthy foods, be physically active, make good decisions, and be a good friend/coworker/human.

Because sleep is so important to me, I protect my sleep schedule fiercely. I'm willing to miss out on other fun activities to get enough sleep. I don't watch a lot of TV, and there's a good chance I will turn down your invitation to get drinks on a weeknight. I know this doesn't exactly make me sound *cool.* But I don't really care—I'd much rather be energetic, relaxed, kind, and healthy than cool!

Sleep also plays a *huge* role in our ability to show up for other people. Sleep scientist Matthew Walker writes in *Why We Sleep* that REM sleep refreshes our brain's emotional circuits and makes it possible to understand and respond to the socioemotional signals that are near constant wherever humans are present. According to Walker, our sleep habits are a core part of the way we navigate social situations and of our overall emotional IQ. He offers two rules of thumb for assessing whether you are getting enough quality sleep:

1. After you wake up in the morning, could you fall back to sleep at 10:00 or 11:00 AM? If so, you are likely not getting enough sleep (or not sleeping very well).

2. Can you function optimally without caffeine before noon? If not, then you are, in Walker's words, "likely self-medicating your state of chronic sleep deprivation." (. . . Woof.)

If you know you're not getting enough sleep or sleeping particularly well, there are plenty of things you can do: watch your caffeine intake, drink less alcohol (especially in the evening), make sure you give yourself two to three hours between exercising and bedtime, lock your phone in a box at sundown every night, and so on. In my experience, the most important thing is to *decide* that sleep matters to you. It's really hard to, say, get up early on weekends, leave a party where your crush is hanging out, or consistently put down your phone and pick up your journal if you don't *really* think it's important that you do. And sleep might not be more important than those things are to you! The point is to figure out how much sleep matters to you—and to understand where that value intersects with the bigger issues that can interfere with sleep (like anxiety, medications, unchanging work/ school schedules, being a night owl)—and then build a routine and a plan from there. It wasn't until I admitted to myself that I was sacrificing something undeniably important to my health and well-being to do a bunch of things that I didn't *really* value that I was able to implement the tips above.

Bathing

I can't remember the last time I took a shower without complaining about the fact that I had to take a shower. I don't really like water or being wet, and I just find showers . . . boring. If you, like me, think showers can go kick rocks, I have some good news for you: You probably don't need to shower quite as much as you think you do! Experts agree that Americans over-bathe.[14] Frequent showering may actually be doing more harm than good, as it can wash away the good bacteria that naturally exist on our skin, dry out and irritate skin, and introduce small cracks that put us at a higher risk of infection. So if you're a shower hater, you can *probably* skip the daily shower and take one every two or three days—which is something! (And if showering every two or three days is still kind of a struggle, I have some tips in Chapter 5, page 120, that might help.)

BE SAFE, PLEASE

I love safety and I will *not* apologize for it. So many "silly" and preventable accidents can seriously derail your life (or just cost you a *lot* of TME), and showing up for your body means doing the basics to protect it. Here are some small things you should be doing to stay injury-free.

Don't text/read while driving.
Please, I'm begging you.

Don't even think about falling asleep or leaving your home with a candle burning.
Gah, I'm getting angry just thinking about this!!!!

Wear your seat belt.
Literally all the time. *Including when you're in taxis or ride-hails.* (The number of people who don't buckle up when they get into a cab never fails to shock me!) The fact that you're just making a short trip in a residential area or in slow city traffic isn't an excuse; according to the US Department

of Transportation, "Seemingly routine trips can be deceptively dangerous. Most fatal crashes happen within 25 miles from home and at speeds of less than 40 mph." So yeah, I'm definitely that person who won't get into a car if there aren't enough seats/seat belts for everyone.

Wear a helmet when you do *any* of the following:

- ride a bike, motorcycle, snowmobile, scooter, or an ATV
- play a contact sport (hockey, football, etc.)
- roller skate, Rollerblade, or skateboard
- bat, run bases, or play the position of catcher in baseball or softball (when I see people near bats/balls without helmets on, my blood pressure *spikes*)
- ride a horse
- ski or snowboard.

I don't care if you think it looks dumb! Safety is no joke!!!

Exercise

Surprise: I don't hate exercising! (I *do* hate that it necessitates more frequent showering.) Finding a way to move your body that you enjoy—or can simply *tolerate*—enough to do regularly can be a big aspect of showing up for yourself. According to the Mayo Clinic, 150 minutes (two and a half hours) of moderate exercise a week can help you feel less stressed, less depressed, and less anxious; it can help you sleep better, make you feel better, improve your cognitive function, and lower your risk of death from all causes. That said, exercising can be a big source of shame, anxiety, pain, and stress, or it may simply be low on your list of priorities. Opting *out* of exercise might actually be how you need to show up for yourself, and that's OK, too. Ultimately, your relationship with exercise and your specific exercise routine (or lack thereof) is yours to define, based on your priorities, values, health history, abilities, current circumstances, and lived reality.

I lost a lot of TME in the war against my body over the years, and I'll never get it back. The only thing I can do about it is forgive myself and try to do better going forward. When it comes to exercise and showing up, here are some of the lessons I wish I'd learned sooner.

1. Exercise doesn't necessarily have to be *fun* from start to finish—some days, working out is *work*—but it shouldn't feel *punishing* either. And the days it feels realllly sucky should be few and far between.

2. "It shouldn't feel punishing" extends to the emotional aspect. Some gyms are fairly hostile places and don't welcome diversity of body size, race, gender presentation, or ability levels. If you feel uncomfortable, unsafe, or just generally shitty at your gym, in a particular class, or with a specific instructor, it's going to be hard to do it regularly. (And even if you do manage to, it's coming at a significant cost to your overall well-being.) It's OK to walk out of a class before it's over; to quit a gym; to stop trying to make yourself like running; and to refuse to entertain the idea of doing CrossFit.

3. Your form of exercise (or exercise in general) doesn't have to be your whole identity—and, in fact, probably shouldn't be. Yes, you should find a way to move your body that is sustainable, but the fact is, our lives, schedules, and interests change; our knees get bad and injuries and pregnancies and surgeries happen; and there will likely come a day when you can't do a particular activity anymore (or simply have to take a break from it). So paradoxically, being open to the idea of changing course when necessary actually makes it *easier* to stick with exercise in *general* throughout your life.

4. Routines and goals are great . . . until they aren't. There have been many times in my life when working out twice a week would have made me feel a little bit better overall, but because I couldn't work out five times that week, or because I knew I had a trip or a busy period coming up (meaning I wouldn't be able to exercise consistently all month) I simply didn't bother at all. I regret this approach! Now I try to plan less and live more in the present. I ask

myself, *What can I do* this *week* (or *just* today) *that'll make me feel better, regardless of what I did last week and what I'll do next week?* And what if that's all I need to worry about for now?

5. If you want to exercise to be physically healthier, Anne Poirier, a strength training and eating disorder specialist, suggests starting with the *why*—that is, what *specifically* do you want your body to be able to *do* that could be achieved through exercise or movement? For example, do you want to be able to walk longer distances without getting tired so you can visit a particular city? Or so you can feel better while on your feet all day at work? Do you want to be more flexible so you can get down on the floor and play with your kids more easily? So you can experiment with different sex positions? Defining your *why* can make it easier to stay motivated, and to work out in a way that feels positive and affirming.

6. Be creative, curious, and willing to change your idea of what "counts" as exercise. Years of reading women's magazines and consuming popular media led me to me believe that exercise only "counted" if it looked and felt a certain way—a way that was absolutely rooted in how exercise would make me *look*. Now I know—not just intellectually, but in my soul—that the amount of exercise necessary for me to attain basic health benefits is not nearly as hard or as time-consuming or as *sweaty* as I convinced myself it was. It can be difficult to open yourself up to the possibility of other forms of exercise that make you *feel good*, that you can *love* and *enjoy*, even if they don't raise your heart rate to a certain level or change your appearance in any way. But discovering those types of exercise can be truly transformative.

These days, I know I'm genuinely showing up for myself through exercise if said exercise is ultimately creating *more* space—not less—for all of the other good things in life I want to experience.

The 2 x 2 x 2 Approach

Anne Poirier recommends a 2 x 2 x 2 approach to movement and exercise to her clients. Here's how it works.

Two days of being mobile.
Twice a week, spend some time moving through the world, in whatever form of mobility is your default. Poirier recommends walking/being mobile because it "promotes independence," a sentiment I love. Note: There's no set duration for this–you can do it for ten minutes, or stop to rest five times throughout.

Two days of play.
Twice a week, do something you *like* to do, that brings you joy and pleasure. It could be walking around a museum or park, playing tag, dancing, or splashing around in the pool. Again, it's not timed and there are no real rules.

Two days a week of functional movement.
Twice a week, do something related to that reason for exercising you established earlier. So if your goal is to be more flexible so you can get down on the floor and play with your kids, your functional movement might be stretching or doing yoga. If you want to be able to be on your feet all day without getting tired, maybe this is when you power walk.

The 2 x 2 x 2 approach invites you to move *most* days, but that movement is less about how you look, or outdated "rules" about what exercise should look like, and more about living a more comfortable, more joyful life.

I Endorse: Body Neutrality

I am happy to see that after a decade messaging around loving your body—messaging that is quite often delivered by brands and/or conventionally attractive women—the term "body neutrality" is on the rise. Because here's the thing: Loving your body is a big ask, particularly if your body doesn't conform to established standards, or if your body has betrayed you in some way. Body positivity sounds great in theory—but given how hostile society can be to people who look or are different, it's understandable to feel insecure, and to wish your body were different.

Anne Poirier says that body image is a spectrum, and that body neutrality can be seen as a resting place within all the noise—the noise of self-hatred, and the noise of "you need to love yourself." She says it can be particularly helpful if the idea of loving your body is so far from where you currently are that you can't really envision ever reaching that point.

Body neutrality invites you to focus on what you can do with your body instead of what it looks like. (And if your body can't do as much as you'd like it to, or as much as it once did, Poirier suggests celebrating what it can do while also allowing yourself to grieve what it cannot.) If you're trying to reach body neutrality, here are some practical exercises that Poirier recommends.

1. Choose an empowerment phrase that "feels OK" (not perfect! just . . . OK!) and that you can repeat to yourself regularly. Some of her suggestions:

   "My body does things for me."

   "My body deserves respect."

   "My body deserves to be taken care of."

   "I'm doing the best I can."

   "I accept myself as I am right now."

   "This is me."

2. When a negative thought about your body pops into your head, reply with, "Thanks for sharing" or "That's not helpful for me right now." You don't have to talk yourself out of the negative thought; the goal is simply to *notice* it.

3. Write a letter to your body or to a specific body part. It doesn't have to be a love letter, either—you're allowed to be critical here. But once you've done that, it's time to write a letter *to* yourself *from* your body (or from that same body part). That's right—you have to ask your body for comment!!! Your body's rebuttal might contain sentiments like "I protected your child for nine months" or "I am strong; I carried you around Paris for a week" or "I let you have orgasms even after you tried to drown me in tequila too many times to count."

4. Close your eyes and think about the people you really like, and list what you like about them. Is their body on the list? Probably not, right? Then think about a few people who really like you, and what they like about you. Do they just like you for your body? Again, probably not, right?

The goal with this exercise is to develop a better relationship with yourself. Noticing, acknowledging, and maybe even befriending your body *as it is* is one of the best things you can do to show up for yourself.

Track Your Habits

If you're trying to take better care of yourself, it's worth documenting what you're doing and how you're feeling. There are many different ways to do this, but my go-to is a monthly habit tracker in my journal. I'm partial to a graph format with the dates written on one axis and the items you're tracking on the other. You can create something like this in your own journal or through a good old-fashioned spreadsheet.

But there's no singular "right" way to track your habits! You could just as easily use an app or a digital or paper calendar. And if the monthly view seems overwhelming, time-consuming, or like it might stress you out more, try tracking at the daily or weekly level instead.

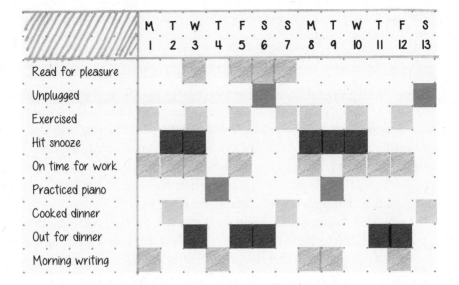

Regardless of your setup, here are the big categories to think about when creating a habit tracker.[15]

What you're experiencing physically.
This might include things like migraines, headaches, nausea, bloating, sleepiness, insomnia, hunger/appetite, periods, hangovers, crying, and breakouts.

How you're feeling emotionally.
Some moods you could make space for: tired, irritable, sad, depressed, angry, sensitive, distracted, happy, content. You may also want to note any days where you experienced *conflict* (with, say, a housemate, partner, or family member).

Daily behaviors that affect how you feel physically and emotionally.
This might include medications, hours of sleep, hours napping, servings of alcohol, servings of caffeine, TV/streaming services, minutes of exercise (and/or particular types of exercise), showering, teeth brushing, chores

(like making the bed), phone use (or certain app usage), time spent in nature, socializing, religious activities, and conversations with difficult people.

As my colleague Anna Borges has reported, checking boxes when you do something healthy for yourself can be motivating, but the purpose of tracking your habits isn't really to achieve your goals . . . it's to be able to see *patterns*. When everything is in a single place, you can start to make connections between, say, drinking alcohol and feeling sad, or getting migraines and getting your period. A tracker also helps you notice *frequency*. It's remarkably easy to tell yourself something isn't a "serious" problem when you don't have the data in front of you; documenting your habits gives you a fuller, more accurate picture of yourself and your life.

If you do decide to attach some goals to these habits, make sure they are realistic and attainable. Otherwise, you might find yourself getting discouraged if you "mess up" early on in the month. The tracker should be less about achievement and more about collecting information. Think of it as a tool that can teach you something about yourself and help you take better care of yourself.

Six Things That Are Definitely Self-Care

1. Eating lunch alone at work
2. Laughing at your own jokes
3. Masturbating
4. Flossing
5. Blocking and reporting trolls
6. Sitting on your bed for an hour in your towel, doing nothing*

* Unless doing this means you're running late for a function or event and thus will feel extremely stressed once you get up and start getting ready

I Regret to Inform You: This Shit Works

I have been writing for a decade about how to live your best life—and reading about it for even longer—so I'm extremely familiar with the suggestions that show up in every single article and self-help book and Reddit thread, regardless of what your specific problem is. Whether you're dealing with a breakup or anxiety or unemployment or bad body image or burnout, the same solutions show up again and again: Exercise. Make sure you're getting enough sleep. Don't drink too much. Meditate. Practice gratitude. Take a vacation. Get off social media. Volunteer. Take your meds. Go to therapy.

If you're the one in need of a solution, this advice can feel incredibly disappointing. It's so frustrating to be told that you just need to start working out when your life is in goddamn shambles. Like, *Don't you think I've thought of that????*

But here's what I've noticed again and again, in both myself and my friends: Just because we've thought of it doesn't mean we've actually fully *considered* it, or that we've made a good-faith attempt to *do* it. And so often, the reason we aren't trying it is because the advice feels simple. Yes, we want to feel better, but we also like thinking of ourselves as complicated creatures whose unique problems couldn't possibly be solved by something as obvious as going to the gym or making a gratitude list every night. We want to believe that our problems are too big for the scientifically backed, tried-and-true, "basic" solutions to fix. Instead of giving the clichéd advice an honest try, we brush past it and seek out alternative options—options that are typically more complex, more expensive, and less tested, but that *do* have the benefit of being new and fun and exciting. Or, worse, we'll do nothing. We'll decide we know more than the experts or the people who have experienced this same thing already, and conclude that we are simply unfixable.

Is that self-sabotaging? Sure. But I think it comes from a place of wanting to protect our tender hearts and egos. It can feel *more* vulnerable to say, "I feel broken but I am fixable" than it does to say, "I'm so broken, I'm simply beyond repair." The former asks something of us and can make us feel small and afraid, while the latter validates our struggle and feels kind of righteous. And when things aren't going our way, that righteousness feels *good*.

To be clear, I don't believe every problem can be solved by working out or drinking more water, nor do I think serious problems or health issues should be met with the ol' "Have you tried essential oils?" sales pitch. But I do think if you are prone to magical thinking with regard to feeling better—and you tend to avoid taking care of your body as a result—it really is worth giving the self-care practices in this chapter a shot. Of course this shit doesn't work all the time, in every situation, for every person. It doesn't even always work for me! But in general, *this shit works.*

Chapter 4
Showing Up for Yourself
Every Damn Day

Showing up for yourself takes place in your *habits*—the behaviors you repeat, often without having to really think about them. But I believe that we *should* be thinking about them. Because the things we do every day—the clothes we wear, the spaces we inhabit, the objects that surround us, the hobbies and activities we partake in—are more than just background scenery. They're . . . it.

Our everyday habits and routines define how we spend the majority of our TME. When they feel right, life feels a tiny bit better. When they are a source of frustration or discomfort or shame, life feels so much harder. And that is true regardless of what is happening with the so-called "big" stuff like your job, relationships, health, finances, and the culture around you. In this chapter, we'll talk about how to notice the way you move through certain spaces every day, and to approach your habits and routines in a thoughtful, considered, *intentional* way—because ultimately, these seemingly small choices, behaviors, and settings are what make up a day, a year, a life.

The Great Indoors

After I moved from Houston to Brooklyn in 2014, my new apartment was quite empty. I barely had any stuff, or any money to buy stuff. (Moving across the country is not cheap.) There wasn't much I could do about this; I accepted that my apartment would simply have to exist in that frustrating post-move transitional state for the foreseeable future. After a few dark and anxiety-filled nights alone in the apartment, I realized I didn't need money to turn my apartment into a *home*. I couldn't buy furniture, but I *could* tape a large empty shipping box shut, set a small lamp on it, and call said box a nightstand. So that is what I did.

Even though most of my belongings remained in storage in Houston, there was something about moving my lamp from the floor next to my bed to a higher surface that made me feel like I was in a home. *My* home. It wasn't a "real" nightstand, but it was a nightstand nonetheless—and one I had chosen solely because I knew it would make me feel a little better. It cost me nothing, but it helped so much, making the overwhelming and terrifying experience of a cross-country move (and a brand-new job) a little less stressful. When I think of what it means to show up for yourself in your home, I think of that cardboard nightstand.

If you don't really care about decor or art or having nice furniture, that's OK! But your domain is your domain! It's the place you can be your truest self: walk around without pants on, listen to your favorite music as loudly as you want, examine every weird spot that appears on your body, talk to your pet like they are a human being. If you don't feel good at home, it's so much harder to feel good out in the world.

Throughout this chapter, I'll use the term "home" and "your place" to refer to the physical unit you call home on a daily basis—whether that's a single room, an apartment you rent, or an entire house. And when I say "space," I'm referring to zones within your home (like your kitchen table, or your bed and nightstand) and other spots where you spend a lot of time—so your desk or office at work, your car, your yard, wherever.

And when I use the word *cozy* here (and throughout the book), I mean "giving a feeling of comfort, relaxation, wholesomeness, pleasure, and intimacy." It's less about things that are physically warm (like blankets and tea), and more about things that feel special, pleasing, gentle, and wholesome, and that make you feel more complete and content.

Your Stuff

A lot of people mock the idea that everything we own should spark joy—the central idea in Marie Kondo's mega bestseller *The Life-Changing Magic of Tidying Up*—but I've actually found it incredibly helpful. It's so simple, but it has been something of a North Star since I read the book, helping me to save money and time and to be a less wasteful person in general. As Marie Kondo's star has risen, I've heard a lot of, "BUT MY TRASH CAN DOESN'T SPARK JOY SO I GUESS I SHOULD JUST GET RID OF IT AND THROW MY GARBAGE ON THE GROUND, HUH????" and I'm just like, *Anyone who thinks a trash can can't spark joy has clearly never owned one they hate.*[16]

You don't have to love your trash can, but I hope you can agree that the things we buy and surround ourselves with *matter*. It's not frivolous to love a particular towel or mug, have extremely strong feelings about light bulbs, or read reviews of laundry baskets before you buy one. (It's also fine to think all coffee makers are created equal or to source your furniture from garage sales.) Like the foods we eat and the people we spend time with, our belongings play a big role in how we feel, so it's worth figuring out what items will make your place feel like *your place*. (And yes, it's worth doing this even if you don't have the resources to buy said items, or to overhaul your entire home right now.) As a beautiful essay on the inspirational website The School of Life puts it:

> The quest to build a home is connected up with a need to stabilize and organize our complex selves. It's not enough to know who we are in our own minds. We need something more tangible, material and sensuous to pin down the diverse and intermittent aspects of our identities. We need to rely on a certain kinds of cutlery, bookshelves, laundry, cupboards, and armchairs to align us with who we are and seek to be. We are not vaunting ourselves; we're trying to gather our identities in one receptacle, preserving ourselves from erosion and dispersal. Home means the place where our soul feels that it has found its proper physical container, where, every day, the objects we live amongst quietly remind us of our most authentic commitments and loves.[17]

To get started, take a little tour of your place! Here are some questions to consider as you go.

What items or spaces make you feel extremely cozy?

These can be *extremely* small—a wall hook, a dish, a particular color. What specifically do you love about them? Pay attention to how different objects feel to the touch; to the lighting (try this during the day and then again after dark); to how things smell; and to what sounds you hear. Note: There might not be that many things that you feel excited about right now, and that's fine!

What items or spaces make you feel angry, sad, embarrassed, or annoyed *or* make your life demonstrably more difficult?

These are the things that you curse on a regular basis, that you're always apologizing for when people come over, or that make your life harder in some way. And the "make your life difficult" question is an important one—if you struggle to fall asleep at night because your window doesn't have shades, that's a problem. Also take note of which of these things bother you because they are broken and need to be fixed, and what, if anything, is just obsolete and could be tossed. Pay close attention to anything that causes you legitimate *shame* or stirs up bad feelings.

Which (if any) of your observations—good or bad—are related to cleanliness or chores?

For example, you might feel good about your nicely made bed or uncluttered kitchen table or feel anxious about the pile of clean laundry that needs to be put away. Speaking of chores, resist the urge to start fixing or tidying as you take your tour! I get the impulse, I do—but if you follow that urge, in a few hours you'll find that your bed is covered with every single item that was once in your closet, and you are no closer to understanding what you like about your home.

Next, think about other homes you've spent time in (e.g., your friends' homes, your family members' homes, and the home you grew up in).

What are the best, coziest things about those homes? Again, be super specific; is it the colors that you love? The windows, the lighting, the floors, the textiles, the plants, the fact that there's always a candle burning? Also think about anything that makes you feel bad or stressed out in those places.

How do you feel about your home's location and style?

You might not be able to afford the exact neighborhood or type of home you want to live in, but thinking through your preferences can still tell you a lot about yourself and help you make more informed choices going forward. How important is it that you live in a bustling neighborhood? What about proximity to a park? Which do you value more—an older building with charming molding or modern amenities like in-unit laundry? Think about what's most important to your overall well-being.

Once you're done with this exercise, you should have a better understanding of what things—big and small—actually matter to you and have an impact on how you feel on a daily basis with regard to your space. From here, the task isn't to go out and buy a bunch of new furniture, or to give up entirely because you can't gut your house right now. It's about understanding what you need and want in *general* so that you can figure out what you can do in the near future and down the line. The goal is to build a home you love and feel less guilty about the things you can't or don't want to attend to right now.

As a next step, make a list of everything you'd like to change or add to make your home feel cozier, and note whether said change will take time, money, energy, or some combination. Then rank the tasks by which ones matter most to you, taking into account how much TME you care to spend right now.

So, your list might look something like this . . .

Very important/tackle ASAP

Install towel rack in bathroom (money, time, energy)
Call landlord to have broken door handle fixed (energy)
Add cozy lighting to bedroom
    Hang the string lights I bought two months ago (time, energy)
    Find and buy a lamp I like (time, energy, money)

Kind of important

Deal with mail pile of shame (time, energy)
Deal with closet of shame (time, energy)
Hang stuff on the walls
    Print photos (time, money, energy)
    Buy picture frames (time, money, energy)
    Hang up said picture frames (time, energy)

Someday

Buy new rug for bedroom (money)
Patch hole in living room wall (time, energy, money)
Buy good knives (money)

And remember: It's OK if your "very important/tackle ASAP" list is short. Maybe all you can do for right now is open the windows to get some fresh air flowing, straighten that pile of laundry so it's not falling over, stick up a Command hook for your keys, and add a better trash can to your wish list. Maybe all you can do for right now is realize that you care a lot about nice lighting and not tripping over power cords, so you'll turn an empty cardboard box into a nightstand until you can afford to buy a real one. Maybe you'll be surprised by how much these small changes can help.

Basically: If you have the means to get a nicer couch and that would make you happier, then do that. If that's a non-starter, maybe just take all of the shit off your couch?

Chores

Speaking of taking the shit off your couch . . . let's talk about chores!

I have a love-hate relationship with chores. I don't love doing them—they are *chores* after all—but I love having *done* them. And even though there are some chores I absolutely hate (read: all the water chores), I still consider chores a crucial part of my showing-up routine.

When my space is tended to, I feel less stressed, more comfortable, more focused, and better rested. Doing chores can also be a form of self-care in a more literal sense—because a clean, tidy home is going to be safer and healthier than one that is not.

The opposite is also true: When my home *isn't* clean and tidy (by my own standards), I feel far less equipped to handle life's daily stressors and to show up for the people I care about. And I know I'm not the only person who feels this way. Doing chores regularly can be a good way to remove unnecessary stress from your life and make your home a cozier, more pleasant place to be. (By the way, if chores are a struggle for you because of bigger issues, feel free to skip or skim this section for now. You might find that the tips in Chapter 5 are more your speed.)

To figure out what your version of a "clean home" and your ideal chore routine look like, revisit some of the observations you noted during your walkthrough in the previous section. Here are some additional questions to consider.

Do you care more about tidiness or cleanliness?

Two very different things! To care about tidiness is to care about *neatness*—so: Items are stored in their proper place and arranged in an orderly manner, and clutter is at a minimum. To care about cleanliness is to care about *filth*—it's wanting a space that is free of dirt, stains, spills, hair, dust, and germs. It's surprisingly easy to care a *lot* about one while barely noticing the other. Think about which one matters most to you, or if they matter equally. (And the answer to this question might be "neither" . . . in that case, try to determine which one is *more* important to you.)

What messy, cluttered, or dirty areas in your home make you feel bad or make life more difficult? What neat, clean, tidy areas in your home make you feel good or make life easier?

Put some thought into what *specifically* makes you low-key mad every single day, what slows you down when you're getting ready and getting out the door, what gets in the way of cooking or preparing food, what causes tension with housemates, and what makes it harder to engage in or enjoy the other things you care about (e.g., hobbies, entertaining, working from home, sleeping). And also think about the things that make you *demonstrably* happier whenever they are taken care of. All this can help you determine which chores specifically feel valuable and pressing to you.

How do you feel physically during and after chores?

Doing chores can be a literal pain. If you have arthritis, asthma, bad knees, or a disability, you might find it difficult to do a lot (or all!) of the chores you'd like to do. In some instances, you may be able to figure out tenable solutions. But you also may not be able to. And that's fine! The point of this exercise is to figure out what makes sense in *your* life.

How do you feel emotionally before and after you do chores?

Rate how you feel about each chore on a scale of 1 to 10 (with 1 being "I will put this off for as long as humanly possible" and 10 being "I love this, I could do it every day!!!"). Do you dread chores more on a certain day of the week (like, say, when coupled with your Sunday Scaries)? Do you hate doing chores before you have people over because you don't want to be rushed—or do you live for the thrill of it? Then think about how you feel after doing different chores. Do you feel proud and accomplished or annoyed that you spent any time on it at all?

How are you feeling in general about the state of your home and your chores routine?

How much time are you spending on chores? How often are you doing them? Does it feel worth it? What's working? What's not? What circumstances and choices have led to the current situation? Are any of those things you can change? And do you actually *want* to change them? And be honest with yourself about that last part. Just because you *could* do chores more often (because there are *technically* enough hours in the week), and think you probably *should* do chores more often (because you feel a lot of guilt about it) doesn't mean you are actually *going* to—because it might mean giving up something else that's a higher priority to you, and you don't actually want to do that.

From here, try to come up with an approach to doing chores that matches your life, and that you feel good about—because once you have an established baseline of what will make you feel good, *why* it makes you feel good, and the best way to go about doing it, you can spend less time beating yourself up over all the things you "should" be doing, and more time getting the damn thing over with and moving on. It might be as simple as figuring out a few smaller tasks that you can do every day (like putting the dishes into the dishwasher immediately after eating, or making your bed right when you get up). Maybe it's doing chores on a different day. (Doing my chores on Friday nights was a game-changer for me.) It could involve researching vacuums and saving up for a good one that you love. Or it might be establishing a robust chore schedule. It's really your call!

And similar to your approach to nourishing yourself (and . . . everything else in this book), your approach to chores should reflect the life you *currently* live. There's truly no benefit to telling yourself you'll clean a little bit every evening if you know you won't; you'll simply feel guilty every evening when you don't do the thing. It's better to be honest with yourself and come up with a plan you can actually achieve. If all you're doing is building a shiny new tool that you'll then use to beat yourself up, it doesn't count as showing up for yourself.

Making Your Space Cozier

Here are some tips that offer the most bang for your buck.

Decor

- Incorporate more colors and patterns that you really like, even in small ways.

- Prominently display the objects that bring you joy, even if they would normally be hidden away (e.g., keeping your beautiful mug on your desk or folding three complementary sweaters nicely and making an ombré stack on your bedroom chair).

- Hang art on the walls; even taping up some postcards or snapshots with washi tape can go a long way.

- Add small lamps and/or string lights, and use those instead of overhead lights.

- Invest in bedding (e.g. great pillows, a duvet you love, a pretty quilt, cozy sheets), which is especially impactful if your bed is very visible in your space or you spend a lot of time in your bed.

- Add more soft things–think: a cozy throw blanket, a fluffy bath towel, or a plush rug.

- Bring in a few plants and/or flowers.

Mood

- Play music.

- Light candles.

- Open the windows.

- Turn off overhead lights.

- Close the blinds/curtains in the evening.

Chores

- Make your bed.

- Tidy your clutter. Sometimes your stuff just has no place to go, but tidying it a bit will help.

- Declutter spots that are super visible or where you spend a lot of time.

- Clean your kitchen sink . . . and then dry it. (The drying makes the entire room look so much cleaner! It's truly wild.)

The Great Outdoors

I have always been what one might call an "indoor girl" and thought of showing up for myself as something best done at home. But that started to change after I read *The Nature Fix* by Florence Williams, which outlines the scientifically backed ways in which nature—trees, water, plants, birdsong, fresh air, an absence of human-made sounds—makes us feel better. I decided to put some of Williams's tips into practice and was kind of embarrassed by how much better I felt, pretty much immediately. It wasn't even that hard! I just had to, like, make a point to look at flowers and trees instead of cars and garbage when I walked around the city. But it turns out, I wasn't alone in my belief that I was too good for nature; Williams says that people routinely underestimate how much better nature will make them feel and blow it off as a result.[18]

Nature is now a *big* part of my showing-up routine; I simply can't deny that it turns me into a much better version of myself. As Williams says, "There are times when we could all be a little less reactive, a little more empathetic, more focused and more grounded. That's where a nature dose can help." Uhhhh, yes! These days, you can regularly find me exclaiming, "Who is she?!" upon seeing a particularly majestic tree (and then whipping out my copy of *National Geographic Field Guide to the Trees of North America* to find out); taking an afternoon break in a park; pointing out fractals in the wild; and walking to the river just in time for sunset.

I was especially inspired by Williams's description of a nature pyramid, which she credits to Tim Beatley, who runs the Biophilic Cities project at the University of Virginia. It's similar to the classic food pyramid and is a handy way to think about how much nature we all need.

THE NATURE PYRAMID

YEARLY — Big outdoor trip

MONTHLY — Spend 1 to 2 days in nature

WEEKLY — Go to a park or waterway

DAILY — Interact with nature

- Thirty minutes a day: lightweight interactions with or observations of nature; think: trees, plants, natural light, fresh air, sunrise and sunset, the moon and stars, and animals
- An hour a week: trips to parks and waterways, "places where the sounds and hassles of the city recede"
- One or two days a month: an excursion to a forest or other immersive natural area
- A few times a year: big multi-day doses of wilderness; think: camping trips, a stay in a national park

If you're not sure where to begin, here are some tips that helped me start using nature as a way to relax and recharge.

Start with your own backyard.
I used to think "nature" was something that happened *elsewhere*—in the woods, at a lake—but it's worth taking a look around the places you spend the most time and seeing if that's actually true. Even though I don't have my own yard in NYC, I do have stunning trees on my block (and I can now tell

you what kind they are!!!), parks within walking distance, and an array of flora and fauna crossing my path every single day.

Make nature come to you.
Bird feeders, bee hotels, and butterfly gardens are great ways to do this. And don't overlook the power of desk plants, aromatherapy, or pumping nature sounds through your headphones.

Learn more about nature.
The more I know about nature, the easier it is for me to observe and appreciate it. Try reading science and outdoor blogs and listening to science podcasts. Or look to Mary Oliver, patron saint of nature poetry. Her poems are so soothing and relaxing; I especially love reading them while outside.

Go to the water.
Even though I don't much care for getting *in* the water, being near water makes me feel better. Spending a day at the beach makes me feel like a whole new person, and simply sitting or walking next to one of NYC's rivers fills me with awe and sends my brain into the "calm alert" zone that feels so damn good.

Getting Dressed

A lot of people think of getting dressed as something we do for other people, but I put it firmly in the "showing up for myself" category. And showing up isn't about dressing up. Sure, it could mean putting on a sequined dress, but it might also mean putting on cozy sweatpants—because one of those feels truer to your real identity and brings you joy, and one of them makes you feel twitchy. Consider a floral dress, a tube of red lipstick, a pair of sneakers, or a trip to the hairdresser; any of these can feel luxurious, beautiful, special, oppressive, uncomfortable, or like an act of survival . . . it all depends on who you are.

When I think about what it means to show up for myself through my clothes (and my hair, makeup, and accessories), I think about *comfort*. Not just physical comfort (though my wardrobe is basically built around my desire to wear flat shoes the majority of the time), but comfort in the sense of feeling confident and at ease with my appearance and in how I move through the world. Wearing clothes you feel truly comfortable in can be difficult, particularly if you have a body that our culture has decided to police more, or if your vision of yourself is at odds with what society has deemed acceptable. But even if you can't wear what you want all the time, it's still worth knowing what genuinely comfortable clothing looks like to you.

We've all had those days where we've worn something we don't *quite* feel at home in. It's that item you didn't *really* love, but bought anyway—because it was on sale, or because it represented the person you hoped to be, or because you needed some new clothes and didn't hate it—and now feel like you have to wear it. Maybe it doesn't *quite* fit right, or has a feature (peplum, a floppy bow) that you dislike. Or you like it as a standalone piece but have no idea what to wear with it, and every time you try to make an outfit out of it, you regret what you come up with. Whenever you resign yourself to wearing it, you think maybe this time will be different. But it's never different!!! Each time you wear it, you spend your day tugging at it, anxiously checking your reflection to see if you look as bad as you feel.

Wearing clothes you don't feel good in is a *huge* distraction. It can be hard enough to get through a day even when you *do* like your outfit! And if you're too hot, too cold, too exposed, or wearing something that's itchy or tight or ill-fitting or just not *you,* it's basically impossible to feel at ease.

So if you're trying to do a better job of showing up for yourself, spend some time thinking about the role your wardrobe plays in how you're feeling on a given day. Here are some questions you might think about.

- How much do you enjoy shopping?
- How much do you enjoy dressing yourself? Do you see it as a creative outlet/something you enjoy? Neutral? Something you dread?
- What items or outfits would you wear every single day if you could?
- What items do you dread putting on?
- What items make you think, "Yay, I get to wear *that* again!"?

- What colors, patterns, and fabrics make you feel cozy inside? Which ones stress you out?

- What seasons or types of weather seem to really agree with you, fashion-wise? Which ones drain the life out of you?

- Do your clothes fit you? (Literally: are they too small, too big, too long, too short?)

- What is the relationship between your clothes and your body? Are you drawn to clothes that hide or "fix" your body in some way? Are you following certain "rules" for people with your body type or who are your age? How is that affecting your wardrobe and how do you feel about it?

- Does your current wardrobe reflect your true style? Why or why not?

- What was the last time your outfit or an article of clothing ruined an otherwise good day (or event)? What were you wearing? What was the problem?

- How often are you willing/able to do laundry?

- Do you have any personal values that influence how you buy clothes, or the clothes you'll wear?

When you're thinking through these questions, try to get super specific—consider not just pants or dresses but underwear, socks, boots, sandals, gloves, pajamas, coats, weekend wear, and the clothes you put on after work but before bedtime. So often, these are the items that make a big difference in how we feel, particularly during seasons with extreme weather. Also think about the role that hair, makeup, and jewelry play in how you feel. Would you be happier if you gave yourself permission to cut your hair short, stop wearing makeup, or wear big-ass earrings every day?

Once you've gone through this process, you'll hopefully have a better understanding of how your clothes are influencing the way you feel, and be able to figure out your core needs and priorities with regard to your wardrobe. Shopping for clothes and getting dressed can be *so* fraught and *so* discouraging—and so expensive, so time-consuming, and so tiring. Figuring out what you feel best in and what you feel terrible in, and then committing to wearing more of the former and less of the latter, can be truly life-changing. It may take a little while to get there, but you can—one pair of comfortable shoes, great pants, and big-ass earrings at a time.

You Probably Need a Hobby

Not to brag, but I am *really* good at having hobbies. It's not that I'm good at all the hobbies I take up . . . but I'm great at *pursuing* hobbies. This is probably because hobbies combine three of my favorite things: learning new stuff, buying new stuff, and—according to every personality test I've ever taken *and* my natal chart—an obsession with self-improvement.

If you don't have a hobby at the moment, might I suggest remedying that? Hobbies provide you with a sense of accomplishment; teach you about yourself; introduce you to new people, concepts, and facts about the world; and give you something to do besides watch the same episodes of reality TV and scroll on your phone.

Hobbies vs. Activities

My friend Terri says that there are two types of people in this world: People who like hobbies and people who prefer activities. I concur! She defines a hobby as something you craft and pursue over time, and an activity as something that doesn't require any real skill and that is typically more of a onetime event (though you can definitely do the same activity repeatedly). To quote Terri: "Lying on the grass in the park on a nice day? Activity! Going to the park every weekend with your Nat Geo field guide to identify the birds chirping loudly overhead? Hobby!" So if hobbies aren't working for you, perhaps consider getting into activities (like visiting museums, going to concerts or shows, reading, trying new restaurants, doing puzzles, or playing games) instead.

Whether you choose a hobby or an activity, the goal is just to develop an interest that brings joy, satisfaction, and relaxation to your free time. Some hobbies that I've pursued in the past few years are making friendship bracelets, embroidery, cross-stitch, dot journaling, painting, calligraphy, making paper flowers, and photography. If you're not into crafts, some other ideas: crossword puzzles, sports (either individually or with a team), book club, playing an instrument, volunteering, trivia, classic movies, or getting more involved in your community.

Finally, remember to let yourself be bad or mediocre at your hobby. Sorry to be all Your Mom's Gruff New Boyfriend for a second, but we can't all be winners—and a little low-stakes failure is good for ya! At the very least, being mediocre at your hobby won't kill you.

✳

As I mentioned earlier, I believe that our habits are . . . kind of everything. Turns out, that's not just true in a feelsy way; it's also true in an etymological one.[19] The word *habit* is rooted in the Latin word *habitus,* which refers to "condition, demeanor, appearance, dress"—so, your inner and outer states of being. Meanwhile, the related *habitare* is "to live, dwell; stay, remain." And *habitus* is the past participle of *habere:* "to have, hold, possess; wear; find oneself, be situated; consider, think, reason, have in mind; manage, keep" . . . which, when you think about it, is kind of an amazing old-school definition of showing up for yourself every damn day.

Chapter 5
Showing Up for Yourself When Shit Gets Hard

howing up for yourself when times are good can be hard enough; showing up for yourself when you're going through a rough patch can feel downright *impossible*. But, of course, that's when you need to show up for yourself the most.

In late August 2015, my husband disappeared. Like, didn't-hear-from-him-for-days, hadn't-shown-up-for-work, I-called-the-police disappeared. After three days, he returned to our Brooklyn apartment. But the next weekend, after he'd spent a few days in the hospital and a couple more on our couch, he left home again—this time for good, though I wouldn't know it was permanent until months later.

Not a single day that followed made any sense. The fact that this could happen—that our seemingly normal life together could fracture so catastrophically, so suddenly, and in such a jagged, unfamiliar way—was shocking, and it was that shock, along with the grief, that completely gutted me. As September turned to October, I lost my appetite and then 10 pounds; all the padding disappeared from my face and left me looking older. Then I began to feel so tender, it was like I no longer had any skin at all.

I knew on some level that I wasn't OK—that *nothing* was OK—but I also didn't know what to *do* with that. So I went to work each day like nothing was wrong (while also doing everything I could to save my marriage). My friends kept reminding me to practice self-care, a well-meaning comment that I found unintelligible. Like, a sheet mask or manicure wasn't going to do a goddamn thing. The truth was, I was scared—of my dark, uncertain future but also of losing myself in my grief. I was afraid if I let myself lie down, even for a second, I wouldn't be able to get back up.

But after three long months of white-knuckling my former life, it finally dawned on me on Thanksgiving: *Oh . . . this is where I live now.* That night, I surrendered. I bought myself two pairs of cozy pajamas—an outfit designed for the sole purpose of lying down. This was when I fully understood what it meant to show up for myself. It wasn't about taking a bubble bath; it was admitting to myself, *Things are bad, and they are going to be bad for a while.* It was dressing not for the life I wanted, but for the life I had.

My new pajamas couldn't save me, or my marriage, which would officially end two years later. But they helped. Because when you feel raw from head to toe, covering your body in something clean and soft and fresh and white feels very, very good. In this moment of trauma, I learned to dress myself by looking to how we dress all wounds. (One first aid website advises: *A little bleeding is OK; it helps flush dirt and other contaminants out of the wound.*) Wearing my winter-white pajamas and wrapped in my crisp and cozy all-white bedding, I was both the nurse and the patient. *A little bleeding is OK.*

It would be awhile before I felt true happiness again, but even on my worst days, putting on clean clothes always made me feel a little bit less bad, a little bit more human. And after months of feeling powerless, suiting up to face my unhappy reality gave me a tiny sense of control.

In that moment, I realized that things are good until they are not, and they are bad until they are not. So often, the bad times happen without any sort of warning. But I found it comforting to remember that the good periods *also* tend to happen without warning. This isn't to say you can't actively work toward improving bad situations; you can. But turning a corner, moving on, getting to the other side, whatever you want to call it, is a complicated thing that is often governed by, I don't know . . . the wind? So instead of trying to change The Big Thing—which was fundamentally unchangeable—I just tried to make myself *comfortable*. I didn't try to feel happy; I tried to feel *less bad*. I accepted beauty and joy wherever I could get it and trusted that these small things would help me hang on until the wind started blowing my way again. And you know what? They did.

This chapter is about doing what you can to feel a tiny bit better as you embark on your journey to the other side of whatever shit situation may befall you.

Let's get started.

Dealing with Bad Times

"Normal" doesn't really exist anymore.

When you're going through a rough patch it can be incredibly disorienting to watch your "normal" life—your routine, your concentration, your favorite things, your stable moods—move somewhere beyond your reach, or disappear entirely. But this is, in large part, what loss *is*. Everything feels different because *everything is different*. You're in a Bad Time; of *course* nothing will be normal.

I know how frustrating that can be. *So not only is this shitty thing happening in my life,* you might think. *But now it's affecting* every *area of my life??? Including the things I enjoy and care about and want to be doing? That's . . . so fucking rude!!!* And it IS fucking rude!!! Truly, one of the worst aspects of dealing with something traumatic or terrible is how *big* it is. Your stress and anger and grief aren't restricted to when you're engaging with the bad thing; you carry it with you everywhere. It might be harder to be good to your friends and your partner, to engage in your favorite hobbies, to excel at work . . . whatever. We all know this on some level, but when it's your turn to go through something bad, it can still catch you by surprise. It's important to allow yourself some time and space to grieve the loss of your old "normal," and to allow yourself to make peace with the fact that things have changed.

Don't look down.

When you're in crisis, there will likely be a lot of big, scary, stressful tasks on your path forward. There will also be a lot of hypothetical questions that make you want to throw up (e.g., "How will I ever introduce future dates to my children?" after a divorce). Thinking about the amount of work—logistical and emotional—that you're going to have to do can be panic inducing. And if you let yourself think about the future too much, or try to game out of every possible outcome, you can quickly find yourself overwhelmed and frozen, unable to do anything, including basic survival tasks.

There will be a handful of top-level tasks that you truly need to handle ASAP without thinking too much about them. But once you've taken care of, say, hiring a lawyer or figuring out your options for taking time off work, there's a limit to what you'll be *able* to do next. In that moment, it's very easy to spin out over of dozens of imagined "someday" scenarios that may or may not ever happen. It feels a bit like being on a tightrope that is stretched across a river of alligators, a big fiery pit, and God knows what else. The other side is so far away, you sort of don't believe it exists.

Should you find yourself in this spot, try to remember this mantra: *Don't look down.* Instead, take one step. Then take another. Don't imagine in vivid detail exactly how bad it would feel to fall into the shark pit or the quicksand or whatever horror you're convinced is waiting for you in the final stretch. Don't think about how many steps you still have to go. Focus on this step— and know that "doing nothing" might *be* the step.

When your thoughts wander to The Big Horrors, reply with a firm, "Don't look down," and focus on whatever is happening right now. Instead of thinking about the next year, maybe let yourself think only about the next month. With practice, you'll be able to limit your thinking to just the next week. Finally, you'll be able to focus on just the next twenty-four hours.

Not thinking about the future after my ex left was hard for me, but it wasn't as difficult as I expected. I realized I had no choice. The alternative— feeling like my heart was going to beat through my chest every day because I was so stressed about what might happen in six months—wasn't practical.

It was also a huge *relief.* It's not like thinking about all the potentially terrible outcomes ever really *felt* good or effectively prepared me for what might come. Focusing on the present moment gave me the brain space I needed to tackle the tasks, big and small, that were necessary to move forward. Once I stopped looking down every ten seconds and quit thinking about the other side so much, I was able to get across some of the toughest stretches.

I had always thought of the phrase "one day at a time" as a fairly empty cliché, but finally, after several weeks of operating this way, something clicked: *Oh, I have to take this one day at a time. There is no other option.* It became the best survival mechanism in my tool kit. So if you're overwhelmed by all of the possible worst-case scenarios, try thinking smaller. Take a tiny next step. When the time comes, take another. And don't look down.

Embrace rituals.

Even if you're really struggling, try to identify potential little rituals in your daily life that allow you to briefly connect to something beautiful, pleasurable, or sacred. Rituals serve to acknowledge the magnitude of your situation and to connect what is happening to you in this moment to the rest of humanity, past and present.

And involving your people in bigger rituals can help you feel grounded and supported. In *The Joy of Missing Out,* Svend Brinkmann writes that communal rituals (like singing "Happy Birthday" or sitting shiva) "are used to focus collective attention on important matters in certain situations. Every individual can seek to cultivate their own small landscape of everyday rituals to endow their lives with form, but this also has to be done at the collective level, where people do things together."[20] So, yeah—go ahead and host a funeral for your pet, have a reverse barn raising after your divorce (where your friends help you pack up your ex's stuff to sell or donate), or throw a big-ass "I'm coming out" party.

Add structure to your indoor/hideaway behavior.

When you're struggling, you'll probably want to spend a lot of time hunkered down in bed or on the couch. And that's fine! But being a little more thoughtful about that time can go a long way. For example, instead of letting

Netflix tell you what to watch for a month straight, you could go through all of the best rom-coms from the past twenty years, or watch every episode of an old sitcom like *I Love Lucy*. Instead of scrolling through Instagram for hours, you could work your way through the entire Harry Potter series on audiobook. No need to get super ambitious here; the point is to look for small ways to upgrade the behavior that typically leaves you feeling sluggish and blah and turn it into something slightly more energizing.

"Healthy" Coping Mechanisms

If you're reading this book, there's a good chance you care about choosing "healthy" coping mechanisms—and it's easy to believe that going to the gym is the "good" or "right" way to deal, while going out for drinks with friends is "wrong." But I think it really depends on the person and the situation; when I'm struggling, I try to remind myself that seemingly healthy behaviors can still be used to self-medicate or to avoid dealing with my problems.

When you're going through a hard time, maybe going for a run *would* actually be the best thing in that moment. But it could be that the "unhealthy" habit of getting drinks with friends would be the better choice. Or maybe neither would! Sometimes, feelings like anger and grief and stress are not a problem that can be solved!

If you can't tell if you're taking a legitimate break from your pain, or avoiding dealing with your life, therapist Ryan Howes suggests having a plan or even a schedule for engaging with whatever is stressing you out. That might mean addressing it daily, or a few times a week, or during weekly therapy sessions. "Having a plan makes a big impact," Howes says. "Any sort of a plan, really. That's the way we regain control. And coping is really about taking back some control."

It's also helpful to remember that some discomfort is to be expected. As Kelsey Crowe and Emily McDowell write in *There Is No Good Card for This*, most of us were taught very early in life that loss is intolerable. Grief and loss are painful, and of course we don't want to tolerate that pain—we want it to go away. But sometimes, you just . . . can't. Sometimes you're just going to feel bad.

When You Can't Do Anything, Clean Your Bathroom

Whenever I'm pacing around my home and/or kind of spiraling, and know I should do *something* but can't decide what it should be, I'll clean my bathroom. I don't overthink it; I just go. And fifteen to twenty minutes later (which is about how long it takes me to clean my bathroom, despite what I like to tell myself when I'm avoiding doing it), my sink is sparkling and I feel better.

Why cleaning the bathroom? Because it tends to be a short and contained chore–unlike, say, cleaning your closet, which you'll start with the best of intentions and then somehow spend seventy-five dollars ordering hangers online before falling asleep on piles of clothes–BUT it's just long enough to help you get clarity on what to do next and to leave you feeling accomplished. It's basically pressing the reset button in a panic moment. It's also one area of your home that could always benefit from a little cleaning!

Tackling Basic Tasks

When you're struggling, everyday tasks (like feeding yourself, sleeping, chores, etc.) can be the hardest to accomplish—which can be *very* disorienting. Like, "Wait, I can plan a whole funeral while eight months pregnant but can't wash my hair or make myself dinner???" But yes—it's a thing! During a rough period, taking care of yourself in the most basic ways might be much, *much* harder than you'd expect.

It can be a huge shock when you suddenly find yourself unable to complete activities that you previously did without a second thought. In my own life, the fact that I could barely feed myself upset me more than the realization that I wasn't going to be on top of my game at work for a little while. Suddenly being unable to do the things that you've always considered basic care can make you feel helpless; it's a very vulnerable place to be, and it can be hard to admit you're there. But if you *are* there, try not to beat yourself up for not being able to do "simple" tasks—because nothing is simple when your life is falling apart, and it's pretty well established that humans struggle to complete basic tasks when they are having a hard time. And "humans" includes you.

Even if you're unable to engage in these behaviors at the level you normally would, it's still important to find a way to do *some* version of them—particularly if you're tempted to deprioritize them and instead look for other, sexier ways to feel better. I know that when you're in crisis mode, you may truly not have the option to do less at work, at school, or as a parent so that you can focus on taking care of yourself. But consider this your gentle reminder that if you're not sleeping or eating or drinking enough water, you're probably not going to be able to manage the rest of what's on your plate. These are the *survival* tasks; they aren't something you can blow off for extended periods of time without consequences.

If you're struggling to take care of yourself and meet your most basic needs, read on for some tips that might be helpful.

NOURISHING YOURSELF

Welcome shelf-stable and frozen foods into your life.
When you're going through a rough time, your schedule, appetite, and energy levels can be unpredictable, which can mean you end up wasting fresh groceries. That's why frozen foodstuffs—like vegetables, fish, potatoes, and pierogis—can be a godsend. They don't require much in the way of prep or cleanup and won't go bad in three days. Along with frozen foods, consider embracing beans, pasta, peanut butter, packaged ramen, and canned tuna. They last a while and have the added bonus of being relatively cheap.

Don't sleep on toast and tea.
Toast and tea are classics for a reason, and there are more options for toast than your standard butter with cinnamon sugar (though I eat that for dinner . . . not infrequently). Lately I've been into toast with tahini, sliced banana, a drizzle of honey, and dried lavender buds (which you can buy on Amazon). It feels fancy but isn't fussy, which is my favorite kind of meal.

Remember, it's OK to eat the exact same meals over and over again.
Once you figure out something that works for you (like toast and tea!), it's completely fine to just stick with it for a while! My go-to meals when I'm struggling (and even when I'm not, TBH) are Sue Kreitzman's lemon butter pasta and Smitten Kitchen's chickpea pasta (see page 295 for links to both recipes); both are fast, easy, inexpensive, and nourishing, and are made from ingredients that will last in your pantry for a while.

BATHING

Remember: You don't have to take a *shower* shower to clean yourself.
If you don't have it in you to take a full shower, you could clean the grossest parts of your body with a soapy washcloth or cleansing towelette to remove odor-causing bacteria. (Grossest parts of your body = "face, underarms, under the breasts, genitals, and rear end," according to dermatologist Joshua Zeichner.) If the idea of washing/drying your hair is what is overwhelming, get a drugstore shower cap and take more body showers.

Put on clean clothes (or clean underwear), if you can.
Humans shed a lot of odor-causing bacteria in our clothes, which is good news if you want to shower less. If you're worried you're starting to smell a little funky, make sure you're changing your clothes and undergarments regularly. One of my firm rules no matter how bad things get is to always swap the clothes I slept in and for fresh day clothes in the morning—even if I'm just getting back in bed. These day clothes don't have to be nice or formal or anything, either. Just clean-ish!

Take a bath instead of a shower.
A lot of people find baths relaxing, but they also serve a practical purpose: cleaning your meatsack! And if you don't have the time or energy or bathtub for a full-on Calgon-take-me-away soak, consider the budget version of it, aka just sitting down on the floor of your tub while your shower runs.

Soak/wash your feet!
God, what a *treat*.

SLEEP

Take note of how much sleep you're getting.

As I mentioned in Chapter 3, it can be very easy to tell yourself you're fine . . . while your actual habits tell a different story. And sleep is foundational to our physical and mental health. So make a point of recording how many hours of sleep you're getting each night, the frequency and duration of naps, and/or notes on how well you're sleeping.

Know that sleeping all the time (or being exhausted all the time) can be a sign of depression.

It can be difficult to realize you're sleeping all the time because of mental health issues because it can feel so *physical*—like, you're *actually* tired, so sleeping feels like the correct response. That's why it's a good idea to track your sleeping habits, and to talk to your health care provider if you are always exhausted or spending a *lot* of time sleeping.

Be even more conscious of how much time you're spending online or streaming shows or movies before you go to bed.

When you're dealing with a lot, zoning out is very, very appealing. And I hate that when you already have so much going on, you have to worry about whether or not you're on Instagram too damn much. But being on your phone before bed isn't doing you any favors, and might in fact be keeping you from a good night's sleep (or just an extra couple of hours). If at all possible, give yourself a hard cutoff time for phone usage and try to find an analogue way to zone out before bed (e.g., coloring, doing extremely easy crossword puzzles, or reading the paperback equivalent of a reality TV show).

If you have to choose between sleep and other things that might make you feel good (like exercise or cooking at home), choose sleep.

Sleep is *so* core to our health and to everything we do—don't skimp on it in the name of other "healthy" activities.

CLEANING YOUR SPACE

When life gets rough, it doesn't take long for our homes to start to reflect that chaos. But it doesn't take a giant crisis to make taking care of your space difficult! *Anyone's* home can be a big ol' mess, especially if you're dealing with anxiety, depression, ADHD, chronic illness, or chronic pain. So if/when you need a little help handling your havoc, here are some of my favorite tips from Rachel Hoffman in her excellent book *Unf*ck Your Habitat*.

Prioritize cleaning things that smell bad or have the potential to smell bad.

So: laundry, the fridge, trash, dishes, litter boxes. If that's all you can do for now, that'll still make a pretty meaningful difference in how clean your place is (and how clean it feels).

Or start by tackling the flat surfaces (in five-minute bursts).

As Hoffman puts it, "tidy up your tops"—it'll give you a lot of bang for your buck. So: Locate the nearest flat surface (like your nightstand or your kitchen table). Got it? Cool. Now set a timer for five minutes and take as much as you can off that surface (and put those things where they belong) in that time. That's it!

If possible, put a garbage can in every room.

Having a trash can near your bed and one by your couch means your side tables won't be sacrificed to greasy takeout containers, snotty tissues, empty Gatorade bottles, and crusty contact lenses when you simply don't have it in you to go to the kitchen or bathroom to toss them.

Recognize when you need help.

When I was eighteen and living on my own for the first time, my dirty dishes became A Problem. I hated doing them (STILL DO! UGGHHHH WATER CHORES!!!) and I let them pile up in the sink for so long that I was pretty sure the dishes at the bottom were growing mold, but I couldn't bear to find out. One day, my friend Amelia came by my apartment, saw the mess, and just . . . offered to do the dishes for me. Like, wholeheartedly offered—because she doesn't mind doing dishes and could probably also see that these dishes needed to be done and I was clearly too stuck in a shame spiral to do it. So even though I felt guilty and embarrassed, I let her do my dishes. It took her like twenty minutes. (She showed me the mold she uncovered and it wasn't actually that bad or scary!) It was so kind and such a huge gift, but also *not that big a deal,* you know? My point: When people offer to help you, believe that they mean it. And if no one has explicitly offered, know that it's *still* OK to ask for and accept help.

Try to have one positive interaction with your home each day.
"Try to do something—anything really—that allows you to interact positively with your home every day," Hoffman says. "Whether that's cleaning, organization, or even just displaying something that makes you happy, aim for getting one thing done every day that makes you feel better about where you live."

Let Yourself Throw Money at the Problem

Money can't solve all your problems or bring back the life you've lost, but it can still help a *lot*—particularly when everyday tasks are turning into giant stressors or huge stumbling blocks. Money can pay for everything from grocery delivery to taxis to a professional house cleaning to the cost of a canceled flight. To paraphrase my friend Meg Keene, there will be times when you think, "I do not care about this thing and I will rip out my eyes if I have to think about it for one more second. Hence, I will throw money at it."[21] When you're struggling, money pays for *convenience,* and the ability to be a tiny bit less stressed out.

Of course, this won't always be an option—it obviously requires that you have money, which not everyone does! But if you *do* have a little money and just aren't giving yourself permission to spend it, remember the classic Don Draper quote that I will now use completely out of context: "That's what the money is for!!!"

How to Tell People You're
Going Through a Tough Time

As a fairly private and generally upbeat person, I spent most of my life staying silent whenever I was going through a difficult time. I actively avoided telling people—particularly my coworkers and casual friends, but even close friends, too—that I wasn't doing well. But there are two big reasons I've started doing it more regularly. First, being honest is a *relief.* Going through a difficult time can feel a lot like carrying a stack of delicate china while walking on a tightrope. What you don't need at that moment is to have to hide how much you are struggling to keep everything from falling out of your arms—or worse, to pretend it's a breeze. You may not be able to set down the china or step off the tightrope right now, but you can at least admit that what you're doing is *hard.*

Second, being honest gives other people an opportunity to show up for you. When you're in the midst of a crisis or low period, it can be hard to remember how much people care about you or to believe that their support will actually make you feel better. And hey, maybe it won't help! But don't underestimate the power of a supportive friend or community; even just a heartfelt "I'm so sorry to hear that" or "That sounds really tough, and I'm here for you" can make you feel a lot less alone and less afraid. Sure, there might not be anything they can do to change or fix the situation, but your candor opens the door for other forms of support, including hugs, cute kitten videos, a few freezer meals, or just extra kindness and grace. You don't have to share your private business with everyone you encounter to feel this relief and support; in my experience, it comes from simply telling one or two people a little bit about what's going on (especially if they are people you see or talk to fairly regularly).

If you struggle with receiving care, consider that when you let people show up for you it's good not only for you but for them, too, and could in turn be great for your friendship. As Shasta Nelson says, "There are downsides to pretending we don't have needs: It denies that we're human, and it robs our friends of the joy of giving. We're not as fun to play with if we only sit at the bottom of the teeter-totter, never giving our friend a chance to push us up."[22]

A lot of us take it as indisputable fact that no one who asks "How are you?" wants a real answer. But . . . is that really always the case? Why have we all decided that this is true? I ask people how they are doing every day, and even if I'm sometimes saying it out of habit, I still want to know. And I'm not unusual in this regard; while there are certainly exceptions to this, it's likely that the people in your everyday life do actually care on some level. But even if the asker isn't consciously looking for the most honest answer, they likely won't recoil in horror when you offer it.

If you're worried about burdening someone who just wanted to exchange pleasantries, that can be mitigated by what you share and how you share it (more on this in a moment). But in the age of perfectly curated and relentlessly positive social media posts, a lot of people *welcome* a conversation with someone who is willing to be vulnerable. If we were all a little more honest in the moments that we're not doing well, maybe we'd all feel a little better.

When you're thinking about whether and how to be more honest, consider two things: what you're comfortable with sharing and your relationship with the other person. Ideally, what you say should match the level of intimacy you currently have. Nelson frames this kind of opening up in the context of what she calls the "frientimacy triangle." The three sides of the triangle are positivity (which in this context means genuine interest, joy, amusement, humor, and pleasantness); consistency (i.e., spending time together, which establishes confidence and trust in the relationship); and vulnerability (sharing more personal details, being willing to be exposed and honest).

THE FRIENTMANCY TRIANGLE

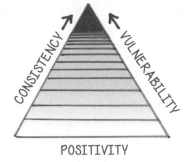

POSITIVITY

Positivity, because it's a baseline requirement, forms the base of the triangle. But in this usage, positivity is not about being intractably upbeat. "Positivity does not refer to what we're talking *about*," Nelson told me. It refers to the joy, interest, humor, gratitude, and warmth that are present in each conversation and in the relationship as a whole. "Even when we're hurting, we can be grateful, we can be curious, we can affirm other people. It's still our job to make sure people leave the conversation feeling valued."

Once a baseline of positivity is established, Nelson says, consistency and vulnerability (the two arms of the triangle) should move upward at roughly the same pace. So if the consistency (the amount of time you've spent together, the length of the relationship, and so on) is relatively low (think of a 2 on a scale of 1 to 10), whatever you share will probably be relatively low in vulnerability as well. You can still be honest with people you have met fairly recently, but recognize that a new friend likely isn't the best audience for every messy detail of your life. "It's always appropriate to share what's going on in your life, but we shouldn't be *processing* with the people at the bottom of the triangle," Nelson says.

Let's say you're going through a divorce. With the friends who are at level 1 or 2 on both consistency and vulnerability, Nelson suggests you might say, "I'm going through a divorce and not gonna lie, it's pretty rough. But I am looking forward to making new friends and keeping busy and trying to remind myself that there is plenty of love and fun to be had in the world." With a level 9 or 10 person—like, say, a sibling you're really tight with or your lifelong best friend—you might share the ways it's affecting your children, your fears about dating again, and the fact that you cry yourself to sleep every night. As for everyone in the middle? Aim to share in a way that gives the other person the information and context you feel is most important (whether that's "I feel sad" or "I need to take a few days off") while still making clear that you don't expect this person to react like a very close friend (or a therapist) would. "Share a little and see how the person responds," Nelson says. "Pay attention to social cues. Are they asking questions? Is it only one-way sharing?"

Nelson says you can practice positivity even when you're down by thanking the other person for listening, giving them permission to be happy about whatever is going on in their own life, being willing to laugh when you can, and remembering to say, "But enough about me; what's new with you?"[23]

If you're worried that being honest about your feelings will make you seem like a Debbie Downer, I get it—I've been there too. These tips have helped me think about my relationships as a *whole* instead of focusing on every individual interaction. When I zoom out to get that perspective, I can see that it's perfectly OK for me to be a little more vulnerable and authentic with my friends—in part because we're all doing our best to bring that genuine positivity, even when things are shit.

Don't Mistake a Level 4 Friend for a Level 9 Friend

During our conversation, Shasta Nelson said something I've been thinking about ever since. We were talking about the levels of friendship, and I commented that most of us probably don't have that many friends at a level 9 or 10–like, not *that* many people would reach that level of intimacy in our lives, right? She replied, "Many of us don't have *anyone* up there." She went on to say that if you don't have a lot of friends in the top tier, it's easy to treat level 4 or 5 friends like they are level 9 or 10 friends–because they are your "best" friends, even if they aren't actually your best friends. It's truly a bummer not to have someone who feels like Your Person, but trying to fast-track friendship in this way tends to backfire. So before you unload on your friends, it can be worthwhile to take an honest look at the relationship. Does the sharing go both ways? Are you Their Person, too? Or are you vaunting them to a higher level of friendship when it's not really appropriate or earned?

If you're thinking that being more open would make you feel better but simply have no idea how to respond to "How are you?," here are some ideas that you can use as a jumping-off point.

💬 What to say

"Eh, I've been better, honestly! I'd rather not get into it, but I'd appreciate any good vibes you want to send my way right now."

"Honestly, it's been a rough few [days/weeks]. I'm dealing with some [stressful stuff in my personal life/family drama/family stuff/health problems/stuff] and could use some good vibes right now."

And try not to overthink the phrase you use to describe the situation here! "Some stressful stuff in my personal life" can cover pretty much everything, and you don't owe anyone a full explanation on exactly what's going on with your latest round of IVF and how it's affecting your body and your marriage. The point is to convey, "I'm not OK and I don't really want to get into why." There are no vulnerability police who are going to throw you in jail for not choosing the exact "correct" phrasing for your specific issue.

If you want to be a little more forthcoming, try one of these:

"Honestly, it's been a rough few weeks; my mom is having some health problems. But I'm hanging in there!"

"Hey, I just wanted to let you know that my mom was recently diagnosed with cancer. No need to worry—she has great doctors and I have a good support system in place. I don't really want to talk about it now, but I wanted you to know in case I seem a little distracted or start taking more time off than usual."

"Hey, I just wanted to let you know that my mom was recently diagnosed with cancer, and her prognosis isn't good. She'll be moving into hospice care later this week. I'm doing my best to keep it together, but I'm devastated. I don't really want to talk about it right now, but I wanted you to know in case I seem [distracted/tired/weepy/out of it/down] or start taking more time off than usual."

(Of course, you can skip the "I don't really want to talk about it" if you're actually comfortable talking about it!)

It's also a good idea to set some boundaries in terms of sharing this information with others. Doing this is helpful for everyone involved—because if your friends know exactly what your expectations are, they are less likely to gossip and less likely to accidentally tell someone what's going on. So you may want to add something like, "So far, the only people I've told are Kai and Alex. I'd appreciate if you kept this between us for now so I can tell everyone else in my own time."

And if it's not something you want to keep super private, you could say something like, "So far, I haven't told a lot of people but I'm not trying to hide it either."

SHARING BAD NEWS FAR AND WIDE

One of the worst aspects of experiencing something terrible is having to manage other people's reactions to your bad news. But even if you know everyone around you will be supportive, having to talk about a painful experience is, well, *painful,* and sharing the news publicly (or semi-publicly) is often what makes it feel real for the first time.

To share bad news with a group, you can modify one of the scripts from above so it sounds more like this:

> "Hi, everyone, I have some bad news to share today: My mom was recently diagnosed with cancer, and her prognosis isn't good. She'll be moving into hospice care later this week. I'm doing my best to keep it together, but I'm devastated. I don't really want to talk about it right now, but I wanted you all to know what is going on."

You may also want to add something like, "I don't need anything right now, but I'm also accepting hugs and heart emojis," which communicates, *I don't want to talk about it, but it's also OK to let me know you read this and that you care.* Most people genuinely just want to know what to do and say and are worried about doing the "wrong" thing; it's totally OK (and, honestly, a kindness) to tell them exactly what you need!

As for the medium, you have a few options. While some people might argue that bad news has to be shared via phone or IRL, I disagree—I think texts, emails, and even status updates are appropriate in a lot of circumstances.

Email might feel formal, but I prefer it to texting for a few reasons. First, people tend to check their email when they are in the mood to read/receive emails. By sending an email, you increase the chances that they will read it at a time that is good for *them,* which means they can respond more thoughtfully. Speaking of responses, sending emails means people are more likely to *reply* via email—which means *you* can better control when you read and engage with these messages.

That said, texts are perfectly fine. A status update (on Facebook, Twitter, Instagram, etc.) can also work if you've already told the people in your inner circle and are now trying to reach a more extended network. And if you choose to share the news digitally, you may want to do it either first thing in the morning or in the evening (outside of common working hours) so that people are able to process the information and properly respond.

If you don't have it in you to communicate the information on your own, don't overlook the power of good gossip when it comes to sharing bad news. Good gossip here means gossip that you've blessed and/or requested—because it means you aren't burdened with telling people over and over again. This might look like asking one really thoughtful coworker to quietly tell all your other coworker pals that something bad is happening, or asking your BFF to be the one to inform your extended friend group about your divorce news. If you go that route, you may also want to ask the intermediary to share your expectations about privacy and further discussion, like so:

"They asked me to share this with you."

"You should definitely still feel free to reach out to them."

"They know I'm telling you but would prefer not to talk about it this weekend at book club."

DEALING WITH NOSY FOLKS

If someone starts asking for a lot of details or trying to engage you in a way that you're not comfortable with (which may or may not be rooted in a genuine desire to help), here are some responses you can try.

💬 What to say

"I don't really want to talk about it, to be honest. Can we change the subject?"

"I'd really prefer not to get into the details. Let's move on!"

"Honestly, the thing I need right now is to talk/think about it less. So, I'd love to hear what's new with you!"

"Oh, that's not a good brunch conversation."

"I'm actually finding this conversation pretty overwhelming and would like to take a break from it, please."

If you can, try to keep your tone neutral; they'll likely be embarrassed, and dealing with their defensiveness or a big wounded shame spiral is the last thing you need right now. Of course, if they really won't cut it out or you just don't have it in you to be gentle, it's OK to be less gracious in your response.

Here's what you might say if a sharper response is called for.

"That's actually a *really* personal question and I don't want to talk about it."

"Wow, that's a really inappropriate question."

"That's a really strange thing to say to someone in my situation."

"That's a really hurtful thing to say. What the fuck?"

[Deep frown, scowl, side-eye, or some other form of body language that communicates "Oh, absolutely no."]

Ultimately, what you choose to share, who you share that information with, and how you communicate it is super personal and completely up to you. Figuring out what level of vulnerability you're comfortable with in different relationships takes experimentation and practice—and might change over time, or depending on what exactly you're dealing with.

Sometimes, being honest can feel like self-care; other times, it might feel like a burden. But when I'm struggling, I find it helpful to simply remember that I have a choice, that I'm *allowed* to give a candid answer to "How are you?," that being vulnerable isn't an all-or-nothing proposition, and that being a little more honest can actually make me feel a lot better.

Accepting Help

If you need to get better at accepting help, you can follow a similar formula to the one I mentioned in Chapter 2. Accept help from strangers when it's offered, and then build up to accepting help from people you know when it's offered. Or, you can take this shortcut: When someone says, "Let me know if you need anything," *let them know if you need anything.*

If you're not sold on this idea, allow me to address some of the common excuses people give for not allowing other people to show up for them.

Reason: "They didn't really mean it."
Counterpoint: They did, in fact, really mean it! But also, what's the worst that could happen if you follow up with, "Hey there, you told me a few weeks ago to let you know if I need anything, and there actually is something I could really use right now"? There's no harm in taking people at their word in this case. If they didn't mean it, well . . . they'll learn a valuable lesson about not letting their mouth write checks that their ass can't cash (and you'll learn a valuable lesson about that friendship).

If you're worried that what you need in this moment is too big or burdensome to ask of this friend, think back to the frientimacy triangle and the levels of friendship from earlier in this chapter. Is this a level 3 friend?

If so, then sure, it might not be the best idea to ask them to come to your doctor's appointment and hold your hand during the exam. But it might be perfectly OK to ask your level 6 friend who has always demonstrated kindness and thoughtfulness to give you a *ride* to your doctor's appointment. Don't get me wrong: It's great to be considerate and think about whether you're asking too much of other people. But so often, this results in our never allowing *anyone* to take care of us, and shouldering these tasks entirely on our own.

Reason: "The thing I need is weird or unconventional and they'll think I'm a freak if I ask for it."

Counterpoint: Humans are smart and capable of nuance. I genuinely believe that most people would rather do the right thing *for you* than whatever society deemed "right" fifty or a hundred years ago. Even if they've never been asked to do something "unconventional" for a friend in need before, they will understand if you say, "This might sound strange, but I could really use someone to come keep me company while I do my dishes and laundry. My place is a mess, I'm overwhelmed, it's giving me a ton of anxiety, and I just need someone to be here with me while I deal with it. I'll treat you to pizza to make it worth your while." They may even be flattered—because you're showing that you trust them and are willing to be vulnerable with them, and letting them know that they too can ask for something unusual when they really need it.

Reason: "I don't actually really need help, I'm fine."

Counterpoint: You're not fine.

HOW TO TELL SOMEONE THEIR "HELP" IS EXTREMELY NOT HELPFUL

When you are going through a difficult time, people will likely attempt to support you. And some folks will, inevitably, get it wrong. If someone else's behavior is making your bad situation worse, the best thing you can do—for both of your sakes—is to gently correct them and communicate that what they are offering is actually not what you need right now. If you want, you can explain why—a generous move that may ensure they don't make the same mistake in the future, with someone else—but you don't have to.

💬 What to say

"I really appreciate how thoughtful you've been since I told you about my situation; it means a lot to me to have a friend who cares about me so much. But right now, I'm feeling a bit overwhelmed by these efforts to make me feel better. Could I ask you to stop fussing over me and instead give me a little space? I promise I'll tell you if I need something."

"I know some people in my situation find anecdotes like the one you just told me helpful, but I find them really stressful and scary. Could I ask you to not share stories like that with me in the future?"

"To be honest, I'm not in a place where I'm ready to look at the positives of this situation just yet. I'm still really hurt and angry, and I just need to be hurt and angry for a while."

"I know you mean well when you say, 'He's in a better place,' but that phrase isn't helpful or comforting to me right now."

"Can I ask you to do me a favor and stop sending me articles about using crystals to treat cancer because 'oncology is a scam'? These articles aren't helpful to me and are kind of stressing me out."

And if it feels right, you can add something like:

"What I do need right now is [a hug/the name of a good lawyer/someone to organize a meal train/not to talk about this when I'm at work]."

In most of these situations, it's best to focus on yourself and your preferences instead of criticizing the other person's behavior. Because in a lot of instances, the person won't have done something universally wrong; they will simply have done something that you don't appreciate. You know what they say: One person's "how essential oils cured my cancer" article from alternativehealingmooncircle.net is another person's treasure!

It might also make sense to ask a trusted third party to intervene on your behalf, particularly when you're dealing with something really serious. That might sound something like this:

> "Hey, Ash, it is so incredibly kind of you to offer to sing at the memorial service on Saturday, but Kyle has reiterated to me a few times that the service is meant to be family only. The best thing you can do to be supportive right now is to respect their wishes."

If the person who is missing the mark is a close friend, you might want to be more direct and vulnerable—because not saying anything can do long-term damage to the friendship, and because you (presumably) do want and need their support in a different way right now. In that case, you might say something like this:

> "Shawn, my miscarriage has left me completely devastated. I'm angry and heartbroken and furious, and hearing you say 'everything happens for a reason' makes me feel the complete opposite of supported. Please don't."

> "I know you're trying to cheer me up by telling me to focus on the positives of getting fired, but it's actually coming across as dismissive because I'm still really upset. Can you please just be upset with me for a little while?"

> "Hey, I know you mean well by sending me these articles related to my diagnosis, but they are actually making me spiral the fuck out. I'd like to request a break from all cancer-related literature until further notice."

They might honor your request! They might not! But at least now you can feel less guilty about ignoring their daily affirmation DMs.

How to Vent Responsibly

When you're going through a difficult time, venting can *really* help. Therapist Ryan Howes says that venting is really about *processing.* You haven't come to any real conclusions yet; you just need to get your thoughts out of your head, and you need a warm body to listen. Venting tends to feel good; it helps us name what happened and give it a narrative structure, which is really powerful. But it's also something that we can easily get lost in, draining our energy reserves and alienating the people who are listening to us in the process.

If you're worried about venting too much and exhausting your friends, here are some tips that might help.

Let people *ask* you how you're doing.

When you're dealing with a lot, it's easy to blurt out the latest update to the first person you see without so much as a hello. If you're worried about falling into that trap, consider holding off until someone actually says, "How are you?" or "How's everything going with [situation]?" Being asked still isn't a free pass to dump on them for the next three hours, but this is an easy way to keep your urge to unload in check, and to make sure your friends are interested in your latest download.

Explicitly ask for permission to vent—even if you just want to vent via text.

If you need a friend to lend an ear, consider requesting it in a more formal way. Scheduling time to talk or text about a specific topic isn't silly; it's courteous. As therapist Andrea Bonior says, "Texting lets us place something—immediately—into someone else's consciousness, whether they want it there, and are adequately prepared to deal with it at the moment, or not."[24] Texting something like "When you have a moment, I'd love to talk with you about the latest in this Sam situation" or "If you're around later and up for it, I'd like to scream about the Sam situation" will go a long way toward communicating respect for their time and energy. (And do be specific about what you want to discuss; just saying "Got a sec?" or "Are you busy?" isn't cool.) It's entirely likely they'll respond, "I can talk now—what's up?" but they'll still appreciate that you asked.

If you aren't looking for advice, *say so.*

In general, our loved ones want to be helpful and offer solutions to our problems . . . but jumping right to solutions can inadvertently communicate "I don't want to hear about this anymore; I want to fix this so you'll shut up about it"—which is maybe not what you want to hear in that moment. So if you know you simply need to vent, or that you aren't in a place to consider what to do next, *tell the other person that up front.*

Don't outright reject all suggestions and attempts to problem-solve.

This might seem at odds with what I said a second ago. And it kind of is! Here's the thing: Wanting to vent and be validated is totally fine. But *only* venting, and shutting down whenever the conversation turns to the topic of possible solutions? Not so fine! It's frustrating to listen to a friend talk endlessly about the same topic, particularly if they are refusing to acknowledge their part in the situation or do anything to feel better. Of course, sometimes there isn't anything you *can* do to make things better. But at that point, talking about it for three hours isn't really making it better either.

Consider the forty-five-minute rule.

A couples therapist once gave me this very good advice: If you're having an argument or intense conversation, take a break after forty-five minutes. After the forty-five-minute mark, she said, people tend to be too emotionally exhausted to have a productive conversation; a twenty-minute break (at minimum!) can help everyone process and reset a bit. Putting this advice into practice made a huge difference, and I now try to apply it to *any* negative conversation. Aside from being good for the listener, it's good for you, too. Because even if you aren't arguing, you're still depleting your energy (and probably starting to lose the thread of the conversation) when you vent for that long. So keep an eye on the clock, and remember: There's a reason most therapy sessions are only fifty minutes long.

Notice if you are repeating yourself.

Ryan Howes says if you find yourself saying the same thing over and over again (or the person you're talking to keeps responding in the exact same way), you miiiight be ruminating, which can be pretty tiresome for the other person. If you're just cycling through the same few exchanges ("This is bad! I'm so mad!" "Ugh, I know! It's so bad!") and neither of you is bringing up new information or insight, consider wrapping it up soon. Of course, there are exceptions to this, and sometimes a situation is so terrible or tragic or unfixable that all you can do is repeat, "This happened and I'm so upset!" while your friend nods sympathetically and says "It's awful; I'm so sorry." But that shouldn't be the norm in most conversations. So if you're just rehashing the same points—or if your friend is looking/sounding bored—it might be time to call it quits.

Try not to pre-vent.

Pre-venting is when someone says, "I'll tell you more about this tonight" . . . and then *immediately* launches into telling you now . . . and then *still* wants to discuss it in full when you see them later that night. It's a variation on repeating yourself, but it can be less obvious because some time passes between the initial conversation and the later one. But if you've already established you're going to talk at not-now-o'clock, try to hold off on emotion-dumping before then. And if you do find yourself getting into the whole story (or, say, 75 percent of it) now, recognize that you don't *really* need to rehash or repeat the same details later.

Consider journaling.

I wrote an entire book about journaling, so I admit I'm a bit biased, but the health benefits of journaling are well documented. Dumping your thoughts on a page allows you get everything out *and* helps you process what you're experiencing. Set a timer for twenty minutes—any longer than that can actually lead to ruminating—and write freely, without worrying about punctuation, spelling, or the "quality" of the writing. Your writing doesn't need to be "interesting" because no one is ever going to read it. (*You* don't even have to reread it later!) You might find you feel a lot better overall, and that your urge to vent to a friend has mysteriously disappeared.

Give your friend time and space to talk about their life.

I'm of the belief that not every conversation with a friend has to be perfectly balanced in terms of who is talking and who is listening. We've all had days when we don't have much to talk about and a friend has a lot going on, and we're perfectly happy to listen while the friend vents, and then end the phone call there! It's fine! But. *But.* If you only ever contact your friends to vent—or if your "How are you doing?" is perfunctory and communicates "I know this is the correct thing to say" instead of sincere interest—your pals are going to catch on. So be sure you're leading with "How are you?" sometimes (*before* you've talked about yourself) . . . and actually listen and engage when they answer. And if you know you're only going to hang out for an hour, remember to cut yourself off after twenty or thirty minutes so they have a chance to talk, too.

Do Even Less

You already know how much I believe in the importance of doing less. When your life is falling apart, might I suggest . . . *doing even less?* The good news about being in crisis is that you're allowed to opt out of normal activities. You are allowed to cancel plans; to ask for an extension on a deadline; to take a day off; to cry unexpectedly; to not be your best self. When you're feeling overwhelmed or guilty, remember: *This is exactly why the phrase "family emergency" exists.* The emergency is here; it's yours and it's happening right now. It's easy to lose sight of this in the moment—to tell yourself that "real" trauma is something that happens to other people and not to you (especially if you don't want to admit that what is happening is really, really bad).

Instead of assuming you'll be able to keep up with your life as normal, try starting with the opposite belief: that you'll be able to do *nothing.* Don't be surprised by the fact that you can do even less right now; rather, let yourself be shocked and proud when you can do *anything.* Lower your expectations, lower your standards, lower your bar. *Do even less.*

Part II

Showing Up for Others

Chapter 6
How to Make Friends

aking friends as an adult is *hard*. You could be forgiven for not expecting this, especially if you had a lot of close friends as a youth, or if you grew up believing that adulthood would resemble *Friends* or *Sex and the City*. But the reality is, having a tight/set friend group as an adult isn't the reality for a lot of people, especially as more of us move farther away from our hometowns and colleges and relocate for work (often repeatedly).

The good news is that you can do hard things, including make new friends! I say this as someone who has moved quite a bit in her adult life and who considers herself pretty decent at making new friends. In this chapter, we'll talk about how many friends you actually need, how to find your people, how to talk to them, and how to connect with them in a more meaningful way.

Before you jump into making friends headfirst, it's worthwhile to think about what you're looking for in new friends—and identify what *you* have to offer. I've found that when I don't do this, I end up wasting TME getting to know people who aren't *ever* going to be my people, or end up in friendships that aren't actually that great for me. Or I'll treat making friends as an all-or-nothing proposition and quickly burn out.

By now, you should be well aware of your needs, your preferences, and your best qualities. From here, put some thought into what you are looking for in a friend—in terms of both personality and the connection. Here are some questions to ask yourself.

What are your other friends like?

Your established friendships provide a *lot* of data, and you can use that information to make better decisions about the people you let into your life. Think about your current friends and the friends you've had throughout your life. How are they similar to you? How are they different? Are they introverted or extroverted? What are their values? How would you describe their lifestyle and their brand of humor? How do they communicate? How do they handle conflict or difficulty? What first drew you to them? What surprised you about them? What do you think made your friendship work? If the friendship is now over, what went wrong? And what do you wish you'd done differently early on?

What do you want and need in a friend?

Do you want a new BFF, or just more casual friends? People you can do activities with? Someone you can confide in? Someone to travel the world with? Are you looking for friends who share your worldview or a particular life experience? Your immediate answer might be, "I don't know, I just want friends?!?!" but try to get more specific, if possible.

Where does making new friends fall in your list of priorities?

Think about what's taking up your TME these days. How important is making friends to you compared to, say, cooking at home, reading more, or spending time with family? It's not that you have to definitively choose one or the other, but some days you might—and in those moments, it's good to know exactly how much establishing new friendships really matters to you right now.

What can you offer a friendship right now?

Revisit the personal values you identified for yourself in Chapter 1. How do those shape what kind of friend you are? Also think about your strengths and weaknesses as a friend. Maybe you're great at organizing and planning big group hangouts, or are *the* friend to call if someone needs help changing a tire, or packing boxes before a move, but are never available for spontaneous hangouts and take a week to text back. Figure out what makes you special and unique, what you're not great at, and what, if anything, you want to improve or change going forward.

I find this exercise useful because humans are often bad at articulating why we like or dislike certain things. For example, most of us would probably say we want friends who are funny, right? But "funny" is subjective; what we mean is that we want friends who make us laugh, who share our sense of humor, and who like the same funny things we do. It's helpful to dig into what, specifically, is your jam, so you can start to identify the people you're likely to connect with a little quicker.

THE "RIGHT" NUMBER OF FRIENDS

You may have heard the term "Dunbar's number" thrown around in the context of friendship. This number—150—comes from Robin Dunbar, a professor of evolutionary psychology at Oxford. According to his research on brain size and social groups, humans can only handle roughly 150 casual friendships at a time, and most of us have between 100 and 300 friends in our social circles.

From there, our social circles tend to decrease in size by a factor of three, and the relationships become increasingly more intimate at these levels. So within that original 150, we'll each have about 30 to 45 people we'd consider *good friends* (people you'd invite to a group dinner); 9 to 15 we consider *close friends* (people you can really confide in and turn to in times of need, and whose death, if it happened tomorrow, would seriously upset you); and roughly 3 to 5 people in our intimate support group. About 60 percent of our time and attention is spent on the 3 smallest groups (the 5/15/45).[25]

With this in mind, it's worth considering whether you actually need *more* friends, or whether you need *closer* friends. If you already have fifteen or twenty good friends, it might make the most sense to deepen your relationships with those people instead of trying to meet an entirely new best friend. Of course, that won't always be an option, especially if you've just moved or if your social network is on the small side. But it's good to remember that casual friends can and do turn into best friends.

A DEEP–SHALLOW COMPANION

Regardless of how many friends researchers say you need or how many you currently have, my theory is that everyone needs one individual to fill the role of what I call your deep–shallow companion. This is the person who is willing to listen to you talk about the most humdrum shit about your day (aka your deep–shallow topics), pretty much every day (and then shares theirs in turn). They let you go on about the traffic you sat in, the errands you ran, the minutiae of your to-do list, or everything Sweetgreen did right or wrong with regard to your salad order. (My experiences with the Sweetgreen app are the *epitome* of deep–shallow talk.) Deep–shallow stories are both too boring and too complicated for most audiences. It's not *real* drama but a five-act Shakespearean play, and it all took place in the self-checkout line at Target.

Deep–shallow is the height of intimacy demonstrated through extremely not-intimate conversational topics. It's a bond and love that is so deeply rooted it can withstand this particular type of shallow conversation. Of course, most relationships include the occasional deep–shallow talk; sometimes, the first coworker pal you see when you walk into the office is gonna hear your terrible commute story, whether they like it or not. But your deep–shallow *person* is the one who you talk like this with daily. It's a role often filled by a parent, sibling, or romantic partner because it requires so much love.

My suspicion is that a *lot* of loneliness stems from not having a deep–shallow companion. Which really sucks! Because if you try to make someone your deep–shallow person and they don't want to be (perhaps because they already have a deep–shallow relationship, because it's too early in the relationship, *whatever*), you probably won't get the attention or enthusiasm you're looking for, which just feels bad. It doesn't mean they don't want to be friends with you or that they don't like you (truly!) . . . but it still stings. Deep–shallow conversations are often when we're our most relaxed and uncensored and real selves; not having a deep–shallow person can lead to feeling very unseen and incredibly alone.

I share this not to call attention to something you feel sad about and can't really fix, but because I know what it's like not to have the words to explain this particular kind of intimacy or describe what it looks and feels like. Sure, you can't conjure up a new deep–shallow companion overnight, but it's helpful to be able to name what you're looking for, and to understand what you're missing if your deep–shallow person is no longer in your life.

THE MYTH OF THE BEST FRIEND

From *Broad City* to *Bill & Ted* to *The Baby-Sitters Club,* there's a well-established cultural narrative about what a best friend looks like. They are wise and funny, honest but always kind. They have known you since you were five years old and you talk every day. They do tequila shots with you after you get dumped and give a perfect toast at your wedding. They know all your secrets and also your mom. They are somehow always around when you are trying on clothes. They are one of the most important people in your life, and they always have your back.

If you don't have the Hollywood version of a BFF, it's easy to think there's something wrong with you—that no one likes you, that you're not capable of making close friends or maintaining friendships, that you're all alone in this world.

I subscribe to the Mindy Kaling sentiment that "a best friend isn't a person; it's a tier." Throughout my adult life, I've had (and have!) multiple best friends. Still, I'm not immune to the idea that I should have a singular best friend who also considers me their best friend. That idea is pervasive, and the pressure is real. But I'm beginning to realize that this best friend is, for a lot of people, a myth. Like, a best friend? In *this* economy???

I'm only sort of kidding. The world is changing in ways that make it incredibly hard to make or maintain a traditional best friendship. When you're moving every few years or #hustling nonstop just to stay afloat, it's difficult talk to your best friend every day and see them every weekend. And even if you live in the same city, well, people have lives! They have partners and families and demanding careers and clinical depression and not a lot of TME for brunching, shopping, or talking on the phone.

I think it's important to remember that, despite the prevalence of the term "best friend," there isn't *really* a shared cultural definition for the term. If you're basing your idea of best friendship on, say, talking intimately every day, and someone else thinks that "I've known her since I was five but we don't actually talk or see each other very often" absolutely counts, then you might not realize that by their definition, you too may have a best friend. Even the idea of closeness in friendship is a moving target. For some people, a "close" friend might be any person they talk to frequently, even if the conversations aren't that deep; others might only apply the term to a person they're comfortable FaceTiming while on the toilet.

If you're feeling like a loser for not having a best friend—whatever that term means to you—know that there is nothing wrong with you, and you're *definitely* not the only one.

Meeting New Friends

Once you've done the work to figure out what you're looking for and what you have to offer, it's time to get to work. Here are some tips for actually meeting the people who have new-friend potential.

Figure out where your potential friends hang out.

If you're trying to make new friends, it helps to frequent places where other people with similar interests are likely to be. When I first moved to Houston, I had the most luck taking classes at boutique workout studios and attending their workshops and social events; the smaller atmosphere made it easier to bond with other people there, and seeing the same people in certain classes each week made me feel more confident about striking up a conversation with them.

Are there any classes where your potential pals might be? Do any of your favorite brands do in-store events? Are you in any Facebook groups where local folks might be interested in meeting up in person? Does joining a social club or coworking space make sense for you? It might take some trial and error (and some time on Meetup.com—really!), but eventually, you'll have that moment when you realize, "Oh! *This* is where my people are!"

Try to become a regular somewhere.

When you frequent the same places or classes, people (including you) start to become familiar faces. And even though you don't *need* that familiarity to start a conversation, it can definitely grease the wheels a bit, and give you the confidence to start chatting.

Related: Don't feel weird mentioning that you've noticed someone a few times. First, they've likely noticed you, too. Second, noticing and remembering people is a perfectly normal thing to do!

Don't write off people who are at different life stages than you.

Whether you're just starting college or sending your third child off to grad school, it's completely reasonable to want to make friends who are doing roughly the same things you are. And I don't want to gloss over the importance of building a community around shared life experiences or identities—those commonalities really do matter. But we miss out on valuable relationships when we write people off for being, say, too old or too young, or for not being parents or not being students. These days, fewer of us are attending religious services, getting to know our neighbors, and engaging in civic activities, which means we have far less exposure to people at different life stages. But talking to people from different generations broadens our worldview and makes us kinder, smarter, and more empathetic.

These friendships are also just *practical*. For example, if you, a thirty-six-year-old parent, need a last-minute babysitter on a Saturday night, who are you going to call? Your thirty-five-year-old BFF with a newborn and a toddler and a super firm bedtime schedule? No—you're going to call me, because I don't have kids and I'd absolutely *love* to hold your baby! Or maybe you'll call the person who has been an empty nester for years, or your twenty-three-year-old former intern. There's a reason that for most of human history, humans have organized themselves in networks that include elders and youths, y'all. And even having a five- to ten-year age difference between you and a close friend can make your life feel significantly better and more complete.

Be prepared to put down your phone.

I get why you'd prefer to connect with people primarily in cyberspace . . . but scrolling endlessly or putting most of your effort into online friendships drains time and energy and can sap your desire to connect with folks in meatspace. So as much as it pains me—an introvert who loves doing *every-thing* online—to admit it, you simply have to be willing to be on your phone a little bit less and in the real world a little bit more when you want to make new IRL friends.

Know that you're going to have to talk to people.

If you're trying to make friends in the wild, you really can't just wait around for someone to talk to you. I mean you *can*—it's your life—but it will be harder and take longer that way. I'm not a particularly outgoing person, but when I'm trying to make friends, I've realized I have to be, like, 15 percent more outgoing than my default setting.

Friendships often begin with good old-fashioned small talk. In *Small Talk: How to Start a Conversation, Truly Connect with Others, and Make a Killer First Impression,* Diane Weston writes that it's a type of communication that "has evolved to turn people you don't know into people you do. It turns a stranger into an acquaintance, and an acquaintance into a friend."[26] Which is true! We express (and learn) a lot more than we think during small talk—and even if we don't, it's still a very necessary step on the path to friendship!

Weston suggests using the acronym ARE to improve your small talk.

Here's how to put it into practice.

A—*anchor.* In this context, an anchor is about where you are and what is around you. So you might comment on the class you're waiting for, the long line at the bar, the weather, the music, or the decor.

R—*reveal.* This is where you use the topic of the anchor to share something about yourself. You might say something like, "I always struggle to get to this class on time because I'm not a morning person." Or, "I love this place; I've been coming here for the past year since I moved here." Or, "I grew up in Michigan, but this weather is still too cold for me."

E—*encourage.* This is where you invite the other person to talk, respond, or reveal something in turn, for example, "What did you think of last week's assignment?" "Do you live around here?" or "Oh, when did you move to the East Coast?"

That's not so hard, right? And once you've made that initial connection, conversation (and the beginning of a friendship) can flow from there. Maybe the conversation will continue. Perhaps it won't—but then you'll say hello and chat with them again the next time you see them. Maybe you'll invite them to join your study group or they'll ask if you'd like to join them at their table or *whatever*. And all you had to do was be friendly!

Don't be a snob.

If you tend to have strong feelings about people's taste in music, books, food, or TV, or care a *lot* about where people went to school or what town they are from, you're going to miss out on a lot of amazing friend opportunities. Before you write people off because their tastes aren't "impressive" by your standards, consider whether this is a deeper-rooted You Problem. One essay I read put it perfectly: "At the root of snobbery is a lack of imagination and confidence about how to decide who in the world is valuable."[27]

On Names and Pronouns

- If you don't know how to pronounce someone's name, say, "How do you pronounce your name?" If the name is hard to pronounce, learn how. Practice at home if you have to. I believe in you!

- Check with people before you start calling them by a shortened version of their name. If someone has made clear they prefer their full name or don't like the nickname you're trying to give them, accept that and let it go. Calling someone by a nickname they dislike or don't want to be called is disrespectful at best, and racist at worst.

- Resist the urge to inquire about a name that seems unusual to you, especially if you're just meeting someone. If their name is *that* unusual, it's likely that the story behind it (or the lack thereof—sometimes, parents just choose names they like!) will come up in conversation at some point. And if it doesn't come up, assume you don't need to know. And in either case: *Move on.*

- If you notice a mutual friend mispronouncing a friend's name, correct that person. ("Oh, it's actually Ay-vuh not Eee-vuh.") Do this repeatedly if necessary.

- Use people's correct pronouns. If someone tells you they go by they/them, not he/him, then refer to that person as "they/them." Do this all the time, even if the person isn't present when you're talking about them. (And don't nitpick the use of the singular "they" in writing, for crying out loud.)

- If someone is getting divorced, it's OK to ask them what last name they'll be using going forward. (Not the moment they tell you the news, of course . . . but it's OK to ask before you, say, mail them an invitation or card.)

- And it should go without saying, but . . . never mock someone's name. It's literally their name!!!

When you're ready to take things to the next level, let your intentions be known.

I've found the easiest way to make friends is to tell people I'm trying to make friends. I also let my current friends/acquaintances know—because I'm definitely not opposed to a friend set-up when I'm looking for new pals. But if I meet someone new who I seem to click with, I'm very comfortable saying, "I'd love to hang out soon! I just moved here and haven't met a lot of people yet!" or "We should get together some time! I'd really love to meet some new friends who are [in my industry/live around here/also parents/ etc.]" There's no shame in wanting or needing to make friends! It's fine!!!

So many people will breathe a sigh of relief at that kind of statement, and confess that they too want to make new friends and have been struggling with it. (It's also just practical when there's any possibility that an invitation to hang out could be misconstrued as asking someone on a date. And on that note: Don't casually use the word "date" in when you're talking about friend hangouts, and don't tell people you're low-key interested in that you're just trying to make new friends! It's confusing!!!)

True story: I recently hosted a party and invited some potential new friends I'd met the week before at a trivia event, and, to my delight, they came! During the party, the trivia peeps were discussing some potential future hangouts and one woman said, "I mean, I'm pretty thirsty for new friends right now, so I'm down for any of these things!" Everyone *immediately* agreed, and the conversation shifted to how hard it is to make friends as an adult, while I secretly celebrated her statement. Inject that honesty, vulnerability, and real-world validation straight into my veins, baby!!!!!

Suggest specific friend date ideas *and* days/times—so you can really commit to making it happen.

Avoid a general, "We should get together some time!" and skip the generic "We should get coffee"—coffee hangouts have a way of getting rescheduled indefinitely and never get on the calendar at all. Instead, try to suggest something more specific.

💬 What to say

"Would you like to get lunch after this?"

"I've been dying to go to the new escape room that opened near the mall. Would you want to go with me sometime this month?"

"Did you see there is going to be a Beyoncé-themed cycling class next Wednesday? I'm planning to go if you'd like to join me."

You can also extend an invite via text, like so:

"Hi! Not sure how you feel about musicals but I'm dying to see the new *Cats* movie this weekend. Would you want to join me?"

And if you have your heart set on coffee, this too can be made more specific! "Have you been to Sweetener? It's not too far from here, and they have the best lavender lattes. We should go after class next week!"

Accept their invitations.

If a new friend invites you to their art showcase, recital, or house party, *actually show up*. Attending an event earns you friendship points regardless of where you are in the relationship, but I swear there's some sort of gold star multiplier applied when you do it early on in the relationship. *Everyone* loves it. It's an incredibly effective way to show interest and enthusiasm in the person, and to learn a little more about them.

Be willing to be spontaneous.

The ideal conditions for making new friends? Casual, unstructured, repeated interactions. Think: shooting the shit, grabbing lunch or drinks, joking around after a class or meeting, and just *chatting*. If you're a big planner like I am, you may find these unplanned interactions difficult. But at least try to be open to the idea, and maybe occasionally say yes when a surprise opportunity to hang out (or extend a hangout) arises. Go along with the group of coworkers who invited you to get lunch; say yes to the person who sends you the "I'm in your neighborhood, want to meet up?" text (or send one of your own); or let brunch flow into wandering through a bookstore and boutiques.

Don't expect friendship to happen overnight.

Yes, some friendships are immediate, but those are rare—most take time to really gel. One study suggests that casual friendships emerge after about 30 hours of interaction, and that good friendships can require around 140 hours—but there are a lot of factors that can influence these estimates, including the number of weeks that those hours are spread out across.[28] And the *way* you spend those hours matters a lot (see the above point about the ideal conditions for making new friends). While you can try to create the right conditions and lean into these moments when they happen, you really can't force or engineer them. Ultimately, making a new friend involves some luck and magic—it requires time and also good timing. So don't get terribly discouraged if you're meeting people you like but don't have a new BFF just yet. You'll get there.

Don't overlook the power of acquaintances.

It's understandable to want to make new "close" friends, but casual friendships are still really valuable. According to sociologist Mark Granovetter, having "weak ties" (think: a friendly crossing guard you chat with regularly, someone you see at the park or gym several days each week) can boost your overall well-being, and make you feel less lonely and more connected to your community.[29]

Miriam Kirmayer, a therapist and friendship expert, says it's in our best interest to cultivate these friendships at the places we frequent—so, work, your kids' school, your place of worship, etc. "We can have friends or acquaintances in different contexts who add meaning to our lives in their own way," Kirmayer told *The New York Times*. "We have an acquaintance at work that we connect and talk about work projects, or dog-walking friends. It helps to have these different kinds of people in our lives to add different kinds of support."[30]

Know when to quit.

While I believe that making new friends is a worthwhile effort, it's still a *lot* of effort, and, like anything else, your heart has to be in it. There have definitely been times in my life when I've felt outside pressure to make new friends, and it got under my skin in the same way it would if someone was constantly telling single me that I should find a partner. It's OK to take a break or to deprioritize making friends for a little while. Making new friends—especially as an adult—is *work*.

Connecting with Your New Friends

So, you've met someone you want to be friends with, and you think they want to be friends with you, too. Great! You did it! This is so exciting! Here are some ways to tend to this new connection and help it grow into a long-lasting friendship where both of you prioritize showing up for each other.

Be generous with attention.

Look, we're all simple creatures: We just want people to care about us and think we're interesting/special. And the entry-level way to communicate "You're interesting and special!" is simply to pay attention. As *Small Talk* author Diane Weston explains it, "Whether you are talking to your partner or someone you're standing next to in line, the thing that most people want is to be listened to. Not just tolerated."

So, how to communicate that you're doing more than just tolerating someone? Start with the basics: Make eye contact with them and don't look at anything else, including your phone; listen to what they are saying (instead of thinking about what you are going to say in response); and respond in a way that shows you heard what they said.[31] I know these seem fairly obvious, but it's surprising(ish) how many people *don't bother to do them*.

While not doing these basics will definitely communicate a lack of interest, the reverse isn't necessarily true—that is, doing these things won't guarantee that you'll seem interested or that people will enjoy talking to you, especially if you're only doing this because you know you're "supposed to." You can make unbreaking eye contact or ask all the follow-up questions in the world, but, in general, humans are able to intuit when someone is insincere or doesn't *really* care about getting to know them.

The best way to show interest is *to actually be interested.* When you genuinely believe that other people are unique, special, and worthy of your time and attention, they'll feel it.

Learn to recognize the difference between a conversation and an interrogation.

Asking people about themselves is a fantastic way to show interest, but I get super-overwhelmed if a new friend hits me with one question after another, and I don't think I'm the only one! Firing off a bunch of questions can also come across as impersonal. It's important to process the other person's answer, and respond to it (even briefly!) before hitting them with another question. Here are two versions of a new-friend interaction to illustrate the difference between a conversation and an interrogation.

Version 1

Tyler: So, what do you like to do for fun? Do you have any hobbies?

Cam: Well, I recently joined my company's softball team, which has been fun!

Tyler: Oh, cool! Had you ever played softball before?

Cam: I played in high school, actually.

Tyler: Nice! What position did you play?

Cam: Second base.

Tyler: Fun! Did you play any other sports in high school?

Cam: Yes, I played basketball until my junior year.

Tyler: Nice, what position were you?

Cam: I was often the point guard.

Tyler: Oh, cool. So, how often does the work league practice and play actual games? Is it a big commitment?

Cam: It's not too bad! We practice for an hour on Monday evenings and then we play on Wednesday evenings.

Tyler: Where are the games?

Cam: We're at Rust Park!

Tyler: Fun! Do you live around there?

Cam: I don't! I live in Burgerville, so I have a thirty-minute drive home from practice.

Tyler: Oh, how long have you lived in Burgerville?

Version 2

Tyler: So, what do you like to do for fun? Do you have any hobbies?

Cam: Well, I recently joined my company's softball team, which has been fun!

Tyler: Oh, had you ever played softball before?

Cam: I played in high school, actually.

Tyler: Nice! How often does the work league practice and play?

Cam: Just one game a week, and one practice a week.

Tyler: Oh cool, that doesn't sound like a huge commitment! My office's team is super hardcore; they have two-hour practices three times a week, and then have games once a week.

Cam: Oh, yeah, I couldn't deal with that. We play at Rust Park, which is near my office, so I can easily go after work, but I live out in Burgerville, so it's kind of a trek—getting home takes me like thirty or forty minutes. Doing that more than twice a week would be way too much for me.

Tyler: Oh yeah, that's a lot.

Cam: Remind me—what neighborhood do you live in?

See the difference? In both interactions, Tyler is communicating interest by asking Cam questions, but in the second example, Cam actually has time to *breathe,* and is given an opportunity to help steer the conversation. While most folks do love talking about themselves, being asked a ton of questions can make them feel like they are being quizzed or interviewed, and can seem unnatural when compared to a true give-and-take conversation between individuals who are genuinely interested in getting to know each other.

Instead of asking tons of questions, try asking for recommendations. People *love* sharing their opinions on everything from where to go on vacation to whether you should break up with your partner. So if you have a low-stakes dilemma or need suggestions, ask your new friends! This can be an especially useful if you've realized that you tend to interrogate people without meaning to, or if your new friends are on the introverted side.

On Touching

It's a good idea to figure out your friends' comfort levels with regard to physical touch early on. You shouldn't assume that everyone appreciates hugs, pats, squeezes, and rubs–but don't assume everyone hates them, either. Instead, start by paying attention to physical cues. Are their arms crossed/do they have their hands in their pockets? Or are they going for a handshake the second they approach you? Do they tense up when you accidentally brush up against them? Are they touchy with *anyone?*

If you're a hugger and aren't sure if they are, too, start with the basic request: "Can I give you a hug?" (I swear, this feels way more awkward in your head than it does IRL!) Or: "I'm a hugger; are you?" It's not weird; it's considerate.

Practice naming your needs early.

If you have a habit of not being vulnerable or saying what you need, a new friendship can be an ideal opportunity to change that—because there's no baggage or ten-year history that will make your setting a boundary come across as unusual or out of character. New friends will just assume you're a confident person who is comfortable sharing your needs. (And if they react badly to this, that's a sign that you may not want to be close friends with them.)

During your conversations, take note of the ways in which you're alike and different.

As you're getting to know people, it can be helpful to mentally note anything they say that communicates a way in which they differ from you—in their personality, tastes, beliefs, values, preferences, or priorities. Most of us take the "treat others as you'd like to be treated" rule to heart, which is a good thing . . . until you're dealing with someone who is the complete opposite of you in a particular regard. In those instances, noticing the ways in which you're different (or appear to be different, based on the information available to you) can help you communicate interest in a more meaningful way; plan hangouts they actually enjoy; say or do things that make them feel more comfortable; and not take it personally if they don't respond to an idea, suggestion, topic, or situation with the same enthusiasm (or outrage!) that you would.

For example, let's say they casually mention—at different points across conversations—that they are introverted, nonreligious, and don't talk to their parents or siblings all that much. Meanwhile, you are a huge extrovert who calls their sister every day and never misses church followed by Sunday dinner at your mom's house. This divergence doesn't mean you can't be friends! It just means that when your niece's baptism rolls around and your family is planning a party for two hundred to celebrate it, you can couch the invite to your friend in the context of, "I totally understand this might not be your thing so feel free to say no, but I still wanted to invite you because we'd love to have you there!"

Remember: Your New Friends Are People

If you're worried about coming on too strong to new friends, it can be helpful to ask yourself if you're interested in your potential new friends as *people,* or as *potential new friends.* It's a small distinction, but it really matters. A *potential new friend* is someone who appears to be sort of . . . your-friend-shaped. They might enjoy many of the TV shows or musicians that are popular with people your age, or, say, appreciate the same types of memes that you do. Great! That's a good starting place! But when you're interested in someone as a *person,* you'll go beyond those shared interests and identify the qualities or characteristics that are uniquely them that you genuinely like and appreciate.

So, if you're interested in someone as a potential new friend, you might notice that you both like *The Real Housewives.* But then let's say you *also* notice that this person is an extroverted trivia buff who remembers everyone's birthday and is obsessed with Shrek memes. And even though none of your current friends are obsessed with Shrek memes, and "likes Shrek memes" isn't a quality you tend to seek out in new friends, you actually really like this about them—especially when coupled with their other personality traits and the interests you have in common. *That* is starting to like someone as a *person.*

There's absolutely nothing wrong with liking everyone as a potential new friend at first—that's how making friends begins! But it causes problems when you find yourself *collecting* potential new friends, and treating them as interchangeable. At that point, it's less about genuinely connecting with people and more about fitting them into the role of Friend that you're trying to cast—which is something folks tend to pick up on and don't respond well to. If you regularly find yourself getting super invested in people you only know on that potential new-friend level, or sending the *exact* same messages, invitations, life updates, and "This made me think of you!" links to *all* of your potential new friends, you might be falling into this trap and need to readjust.

Your new friends are people—but your new friends are also *just* people. When you're stressed about striking up a conversation, asking them to hang out, or going to their house party, remember this. They are human beings who are probably just as nervous and uncertain as you are. I'm realizing that so much of being a person in the world is believing that you're the aberration—that everyone except you has it all figured out; that they all have access to something you don't; that you're broken and in need of fixing. But you're not insufficient; you're good. We're all good.

Chapter 7
The Care and Keeping of Friends

'm a big believer in the idea that we should give our non-romantic relationships the sort of attention, care, and mental energy that we give our romantic ones. I would like to see more women's magazines devote as much space to the topic of friendship as they do to romantic relationships. "101 Ways to Please Your Friends This Weekend!" "*Exactly What to Say to Blow Your Friend's Mind Tonight!*" But at minimum, we should be thinking about our close friends *at least* as much we think about our crushes, our favorite sports teams, or reality TV celebrities.

While I think that we as a culture are starting to recognize that friendships do deserve real time and attention, I don't know that we've totally figured out what that means, practically speaking. So in this chapter, we'll talk about how to do just that—how to have better conversations and hangouts, ways to make your friends feel seen and understood, tips for keeping in touch with people, and how to be more vulnerable within your friendships. I might not be able to give you 101 ways to please your friends this weekend, but I think we can get pretty close.

Showing Up for Friends Every Damn Day

Good interactions with friends are one of life's greatest joys. And while it's easy to be *bad* at conversations with friends, it's not *that* hard to be good at them, either. Regularly showing up for friends is about being mindful of what you say (and don't say), what you share, and when you share it.

EXPRESSING GENUINE INTEREST

Come to conversations prepared with things to talk about.

You don't need to make a twenty-minute PowerPoint presentation before a coffee hangout, but in the hour before your visit, you may want to think of some answers to the inevitable "What's new with you?" question. If you're drawing a blank, think about what you've enjoyed recently (books, podcasts, movies, new recipes); any noteworthy purchases you've made since you saw them last; any new trips/vacations you're planning; and anything on your calendar for the next month or so that you're excited about.

Ask and remember the names of the coworkers and colleagues they talk about the most.

This tip—my friend Gyan's suggestion—isn't something I'd necessarily do during a first hangout, but it's worthwhile if you're a bit further along in the friendship process. Not only is it logistically easier, it communicates, "I am invested in you and your stories." (Bonus: Ask to see photos of the main people in their life. It's more fun and will help you remember the people better.) I always think it's cute when a newer friend asks me about one of my other friends by name or says, "You don't have to keep saying, 'My coworker, Casey.' I know who Casey is." It's a sign they've been paying attention.

When you're catching up, ask them how their parents/siblings are doing.

I like this question because a) I tend to care about my friends' families, and b) it's a really effective way to get to know a friend better. If, for example, they are having a lot of conflict with their sibling, or their relationship with their parent is strained, that's a big deal! And even if things are good, you'll still learn a bit more about your friend through their answer.

Make a point to research or engage with their interests in your free time.

If they keep talking about a comic book or podcast they are into, or they recommend a recipe or product, check it out after your conversation. You might discover that it's not really your thing, which is fine—you don't have to join their fandom to further the friendship. Even saying something like, "I looked up that wild Wikipedia entry you mentioned the other day and—WOW!" communicates "I am listening to you and I am interested in you."

Take an interest in the things your friend cares about, even if the topics aren't exactly your cup of tea.

Sure, *Steven Universe* fanfic might not be *your* thing, but if your friend brings it up, you can still say, "Confession: I've actually never watched *Steven Universe!* What's it about?" Or "Oh, I don't know much about writing fanfic! How did you get into it?" Or "I don't know anything about *Steven Universe,* but holy shit—this fanfic forum drama you're describing sounds *wild!* Please tell me everything." You don't have to be friends with people you don't share any interests with or who relentlessly blather on about topics you couldn't care less about, but learning about new topics from people you like is *fun.*

Commit to being with the person or people you're with.

A couple of years ago, I took a trip with a friend I rarely spent time with in person. We'd been looking forward to the trip for a while, so I was dismayed that she checked her phone *constantly* during the trip. I'd be in the middle of telling her a story over breakfast, and I'd realize she'd gone quiet because she was scrolling through one of her feeds. (Yes, *while* we were eating in a restaurant!) Or she'd say she needed to check her email for work, but a minute later was in her Instagram DMs, where she would then stay for . . . a while. I was hurt and also just annoyed. We'd planned this trip specifically because she said that she missed me and wanted to see me. The phone—which had always been central to the way we stayed in touch—had become a genuine barrier to connection.

Look: I'm not the phone police; I don't care if people check their phones sometimes when we're together. It's not the end of the world if friends occasionally lounge around and scroll through their phones together. But it *is* frustrating when that crosses from "Sorry, I just need to respond to this text from my mom" to "I'm totally zoned out scrolling through Twitter and don't even realize that I'm now ignoring you" territory. And it's especially annoying if you don't get to see the person very often, or if booking time together is kind of an event.

What constitutes "good" phone etiquette in a given group really depends on the people, but these days, I err on the side of caution because I've found myself feeling pretty bummed and disappointed by friends who are clearly more interested in their phones than in me. And it's so easy to tell yourself that your friends don't care if you check your phone frequently—even if they very much do care.

What to Say to a Friend Who Won't Put Down Their Phone

- Be direct! Keep your tone neutral and gentle and say something like, "Hey, I'm here to hang out with you. Can you put your phone away for a bit and just be here?"
- Try to get ahead of it. When making plans, you could say something like, "Can we agree to turn our phones off and put them away for this hangout? I've been doing that with friends lately and I'm really loving it."
- Stop talking (even if you're in mid-sentence!) and wait until they are done. If they tell you to continue talking because they believe multitasking is a real thing, don't—just wait in silence until they are done.
- If it's been going on for a while, direct your gaze to their phone and say, "Is everything OK?"—meaning, if it's not urgent, they should cut it out.

Try to talk a little less about other people and a little more about your friend.

In *We Need to Talk,* Celeste Headlee writes, "Research shows we spend about 60 percent of our time in conversations talking about ourselves." OK, not great, we should all definitely work on that! But then she goes on: "Most of the remaining time is spent talking about a third person, *not the person we're talking to.* One study found that 'most social conversation time is devoted to statements about the speaker's own emotional experiences and/or relationships, or those of third parties not present.'"

My reaction to this was astonishment, immediately followed by, "Actually, yeah, that checks out." It also made me realize exactly what had been bothering me about certain conversational patterns I was in with friends. It wasn't talking too much about *them* that was making me feel a bit miffed. It was that we were talking extensively about their coworkers or our mutual friends, so I wasn't really getting a chance to share *my* stuff. It wasn't intentional—my friends are very conscientious and self-aware—and the tenor of our convos wasn't negative or gossipy (quite the opposite, in fact). But the conversations were still leaving me feeling kind of disappointed, and I finally understood why: We were dedicating too much airtime to people who were not us.

This isn't to say you can *never* talk about other people; there are a lot of great discussions to be had about mutual pals, family, celebrities, and politicians. But since learning this, I've been paying closer attention to the ways in which conversations are often *dominated* by talk about not-present third parties, and trying to reel it in when it's happening at the expense of talking about the person I'm with.

Build a routine.

If you want to see your friends regularly, consider setting up a standing hangout day/time. Even if you have to reschedule occasionally, it's still helpful to have *something* on the calendar holding you accountable. You could also opt to always do the same activity or meet at the same place so you don't have to do the extra work of figuring that out each time. It's OK—nice even!—to build intimacy through routine and familiarity.

KEEPING IT (SOMEWHAT) POSITIVE

Keep complaints and criticism in check.

You don't have to be relentlessly positive with your friends; in fact, being cheerful all the time can ultimately come across as out-of-touch or dismissive. But being around endless complaining is *exhausting* and can still bring the other person down. For example, if your friend selected a restaurant for lunch and then the server was rude, your order came out cold, and you never got your drink, and you just keep repeating "Ugh, this sucks" and "I'm so disappointed" and "I can't believe how terrible that service was" over and over, it can start to feel like criticism to your friend, who feels responsible for your displeasure, even if it's clearly not their fault. Remember: If you have a complaint, you have a *request*. So take your request to the appropriate party and then move on!

Be mindful of how you talk about other people/other friends in front of them.

No one wants to open up to someone who is insensitive, judgmental, or gossipy. If you're constantly sharing other people's business, talking shit about mutual friends the moment they leave the room, or just being snarky, it makes everyone trust you less. On more than one occasion, I've had friends say *really* unkind things about other people and not realize they were insulting me in the process. It made me feel like I couldn't trust this friend, and it fundamentally changed how I viewed them and our relationship.

Remember that intimacy isn't transferable.

Just because a friend loves you and feels super comfortable around you, and you love and feel comfortable around your significant other, it doesn't mean your friend wants to open up to your S. O.—or that your S. O. wants the friend opening up to them. Remember that your friends might not want to discuss personal topics while your partner is around or be OK with your sharing the things they told you in private with your partner later. And if you want to be close to a friend's S. O., you have to do the work to build trust and intimacy with them as an individual.

Believe what they tell you.

If a friend is telling you about a personal experience, avoid interrogating them or taking the devil's advocate position. (The devil doesn't need more advocates!!!) Become known as the friend who says, "I believe you," *especially* if your friend has never given you any reason not to believe them. (Which is the case more often than not!) This includes the seemingly small stuff too—like, don't continue to hound people about whether they are *really* allergic to perfume, cilantro, weed, or whatever else.

Don't pressure them to do things you know they don't want to do.

If your friend tells you that the project they've been assigned to at work is confidential, don't bug them (not even "jokingly") to tell you what it is. If you know that they are vegan, don't continue to ask them if they've changed their mind and want a big beefy hot dog. If they say they aren't at liberty to share information about a mutual friend, drop it. Bugging a friend to break confidences or go against their values isn't cute; it's disrespectful.

Figure out how to talk about money

Imbalances in income, wealth, debt, vacation time, and/or personal money principles can really wear on friendships. And because money is so tied to morality and self-worth, it's not always easy to communicate our financial circumstances, beliefs, and boundaries with pals. But money comes up a lot—directly and indirectly—in friendship, so it's worth figuring out what everyone is comfortable with, and approaching these topics with an extra level of thoughtfulness.

I've found that it's helpful to be proactive when it comes to talking about money. This can easily slip your mind if you're not the one who is particularly worried about their budget, so try to make a habit of the following:

- If you're making group plans, ask everyone to share their ideal budget/range for lodging, activities, etc. before you do any research. (Ideally, they'd share this info privately with the main organizer, but it may not always be possible.)

- If you're willing to pick up the tab for dinner or drinks, say "my treat" when you invite your friend so they don't stress about it (or decline because they can't afford it).

- If you're assuming you'll split the cost of something evenly, make sure they are on the same page.

- Ask them how much they are willing to spend on tickets to an event before you make the purchase, and be clear about the date by which you expect them to reimburse you.

- Remember to suggest free activities from time to time, and be kind if they tell you that they can't afford the upgrade you'd really love to splurge on.

- Lead by example: Be willing to say something is too expensive for you, so they know they can do the same.

Ultimately, just be mindful of the fact that a lot of people won't tell you directly that they are broke—and know that even people who have money will likely notice and appreciate your being thoughtful and considerate about others' finances.

HONORING YOUR FRIENDS

Establish shared traditions or shared languages.
Plan a weekend trip every summer, agree to see every new *Star Wars* movie together, write them a letter each year on their birthday, and so on. You can also develop your own shared language for things that come up a lot in conversations. Designating a phrase, acronym, or emoji to reference an inside joke or signal "I'm too busy to talk but am thinking of you!" can go a long way to deepen bonds.

When you're attending their event (like their birthday party or their improv show) wear their favorite color, or an outfit you know they like.

When I was in college, my mom—who cares *so little* about fashion and cloth-ing, and who is not a fan of the color pink—would wear her one pink T-shirt whenever she came to visit me. I knew she chose it specifically because I liked it, which made me feel seen and appreciated and genuinely happy. More recently, I long-distance came out as queer to her, and the next time I saw her, she just so happened to arrive wearing an Elton John concert T-shirt, which I am 150 percent sure was not an accident.

Take photos of and with them.

Having a couple of photos of yourself that you really like is *such* a treat. But a lot of folks don't have any, or have a bunch of selfies they secretly feel kind of self-conscious about. So if a friend is having a great hair day or wearing an awesome outfit, tell them that, and then offer to snap some pics of them. (And take the time to get a shot that they are actually happy with!) And try to take more photos of your people in general when you're together. Not for posting on social media—just to *have.*

Support their goals.

Showing up for friends means not begrudging their efforts when they are ac-tively trying to change for the better. And if you're feeling snarky or dismis-sive about your friends' efforts to improve, remember that it probably has a lot more to do with you than it does with them, and it's your responsibility to figure out what's got you feeling A Way.

Don't put your friends on a pedestal.

Admiring and looking up to your friends is a wonderful thing. But pedestals erase an individual's humanity and ultimately create distance. According to therapist Andrea Bonior, "Putting a friend up on a pedestal means that it will be difficult for you to show your real self to them, and it will be hard for you to be realistic when they need help with their own vulnerabilities."[32] If you've ever been on the other side of it, you probably know that it doesn't feel great to have a friend who looks up to you a little *too* much. "As much as it may feel good to have some admiration, there's something unnerv-ing about feeling like someone can't handle the 'real' you," Bonior says. So celebrate the shit out of your friends, but take note if you constantly feel like they are too good for you, and try to get to the root of that feeling before it begins to interfere with the friendship.

Ask for permission before sharing their good news with others.
I have a *lot* of thoughts on sharing people's bad news without their permission (more on that later!) but I think it's equally important to check that you're cleared to share good news about them. (Because maybe they want to be the one to communicate the news of their job offer or engagement to your friend group!) In general, it's wise to think of people's stories as theirs, not yours.

Celebrate their wins like they're your wins.
Being truly happy for other people is a beautiful thing, and it feels great to know that your friend is truly thrilled for you. So get everyone together for a spontaneous celebratory drink, buy them flowers, or just send them a thoughtful text that communicates "I'm so happy for you; you are wonderful and deserve nothing but good things."

Good Group Hangouts

When I was in college, several people I knew were members of a Facebook group called "All We Do Is Have Blasts." The first time I saw it, I remember thinking it was ridiculous and also made perfect sense. When I'm with friends, all I want to do is have a blast! Who doesn't?! A good gathering with friends—the kind when you find yourself smiling the whole way home, or replaying your favorite moments the next day—is one of the most sustaining, fulfilling life experiences.

While you can't necessarily engineer the perfect blast, you *can* be intentional and thoughtful about your hangouts. Whether you're meeting two friends for coffee, or heading on your annual long weekend at the lake with fourteen people, four babies, and two dogs, here are some tips to keep in mind.

Think about the purpose of your hangout.

In *The Art of Gathering,* author Priya Parker recommends deciding *why* you're getting together before you plan anything. Having an established purpose makes it easier to decide who to invite and what your activity will be, and helps you navigate issues like budget and the presence of +1s, kids, and phones. (Think about it: A book club, birthday, baby shower, and bachelor/ette party all tend to have fairly different expectations. And a casual hangout at age twenty-one might have a *very* different purpose or look quite different from a casual hangout at forty-five.) You can figure this out yourself (if you're the host) or decide as a group, and make it explicit (by, say, putting it in the invite) or just keep it in mind as you plan.

Be thoughtful about the invite list.

Showing up for one person sometimes means shutting the door on someone else. (This is particularly true when there's tension or mistrust within a friend group, which we'll dig into in Chapter 10.) This isn't carte blanche to be a cliquey little a-hole or, you know, a bigot. Exclusion should be done thoughtfully and sparingly, and with the utmost discretion—you should be mindful about how you talk about it in front of other friends, and if/how you post on social media.

Deciding who to invite or to exclude in the name of showing up can be difficult; it's an instance where you have to draw on intuition and lived experience to decide what's right. If you're struggling, it's helpful to consider how critical *intimacy* and *self-expression* are to the hangout. For example, a book club that has been meeting every month for the past fifteen years likely has a high level of intimacy that may evaporate if a new person enters the mix—so you probably shouldn't be casual about adding new folks. But a newer book club where the participants don't know each other very well doesn't rely on intimacy as much to be fun or engaging, so the scenario might be "the more the merrier." Meanwhile, a queer book club is centered, in part, on *self-expression,* so inviting people who would hinder that self-expression—or simply not make everyone the *most* comfortable— could be a problem.

Of course, not all hangouts will have such clearly defined purposes, and some people in the group might feel a higher need for self-expression or intimacy at a hangout than others. It's helpful to think about these two needs when making the guest list, and to remember that if you're trying to show up for everyone, you may not be able to truly show up for *anyone*.

Remember to honor the labor of showing up.
The labor of showing up is the (often invisible!) work of caring—thinking about other people's feelings, comfort, needs, and preferences, and *knowing what to care about in the first place.* The labor of showing up is sending thank-you notes; it's figuring out whose house the family will be going to for the holidays; it's researching a venue that can hold a group of your size; it's planning the group vacation; it's RSVPing; it's coordinating the office potlucks; it's choosing, buying, and wrapping the gift for the birthday party your five-year-old is attending. It's what has historically been treated as "women's work," and, as a result, is often undervalued, overlooked, and ignored.

In the context of group gatherings, the labor of showing up might look like . . .

- recognizing the need for a celebration or gathering
- starting the spreadsheet, Google Doc, or email thread
- bugging people to update/read the spreadsheet, Google Doc, or email thread
- coordinating people's schedules and choosing a date that works for everyone
- calling a restaurant or venue to make a reservation for the group
- taking everyone's preferences into account when planning an event (remembering who is vegetarian, who despises karaoke, who is on a tight budget, etc.)
- being aware of any people in the group who don't really get along or just aren't the best of friends

- responding to any requests related to a group hangout (e.g., sending your T-shirt size and money—on time!!!—to the person planning your friend's bachelor/ette party).

When you don't do any sort of labor within your friendship and/or fail to acknowledge that your friends *are* doing that work, it can lead to hurt feelings and resentment. And, as my friend Terri has said, just because your friend seems to enjoy doing it and is good at it, you don't get to opt out entirely! You should still offer to help out so they can take a break occasionally, or offer to share the work by doing something similar in scope that still needs to be done. At the absolute minimum, you can do two things for a friend who takes on the labor of showing up: 1) *respect* the work, and 2) *honor* the work.

Respecting the work means *paying attention* and giving the person coordinating the event whatever they need to make planning easier. It's reading the email about the lake trip and responding in a timely manner. It's sending your RSVP or paying for your share on time. It's *not* staying silent while everyone researches potential themes and T-shirt designs, and *then,* once they've all decided on a hoedown theme and red tank tops, chiming in with, "Y'all: What if we did a '90s party and got matching purple hoodies?"

Honoring the work is even easier: It's just *saying thank you.* "Thanks for setting up that spreadsheet!" "Thanks for taking the lead on this!" "Thank you for calling and making that reservation; I really appreciate it!" "Thank you for researching all the different T-shirt options and prices." "Thank you for organizing this; it was so fun." It's truly that easy! Be as generous with your appreciation as your friend was with their time and energy.

A Modest Proposal: Take Notes When Hanging Out with Friends

I've been invited to join my friend Julia's Ladies Article Club on a few occasions when I've visited her, and it's always such a treat! One of my favorite aspects of this hangout is that someone always takes notes during the gathering. The note-taker writes down anything that comes up in conversation that warrants some kind of follow-up—so basically, if someone mentions a product or a recipe or a podcast episode or a good Instagram account, the note-taker adds it to her list. Then she'll start an email thread with everyone later on to collect/share the items mentioned.

I've always thought this idea was *so* smart and efficient, and I've started doing it more when hanging out with friends—even just, like, during a coffee date. I like doing it because it's practical, but also because writing these items down in my journal creates a mini diary entry about the hangout/the conversation.

I was recently at my friend Emily's apartment for a little friend dinner party, and when she mentioned a book she liked, I said, "Wait, I'm going to write down the stuff we talk about so I can look it up later." I pulled out my notebook and pen, and another friend, Jess, said, "Welcome to Rachel's meeting," and everyone laughed. AND YET! An hour or so later, Emily asked me where my pullover and my socks were from, and when I told her, she said, "Wait, I want to write all this down," and took out her phone and opened the Notes app. And later that night, after we'd all gone home, Jess texted the group and said, "Who is sending out the meeting notes?" And we all shared the things we'd discussed and made a note of!

I always think I'm going to remember all the things my friends or I mention when we're hanging out, but when you're with smart/well-read/interesting people, that's basically impossible. Just take notes!

Keeping in Touch

Keeping in touch with friends *should* be easy. After all, we've got a device that allows us to do so on our person pretty much all the time. And yet. *And yet.* It recently occurred to me that I was actually much better at keeping in touch with people* before the rise of smartphones and apps, and I don't think that's a coincidence. Of course, there are other reasons I was better at keeping in touch back then: We were younger, so we had fewer responsibilities and more time on our hands, and, at the time, I think *everyone* was less resistant to phone calls. But I also know that my iPhone is, in part, to blame! I can no longer tell myself that liking a friend's pic is the same as *keeping in touch*—or, at least, it's not enough when it comes to the people I care about most. If I want to be a part of people's lives, I've realized, I have to do the work. Here are some tips that I've found helpful.

Stop putting it off.

Falling out of touch with a friend is a vicious cycle; the longer you let time pass without a good update, the harder it gets to pick up where you left off. Because so much has happened since your last chat, the mere *idea* of downloading the past four months of events can be exhausting.

But if you *have* let too much time lapse, all hope is not lost! If you want to maintain the friendship, just suck it up and commit to a *big* catch-up session (think: a LONG phone chat, a day or weekend spent together IRL, a long-ass email where you give the backstory and context for what's currently happening in your life). Once that's out of the way, commit to talking more consistently going forward.

Make time for them.

Remember Shasta Nelson's frientimacy triangle? Of course you do! And remember that consistency is one of the main components? Of course you do! (But if you don't, turn back to page 125.) That consistency can't happen if you don't set aside time for it.

---

* By the way, keeping in touch doesn't only apply to long-distance folks; it's necessary in any situation where you won't cross paths with a friend somewhat naturally (like at work or at school events) fairly regularly.

A lot of us fall into the trap of staying in touch in small ways that *feel* meaningful (liking social media posts, occasionally texting articles or memes) and that don't take a lot of time. It "costs" less time and energy, sure—but that's because it's a lower-quality conversation. After all, sending links or hitting "like" isn't the same as both of you sharing updates about your life. So try to think of these as supplementary interactions, and then regularly make time for the meatier, more meaningful interactions.

Of course, finding time for this is easier said than done. Having time for catch-up sessions might mean that something else you enjoy doing (*cough* *watching every single Instagram story* *cough*) has to go, and it can be helpful to return to your list of priorities here. But it *also* might mean you can't stay in touch with everyone you're fond of or you'd like to be close to. Remember Dunbar's numbers; most of us can really only manage three to five super intimate relationships at a time (and that includes family members!), and nine to fifteen close relationships. It can be hard to admit that you can't actually be best friends with everyone, but . . . you can't! Admitting and owning your limitations is a major part of showing up.

Find a method of communication that works best for the two of you.
Every relationship is different, with two people who bring unique circumstances and preferences that will affect how you'll communicate. Your time zone, work schedules (and types of work), daily routines, internet/cellular connection, physical abilities, and access to privacy can all influence which communication form will be best for a particular relationship at a given time.

Here are some of the ways you might converse/interact with a friend.

- IRL hangouts
- Phone calls
- Voice memos (like voice mails, but somehow less hateful???)
- Video calls
- Emails
- Letters

- Instant messages
- Text messages (which can either be asynchronous *or* happen in real time, more like instant messaging)
- Group chats

But also: Be creative! Perhaps talking on the phone while sitting around the house doesn't work for you but voice chatting while you play a video game together is perfect. Maybe instead of sending a friend an email, you send them a Google Doc so they can easily comment on or reply to the things you're sharing in-line. The point isn't to do what other people think is "right"—it's to find a method of communication that achieves the intended goal.

And once you're doing meaningful check-ins consistently, you may want to establish a low-hanging-fruit way to chat with each other day to day. Something as simple as Snapchatting (yes, Snapchat!!!) each other pics of your breakfast and outfits every morning can be a surprisingly effective way to feel more connected.

If you're not really a phone person, consider talking on the phone.
These days, I—like many people my age—am not much of a phone talker . . . which is wild, because I love talking, and I used to *love* talking on the phone! Most of my current excuses are situational (talking on the phone while walking on a crowded city street is hard; my apartment doesn't have great cell service), and while they are valid, they aren't exactly deal breakers. Also, talking on the phone is just more efficient than texting or emailing or instant messaging (especially now that we know how bad/inefficient multitasking is).

Anyway, my phone call–loving (and text-loving!) friend Terri has taught me the important lesson that some people are *great* on the phone (and not great at texting), so I've been making more phone calls. And it's been great! (But do consider giving any text-loving friend a heads-up that you're going to call them more often, so they don't see their phone ringing and assume it's a butt-dial, or that someone died.)

So, if you're able to talk on the phone, maybe do that! It's better than losing lifelong friends because they can't chat on Google Hangouts all day at work.

Don't hesitate to set up standing days/times to talk.

If you and your friends tend to play a lot of phone tag, it might be wise to put your catch-up sessions on the calendar in advance. If that isn't possible, you can still try to get a general sense of what works and what doesn't work with their schedule. For example, if your friend works 9:00 to 5:00 every weekday, calling them to catch up at 3:00 PM on a weekday probably doesn't make sense. (This seems fairly obvious, but you'd be surprised how many people do it anyway!) But if you know your friend has a forty-five-minute walk home every day, you might find that a random Thursday evening when you have some unexpected down time is the perfect moment to call—even if you haven't already planned that you're going to talk then.

Make your text conversations more meaningful.

If, for whatever reason, texting is the best way to stay in touch with someone, you can make those conversations more productive and effective. First, try aligning with your friend on how you view texting. If you have more meaningful conversations when you're both present (like an instant-message conversation), treat it like an instant-message conversation! That might mean you only do it when you're both in the mood and available, and it might require a more formal start to the conversation—such as asking them if they are around and have a second to chat. On the other hand, if both of you want to treat it as an asynchronous form of communication (more like email), it might be OK to send each other longer updates and messages, knowing there's no expectation of an immediate response.

Second, aim to communicate *effectively*. That doesn't always mean *fast*; in fact, the desire to compose a reply too quickly can lead to a lot of difficult-to-parse abbreviations or shorthand, which can ultimately hinder the conversation. Instead, focus on ensuring that the other person understands you. So: Use punctuation and capital letters, correct any typos, and do the work to make sure your tone is really felt (even just via emojis). And instead of simply sending a link or a photo, also add a message with your thoughts or that explains why you're sending it. This might sound obvious, but a lot of people don't bother, and it *really* makes a difference.

I'm also a fan of "texting" via my computer, which can often be done even if the other person is messaging you from their phone. My wrists quickly start to hurt when I type long messages on my phone, which makes a thoughtful, meaningful conversation difficult. But if you're using Facebook Messenger, WhatsApp, Slack, Google Hangouts, or iMessage (and you have a Mac computer), using a computer is an option. (And if it's someone you really want to stay in touch with, it might be worth switching the conversation to a different platform to make this possible.) Basically, doing this allows you to treat texting more like email or old-school AIM, and to be a little more engaged and communicative than you would be on your phone.

Try not to rely solely on social media for updates.

We all know that social media updates provide a snippet of our lives that never tells the whole story. Yet we're often still content to get a *large* portion of our updates about our friends from social media!!! So consider this a gentle reminder that getting updates mainly from social media really isn't enough.

If you're using social media to stay in touch, be *intentional* about it. That might mean setting up a private Facebook group for your closest friends, where you can all share honest updates without it being super public. It might mean using the "close friends" feature on Instagram more, so you can share the unfiltered version of your life. It probably does not—and I'm just spitballing here—mean scrolling through your feed for hours, looking at influencers, bra ads, and random people you went to high school with or met once at a party ten years ago.

I think of social media updates as a jumping-off point that tells me something about a friend's life that I can then ask them more about later. If I see a friend's vacation photos, I can glean some top-level information (where they were, who they were with, the activities they did, how the weather was) that means I don't have to ask a million basic questions later. But I'll still ask them about it and give them space to tell me more about the trip the next time I chat with them. Saying something like, "How was the trip? I saw your photos on Facebook!" communicates, "You don't have to repeat anything you already posted publicly*...but I'm still interested in hearing about your experience, including all the details you didn't share."

Pay attention to the weather in the city.

This tip comes from my friend Gyan, an Australian living in the US, far from most of her closest friends. "The argument that talking about the weather is lazy or boring is to ignore the fact that the weather is something we all deal with literally every single day," she says. "Weather influences our outfit decisions, weekend plans, and daily commute—it's a big deal, and I'm not ashamed to admit that it's often one of the first things my friends and I talk about. I live in an opposite climate to most of them, so when it was snowing in New York and they were melting during a Sydney heat wave, we empathized with each other. Watching the forecast of my friends' hometowns offers a tiny daily insight into the lives of my favorite people, and I highly recommend it."[33]

Ask to see photos of the people they talk about the most.

I mentioned this earlier as a nice way to show up for all of your friends, but it's just the practical choice in a long-distance friendship. When you'll likely never meet any of the people you're hearing so much about, or when your friend has three different coworkers named Ali, it's *so* helpful to be able to keep everyone's faces in mind.

If possible, connect with a few other people in your friend's location.

If your friend just moved across the country, it's not a bad idea to, say, get their spouse's contact info, or get the number of the new work BFF you met on your recent visit. You don't have to talk with these people regularly; it's just about establishing a lightweight connection in case you ever want to plan an IRL surprise for the friend, or in the event that you haven't heard from the friend and are suddenly very worried about their well-being. One of the biggest downsides to maintaining a long-distance friendship is that it

---

* If you're the type of person who thinks it's "weird" to admit you saw photos/updates/information a person posted publicly on social media, know that it's extremely fine to do this! It's not "stalking"–the person shared this so people would know about it!

makes noticing patterns (and responding) more difficult; having a connection to someone "on the ground" can help offset this.

Do activities "together" even if you're far apart.

This could mean reading the same book, watching the same TV show, going to see the same movie on the same day, or cooking the same recipes. It's not the same as doing it together, of course, but it still feels pretty darn good and allows you to continue to inject new experiences into your relationship.

Make plans for the future.

Doing this is a clear sign of commitment, which can be incredibly reassuring if you're worried your friend is going to drop off the face of the earth after moving to a new city. So start thinking ahead! Maybe you'll commit to flying across the country on each other's birthdays every single year . . . but it also doesn't have to be that deep! You could take some of the advice above, but instead of planning to read a single book "together" right now, you could start a virtual book club where you read a book "together" every other month, or every three months.

Remember that it's OK to give up.

If you're really struggling to connect with a friend—literally or figuratively—it might be time to ask yourself whether you truly *want* to. Not all friendships are forever friendships, and some friendships are helped a great deal by proximity or exposure or being at a certain life stage. It can be a bummer to realize that, and it might leave you thinking, *Was this just a friendship of convenience?* But I don't think it necessarily means the friendship wasn't real; it's just that some friendships simply can't overcome *inconvenience,* and you had no way of knowing this until one of you got a new job or moved away. Be grateful for the good things this friendship brought into your life, accept things as they are (instead of what you wish they could be), let go of your guilt, and put your precious time and energy into someone or something that makes you feel as good as that friend once did.

Embracing Vulnerability

Remember the positivity-consistency-vulnerability pyramid from Chapter 5? Well, it's not just for hard times or for new friends; it's also helpful when it comes to taking established relationships to the next level. That's because vulnerability is a big factor in what separates acquaintances, good friends, and close friends. If you never allow your friends to see your true self, they will never get to know the real you.

Many of us are afraid of sharing TMI (too much information) with our friends. But in some relationships, the problem might actually be sharing NEI—not enough information. Because when you refuse to share anything messy or private or embarrassing about yourself, you downplay your own humanity and erect a wall between yourself and others. After all, it's hard to feel comfortable being your true, imperfect self around people who never ever seem to make mistakes.

It's also not unreasonable for kind, thoughtful people to interpret your lack of vulnerability as a Them Problem—even if it's not—and assume you don't like them or trust them. Refusing to open up to the friends you've known for a while (and who are slowly opening up to you) can, over time, begin to communicate, *You aren't in my inner circle* or *I didn't want to turn to you for support in this moment.* Which: fine! You're allowed to be choosy about who you share private information with and to keep big life news quiet for practical, logistical, or personal reasons! But if you're *regularly* keeping significant information from your closest friends—those you purport to trust and care about—it can chip away at the trust and honesty in the friendship and stand in the way of real, meaningful connections. If you know that your friendships could benefit from a dose of vulnerability on your part but don't know how to make it happen, here are some tips that may help.

Name your wants and needs.

Your needs and desires are a huge part of who you are, so communicating them is a crucial part of allowing others to fully know you. Revisit the list on page 26, and think about what needs you're currently comfortable sharing with different friends. Are you OK sharing what you need from *other* people with your friends? (Think: what you want and need from your family, your other friends, your romantic partners, your coworkers, the bartender who is currently serving you drinks, etc.) Do you feel like you can talk about your hopes and dreams with them? And are you able to share what you need *from them* with them?

By the way, if you're not used to thinking about what you want and need from a friend, it might look something like needing . . .

- to change the topic during a conversation
- to choose a different time/date/location for your next hangout
- more/less physical space
- a different form of communication, or a different frequency of communication
- more/less attention
- a different form of support when you're going through a hard time
- for them to take the lead on making plans, show up on time, or stop flaking on you.

And if you haven't been naming any of these needs, think about why. It could be a Them Problem . . . or it could be a You Problem.

Them Problem: They've reacted badly or been nasty when you (or other people) have expressed a similar want/need in the past; they are highly critical in general and tend to judge or shame people.

You Problem: You don't know what you need; you think they'll like you less if you're honest about your needs; you want to be seen as perfect; they haven't already magically guessed what it is you need, and that annoys you; you believe they'll criticize you for your behavior, and you kiiiiinda know they'd be right.

If it's a Them Problem, it could be time to evaluate this relationship as a whole. If it's a You Problem, consider being more vulnerable with them. In either case, you can test the waters by being more honest about a need that is low-stakes, and one that you're not terribly emotionally invested in. Once you've established that they aren't going to dump you simply because you told them you're hoping to get promoted at work soon, you can start sharing the needs that feel scarier.

Initiate new activities and topics of conversation.
Going outside the established routine of a friendship—by expanding your chosen activities, topics of conversation, or forms of communication—can be *really* scary! "We can feel nervous about intruding into each other's lives, scared to want something they don't," *Frientimacy* author Shasta Nelson says. "This can then trigger feelings of rejection, and fears that we're too needy." But refusing to put ourselves out there all but ensures that the relationship will never level up.

So take a deep breath and invite your work friend to the concert you're dying to get tickets to, ask the friend you text with a lot if they want to catch up over the phone, or ask the friend you only ever get coffee with if they'd like to go shopping with you. Even if they say no, the act of asking still matters. And while you're at it, gently introduce new topics of conversation that go beyond the subjects you usually cover when you hang out. Dipping a toe into topics like sex, money, religion, death, and/or family drama is scary, particularly if you really like the friend and want them to like you. But realizing you can talk to a new friend about these topics is a big deal and can be incredibly affirming.

Invite your friends into your home—even if your home isn't clean.
Allowing a person to come into your home is a very vulnerable act; doing so communicates: "I will let you see me in my most private and safe space, and I trust you not to harm me here."[34] And this is heightened when your home isn't party-ready—when there are dishes in the sink, when your bed is unmade, and when there are piles of laundry everywhere.

Show effort.

People—particularly women—are often expected to do *everything* (choose outfits, make friends, get a promotion, have a clean house, raise children, have perky tits) without ever breaking a sweat. To make an effort is to admit you want or need something—that your life isn't exactly where you want it to be. It's difficult to do this because people aren't always kind when they realize you're trying *really* hard to do a good job or achieve a goal or be liked. But that's exactly why it's a good idea to make a habit of being honest about your effort in the context of vulnerability! When you show your work—and not in a humble-brag sort of way, but genuinely—you allow people to get a better sense of who you are and what you need. And you allow them to cheer you on as you try, and console you if you fail. By showing your effort, you give them the space to be honest about their efforts, too.

Go ahead and admit "This is hard for me to talk about" or "I don't share this with many people."

Even though it might seem obvious to you that you're being vulnerable, it's a good idea to be explicit about it, particularly if you're talking to a newer friend. We all have different comfort levels when it comes to sharing personal information. For example, you might be panicking inside as you prepare to tell your friend you are starting therapy, and they might react as if it's the most normal thing in the world—because *they* don't feel embarrassed about going to therapy. When you name your struggle, you communicate that you want the other person to show up for you—something that is good for *both* of you. It also holds you accountable; once you admit what you're doing to yourself, you can't play it off as no big deal later on (or if they react badly/reject you). Also, naming your behavior can be a good gut check; it forces you to stop and ask yourself if you really want to share this information, and whether it's appropriate to share with this particular person right now.

Be open about the things you like and love, and share your wins.

It's worth remembering that vulnerability isn't just being honest about the shitty stuff; it's also about sharing the good stuff. Communicating excitement or success can be scary—like you're a middle schooler who is about to get their chair kicked out from under them, perhaps as punishment for "bragging." Being earnest feels way more vulnerable than being apathetic or disengaged or ironic . . . but I also can't imagine going through life any other way. And true friends will *want* to hear this stuff. Sorry to be all teacher-in-an-after-school-special, but the people who judge you or mock you when you talk about things you're clearly excited about aren't the people you're meant to be friends with. It's not corny; it's just true.

Apologize.

We'll get more into how to apologize well in Chapter 10, but I'm mentioning it here because it's one of the purest forms of vulnerability. If you never apologize to your friends—even after they express anger or frustration—it might be a sign that you aren't willing to be vulnerable.

Make sure they are being vulnerable, too.

Vulnerability can't be a one-way street; if only one of you is sharing regularly, that could be a sign that something is amiss. If you're being vulnerable and they aren't, it could be a Them Problem, or it could be a You Problem.

Them Problem: They struggle to open up to people; they are worried you'll think less of them, even though you've never given them a reason to think that.

You Problem: You're sharing too much, too soon; you're misreading their interest in you or their investment in the friendship; you haven't shown them that you're really trustworthy; you're actually not offering true vulnerability.

Of course, you can't force anyone to open up to you if they don't want to! But if you want to improve your friendships, it's a good idea to periodically take stock and see if you appear to be on the same page, vulnerability-wise.

Beware of inauthentic authenticity.

I first came across the term "inauthentic authenticity" in Martin Lindstrom's book *Brandwashed*. He talks about it in the context of retailers like Whole Foods. Think about their chalkboard signs with "messy" handwritten prices and the "rustic" wooden crates meant to invoke a roadside mom-and-pop fruit stand . . . even though the produce came from a big-ass farm hundreds of miles away. I often think about this in the context of friendships—because I've noticed a lot of humans exhibiting *the exact same behavior.* It's incredibly frustrating to have a conversation with someone who is performing vulnerability, and doing so ultimately harms the relationship in the long run. If you find yourself "opening up" about supposedly "vulnerable" topics or "flaws" that you actually *personally* feel safe sharing or are relatively confident won't change someone's opinion of you, and you're doing it in an attempt to seem closer to the person than you really are to get them to open up to you or to fast-track an intimate friendship, you miiiiight be doing it wrong and falling into the inauthentic authenticity trap.

Be generous in telling them how you feel about them.
"I really miss you." "I'm worried about you." "I appreciate you." "Your friendship means so much to me." "I love you." And, as my friend Gyan has taught me, "Be specific with your compliments. Your friends deserve to know exactly why they're important to the world."

Chapter 8
The Art of Noticing

eing noticed feels *good*. Think about a time when someone remembered your favorite color; referenced a joke you'd made earlier; followed up on something minor you mentioned the last time you saw them; or complimented you on a seemingly tiny detail that you put a ton of thought into. It's thrilling, right? Being noticed can genuinely make someone's day, foster warmth and positivity, and turn casual pals into close friends.

Noticing isn't about obsessively reading into every little thing someone does; it's about learning to really see people—their values, behaviors, preferences, emotions, needs, boundaries, experiences—and being able to recall what you saw. When you follow noticing with processing (the second step of showing up), you can start to pick up on patterns, which can tell you a much bigger story about a person or situation. Together, noticing and processing set the stage for naming and responding—using what you've gathered to honor, validate, and take action.

One of the definitions of "notice" is "to treat with attention," which I love. It *is* a treat! It's exuberant, joyful, generous curiosity, and it's at the heart of showing up.

How to Notice Everything
(Or Just . . . More Things)

Being good at noticing doesn't mean becoming some kind of observational savant with a photographic memory. It's mostly about knowing *what* to notice and making a *point* to notice.

Noticing starts with mindfulness.

If you want to get better at noticing, start by being fully present. Instead of getting lost in thought, aim to fully engage with what is happening in front of and around you. The goal is to be a little more aware of what you're seeing, hearing, and feeling.

If you're struggling to understand mindfulness, Susan David makes a suggestion in *Emotional Agility* that I found helpful; she recommends making sense of mindfulness by looking at its opposite: mind*less*ness. Mindlessness is, she writes, "the state of unawareness and autopilot. You're not really present. Instead you're relying too heavily on rigid rules or shopworn distinctions that haven't been thought through."[35] Mindlessness can look like entering a room and not being able to remember why you did, forgetting someone's name as soon as you hear it, and not being able to remember if you locked your door when you left your home a minute earlier. Mindfulness, on the other hand, means attending to what's happening and really taking it in.

I've found that embracing mindfulness takes commitment and practice—and a willingness to put down your phone. Meditation, spending time in nature, and monotasking helped me the most. But from there, it's about just doing the thing. If you want to be more mindful in your friendships, try this exercise: Aim to observe one new detail every time you hang out with a friend. It could be the shape of their nails, where they part their hair, a word they use a lot, or something about their values or preferences. (But don't comment on what you notice! Just quietly observe.)

Know what you're looking for.

The point of noticing is to better understand who your people are and what they need. That means being able to identify things like . . .

- basic details (where they are from, when their birthday is, who the most important people in their life are)
- important life experiences and things they consider core to their identity
- their sense of humor
- their preferences
- their priorities
- their values
- their routines
- their physical appearance
- how they are likely to react in various situations
- how they are feeling in a given moment
- what they want or expect from other people—in general, and in specific situations.

If you think you could stand to get better at picking up on the above, here are some high-level tips to keep in mind.

1. **Notice what people say.** Sometimes, noticing is fairly easy—because people will just tell you. Make a point to notice words that explicitly tell you who they are ("I'm from Michigan," "My birthday is in August"); what they are feeling ("I'm upset," "I'm hurt," "I'm stressed"); and their preferences ("No, thank you," "I love green"). Also take note of any topics they seem to have very strong feelings about or be well-versed in. If someone perks up at the mention of musicals or has a lot to say when a certain political subject comes up, it might be because this is very much Their Thing, or because it relates to their identity in a meaningful way.

2. **Notice how they say it.** Mood and tone communicate a *lot,* so make sure to note how people are communicating. Flat, one-word responses ("Ugh," "Hmm," and "Sure") can mean a person is not interested or enthusiastic and is trying to communicate that while still being nice. And if someone says, "I'm fine," sarcastically, they are . . . maybe not fine?

3. **Notice what they do.** To get to know your people better, make a point to notice their daily/weekly routines—the days they work out, their preferred routes, the shows they watch without fail, their favorite way to spend a Saturday. This can reveal basic details and tastes, but also their priorities and values. For example, if they often mention commitments at their place of worship, seeing the same friends every weekend, cooking every evening, or going to the gym every morning, that gives you a sense of who and what is important to them.

4. **Notice what they *don't* say and *don't* do.** If a friend never drinks alcohol, swears, eats meat, or responds to texts in a timely manner, that's very good information to have! At a basic level, it means that adding them to a group text about your upcoming "Fuck Yeah, Beer and Bacon" party is probably not going to make them feel terribly seen. But on a more serious note, if there's a topic that people never seem to talk about, or stay quiet about when other people are enthusiastically discussing it, there may be a reason. Observing this isn't license to pry; it's just good to be aware of the tender spots. For example, if a friend never talks about their family, it may be because there's a strained relationship there. So instead of, say, barraging them with questions about their Thanksgiving plans, you might go with a more low-key, "What are you up to over the long weekend?"

5. **Notice how people look.** This isn't about creepily ogling people's bodies; it's about paying attention to their physical presentation. You might observe what colors/styles of clothing they are wearing, if their clothes are clean/neat/well-fitting, whether they are wearing any accessories (glasses, slip-on shoes, earrings, a wristwatch), how they've done their hair, or the presence/style of makeup. You don't need to comment on it (be cool, guys!!!); it's all just data that that may tell you a story at some point.

You don't have to do everything on this list, and you certainly don't have to do it for every friend, all the time. The point is just to have an *idea* of what noticing can look and feel like and to practice it regularly, until eventually it becomes second nature.

How to Remember Everything
(Or Just . . . More Things)

Once you've started noticing things, you'll need to *remember* them later—which might not be as hard as you think! Joshua Foer, science journalist and author of *Moonwalking with Einstein*—oh, and the winner of the 2006 USA Memory Championship—has said that people with the "best" memories don't have an innate skill; they just *really care* about remembering information. According to Foer:

> Great memories are learned. At the most basic level, we remember when we pay attention. We remember when we are deeply engaged. We remember when we are able to take a piece of information and experience, and figure out why it is meaningful to us, why it is significant, why it's colorful, when we're able to transform it in some way that makes sense in the light of all of the other things floating around in our minds.[36]

If you want to get better at storing and recalling important little details about your people, here are some practical tips to try.

Tell someone about it.
Recounting information to other people is a great study trick, and it works here, too. Obviously you shouldn't recap your friends' personal business to others, but repeating small details—like their spouse's name, how many kids they have, their hometown, and so on—to your roommate or spouse when you get home from your hangout will help you remember it.

Put their birthday and other meaningful days in their life (wedding anniversary, kids' birthdays) on your calendar.
Don't rely on Facebook to tell you when their birthday is; write it down somewhere!

Bonus tip: Make note of any dates that are tied to grief. If it's a closer friend, you might want to reach out on those tough anniversaries and let them know you are thinking of them. And regardless, it's helpful to know when those dates are approaching. You can keep an eye on your friend's overall well-being and be ready to offer a little extra attention and support.

Borrow a cute idea from the Dutch and get a birthday calendar.
Unlike a traditional calendar, a birthday calendar doesn't have the days of the week on it so it can be used in perpetuity. The idea is that you write important dates on it and use it year after year. Apparently you're supposed to hang it in your bathroom, but really, any spot in your home that you frequent is probably fine. (If you search Etsy for "perpetual calendar" or "birthday calendar," you'll find several options.)

January	10 _____	21 _____
	11 Sam _____	22 _____
1 _____	12 _____	23 _____
2 _____	13 _____	24 Harper _____
3 _____	14 _____	25 _____
4 Ryan _____	15 _____	26 _____
5 _____	16 _____	27 _____
6 _____	17 _____	28 _____
7 _____	18 _____	29 _____
8 Devin _____	19 _____	30 _____
9 _____	20 _____	31 _____

Utilize the "notes" section of their contact card in your phone.
This is a great spot to record details like their favorite color, the names of their seventeen nieces and nephews, birthday gifts they'd like, etc. You can also write this info in one of the thirty pretty notebooks you bought but now don't know what to do with. An encyclopedia of friends!

Ultimately, you should find a technique that works for you; the "best" option is the one that you'll actually use. Or perhaps the best move is simply deciding that remembering information about other people and their lives is important.

Spotting Red Flags and Warning Signs

If you're interested in really showing up for other people, it's worthwhile to familiarize yourself with common warning signs that a person is struggling. This is the whole point of noticing and processing—ideally, you'll be able to identify patterns, recognize what those patterns might mean, and respond appropriately.

Of course, every situation is different, and the ways that, say, an eating disorder manifests can be quite different from the way postpartum depression presents. But many bad circumstances do share common symptoms, and not all of them are obvious or widely known.

To be clear, none of the behaviors below calls for an intervention. But they *can* begin to tell you a story, especially when you notice several of them, or when they are coupled with other behaviors that ping as unusual or strange or off.

MENTAL/BEHAVIORAL

- Extreme mood changes or emotional reactions
- Prolonged or strong feelings of irritability or anger
- Avoiding friends and social activities
- Apathy; lack of motivation; seeming "spaced out"
- Appearing fearful, anxious, or paranoid, or acting secretive
- Difficulty concentrating or focusing
- Excessive worry or anxiety
- Constant negativity
- Excessive rumination
- Inability to handle stress
- "Joking" about hating yourself and your life
- Fear about making a romantic partner angry

PHYSICAL

- Feeling tired and low-energy all the time
- Having trouble sleeping
- Sleeping a *lot*
- Multiple physical ailments without obvious causes (like an upset stomach, constipation, or constant headaches)
- Getting sick all the time
- Lack of interest in sex
- Unexplained marks or injuries
- Weight loss or weight gain

HABITS

- Keeping unusual hours (e.g., regularly sending you texts or work emails at 4:00 AM)
- Shopping excessively
- Obsession with food and/or exercise
- Neglecting personal hygiene
- Ignoring household chores
- Changes in eating habits (increased hunger or lack of appetite)
- Unexplained financial problems
- Changes in school or work performance
- Drinking or doing drugs excessively (the Centers for Disease Control defines binge drinking as four or more drinks for women and five or more drinks for men in about two hours)
- Reckless or self-destructive behavior
- Odd, uncharacteristic, unusual behavior

If the red flags are piling up, it might be worth having a conversation about that; we'll cover the responding aspect of this on page 217.

Noticing That Someone Might Need Immediate Medical Attention

We've all heard stories of people who have experienced a major illness or injury but told themselves they were fine and didn't need to go to the doctor ... until another person insisted they get help, thus saving their life (or significantly improving the outcome). This is showing up for someone in a profound way, and while I hope none of us ever has to be that person, I also hope that we are all equipped to do it should that day come. Along with being able to recognize signs of emotional problems, you should also get familiar with the signs that a person is in trouble physically and needs medical attention ASAP.

SIGNS OF ALCOHOL POISONING

- Confusion
- Vomiting
- Seizures
- Clammy skin
- Slow breathing (less than eight breaths a minute)
- Irregular breathing (more than ten seconds between breaths)
- Blue-tinged or pale skin
- Low body temperature (hypothermia)
- Passing out (unconsciousness), unable to be awakened

SIGNS OF A DRUG OVERDOSE

- Shallow breathing or not breathing at all
- Snoring or gurgling sounds
- Very sleepy or unable to talk
- Disorientation/confusion

- Floppy arms and legs
- Blue-tinged lips or fingertips
- High body temperature (hyperthermia)
- Chest pain
- Hallucinations
- Passing out (unconsciousness), unable to be awakened

SIGNS OF A HEART ATTACK

- Pressure, tightness, pain, or a squeezing or aching sensation in the chest (that may also extend to the arms, neck, throat, jaw, or back)
- Nausea, indigestion, heartburn, or abdominal pain
- Shortness of breath (like they've just completed an intense workout when they haven't done . . . anything)
- Cold sweat
- Fatigue
- Extreme exhaustion or unexplained weakness
- Lightheadedness or sudden dizziness

SIGNS OF TRAUMATIC BRAIN INJURY

- Headache that gets worse and doesn't go away
- Weakness, numbness, or decreased coordination
- Repeated vomiting or nausea
- Clear fluids draining from the nose or ears
- Slurred speech
- Looking very drowsy
- Losing consciousness (for a few minutes or a few hours)
- Weakness or numbness in fingers and toes

- One pupil dilated more than the other
- Dizziness or vertigo
- Convulsions or seizures
- Inability to recognize people or places
- Difficulty thinking, remembering (new or old information), or concentrating
- Feeling "slow"
- Getting increasingly confused, restless, or agitated
- Agitation, combativeness, or other unusual behavior

SIGNS OF A STROKE

- Sudden numbness
- Sudden confusion
- Sudden trouble seeing
- Sudden trouble walking
- Sudden severe headache

The American Stroke Association uses the acronym FAST to help people remember the signs of a stroke.

Face drooping
Arm weakness
Speech (slurred, or just trouble speaking)
Time to call 9-1-1 (for any of these symptoms, even if they go away)

So, some common themes here, right? Headaches, confusion, dizziness, difficulty breathing, difficulty talking, loss of consciousness, bad coordination, and extreme fatigue or weakness are . . . not great! Take this shit seriously, whether it's happening to you or someone you care about.

The Importance of Patterns

Once you've noticed something (words, reactions, an emotional or physical state), the next steps are *processing* and *naming*. Processing is using the knowledge you already have—about the other person, about certain behaviors, etc.—to analyze what you've just noticed. Naming is identifying the "what's really going on here"—the behavior, the need, the narrative of what actually happened—and recognizing its legitimacy. Naming might happen in your head ("This person seems insecure") or out loud ("What you're describing sounds really scary"). Naming is how life experiences begin to take shape and make sense, and can be a way to validate others and help them feel supported. (By the way, noticing, processing, and naming often happen quickly and almost simultaneously.)

The goal of noticing, processing, and naming is to spot *patterns*. (This applies to showing up for yourself, too.) Recognizing patterns will help you fully understand and see people, and get a sense of their baseline, everyday self. Once you know what your people are like when they are content or happy or "normal," it'll be easier to recognize when something is off, and to respond appropriately. (Remember, responding is the final step of showing up.) For example, if your friend who has faithfully gone to spin class three mornings a week for years and eschews alcohol is suddenly drinking heavily and skipping their morning workouts, you might decide to reach out and ask them how they are doing. But patterns aren't just valuable when times are bad. Observing that someone loves a certain type of trivia or joke format might give you a new way to connect with them or make them laugh or give them a gift. It's also just *practical*. If you notice that your friend values going to bed early or spends every Sunday with their parents, that might inform when you call/text them or plan hangouts.

If you're trying to show up for people, observing patterns will take you far—maybe farther than anything else in this book. The more your words and actions are rooted in who they are and what they need, the more seen, known, and loved they'll feel.

Chapter 9

When They're Going Through Hard Shit

The thing about life is that while it is *great,* it's also terrible and unfair and cruel. If you're lucky enough to have avoided trauma and tragedy in your social circles until now, I'm sorry to say that it won't stay this way forever, and the best you can do is prepare. It's sort of like living in hurricane or earthquake country, or even flying on a plane—you can *hope* disaster doesn't befall you, but you should also have a working knowledge of what to do if it does.

When a friend is going through a hard time, you likely won't be able to make the situation better. But you can help them *survive.* You can honor and validate their loss; bear witness to their experiences and pain; let them know that they are cared about and valued; and remind them that they are not alone. And you can *not make things worse.* (A lot of the advice in this chapter is rooted in that humble goal!) Even if you can't make the situation better for your friend, you may be able to make them feel a little less bad.

But! Before you can do even that, there are a couple of "showing up for yourself" principles that are important to keep in mind.

First, know that showing up for others might make you feel quite vulnerable. Because even though it's ostensibly something you do for other people, it can still feel risky! No one wants to look foolish or come across as lacking self-awareness. There have been times when I've considered showing up for someone in a small way and then balked—because I was afraid of looking like I didn't understand the relationship, or of misreading my own ability to make someone feel better. My thought process was basically, "Who am *I* to send this person a SYMPATHY CARD?" which is completely at odds with my own well-established beliefs about sympathy cards and grief! I don't know how to explain it; I just lost my nerve! I really regret not reaching out in those moments, and now I try to push through my fear and trust that doing something gentle and small is better than doing nothing. Taking that risk is what showing up for others is all about.

Second, you should only give what you actually *have*. When a person you care about is struggling, of *course* you want to do everything you can to make them feel better. But first, stop and think about what you specifically can truly offer in this moment. You shouldn't go into debt (emotional or financial) when you're showing up for someone else. (And really, the other person probably doesn't *want* you to do that.) Give what you have, and trust that that will be enough.

Showing Up in Hard Times: The Basics

Being equipped to show up for others means knowing the basic responses and etiquette that apply in *most* difficult situations. (We'll get into how best to respond to specific big common events on page 221.) Regardless of what the person is going through, the following tips are a good place to start.

Keep your focus on them.

When listening to a friend in need, it's crucial to *actually listen*. That means listening to *hear,* not listening to *respond.* It's not that sharing your thoughts isn't helpful; it's just that it's so easy to dominate the conversation without even realizing it. And what feels like being empathetic to you might feel like being silenced to them.

In *We Need To Talk,* Celeste Headlee cites sociologist Charles Derber's description of two types of responses that exist in conversations: the *shift* response and the *support* response. The shift response draws attention to you; the support response keeps attention on the other person.[37] Here's what the two responses might look like in practice.

The shift response
Friend: I'm so exhausted all the time.
You: Ugh, me too. I haven't been sleeping well at all lately.

The support response
Friend: I'm so exhausted all the time.
You: Oh? Are you not sleeping well lately, or do you think there's some other cause?

Offering more support responses and fewer shift responses is a good conversational habit in general, but it's especially wise to be conscious of this when your friend is going through a tough time.

Resist the urge to say, "I understand," or to share your version of a similar-seeming experience.
It can be really difficult not to jump in with your own stories, particularly if the person is going through something fairly unique, or if you're genuinely trying to demonstrate that you get it. But try to pump the breaks. In your attempt to empathize, you run the risk of totally missing the mark and, say, equating the death of their child with the death of your pet goldfish.

If you are confident you've had a similar experience that they might want to hear about, maybe say something like this: "I lost my mom to cancer when I was fifteen, and while I know I'll never understand how you feel right now, I am here if you ever want to talk about losing a parent." The key is to let *them* decide if the experiences are similar enough to bond over, and to frame it as "this is something we can talk about later" instead of derailing the current conversation to talk your experience.

When in doubt, *ask*.

It's truly OK not to know what to say or do in response to a friend's terrible situation. *They* might not even know what they want you to say or do. So if you're not sure, ask. Here are some questions that you might want to ask in these moments.

"How can I best support you right now?"

This is my all-time favorite question when a friend is dealing with something difficult (or is simply stressed out). I like it because it communicates "I am here for you" while also saying "and I care about you enough to get this right." It acknowledges that everyone is different and invites the individual to tell you what they need from you personally. It also shows humility; when you ask this question, you communicate "I don't necessarily know best, and I'm open to feedback." Finally, it gives them an opening to subtly steer you away from any of your default responses that aren't going to be helpful to them at the moment (e.g., they can say "I need you to be my rock" if they know you tend to get really emotional).

"What are you in the mood for right now?"

This question gives your friend permission to set the tone of the conversation or hangout, and gives them the gift of control. They may not realize that they get to have a say in how they cope, so let them know that you're here for them whether they're in the mood to talk, laugh, cry, yell, vent, scream, do research, be cheered up, be sad, continue on with your original plans, get a manicure, pretend this isn't happening, or whatever.

"Do you want to talk about it?"

This is my go-to response immediately after a person has told me something shitty that just happened to them. What I'm really saying is, "This sounds bad. I'm here for you, but I'm going to make sure a conversation with me is what you want/need right now before I launch into it." Occasionally when I do this, the person will realize they actually don't want to talk about it, or will say they want to talk about it at some point later, but for now, they'd prefer to stay focused on the task at hand. Which: great! I'd rather give them a moment to think about what they really want to do instead of replying in a way that gets them all fired up and emotional before they even realize what is happening.

"Oh, gosh; how are you feeling about it?" or *"Oh! How are you feeling about it?"*

I say this when I need a liiiitle more information. A lot of people (myself included!) have a habit of telling others what happened but forget to say how they feel about what happened. I don't want to be the friend who says "Oh no!" in response to a wanted pregnancy, or who mistakes a demotion at work for exciting job news. I'd prefer not to take the risk when it's so easy to do a quick check-in before I start emoting.

"Do you want my thoughts/advice on this, or do you just want to vent? I'm totally here for you either way."

This is a good option if your friend isn't telling you what they need from you in this moment, or if you tend to be a fixer and advice giver.

"How are you doing/feeling today?"

This question acknowledges that bad times aren't static; a lot can change on a daily, weekly, or even hourly basis. It also lets people decide to tell you about their morning instead of, you know, the past three months of hell they've been going through.

"Are you OK to keep talking about this, or would you like a break?"

Remember the forty-five-minute rule from Chapter 5? This is how it looks when you're on the other side of it! I keep this one in mind when my friend and I are having a particularly heavy conversation and the friend is visibly distraught or drained. Note: This is not something you should say to hint that you'd like to wrap up the conversation; if you're getting tired or burned out, it's best to skip this question entirely. Only ask this if it's coming from a place of genuine care.

"Would you prefer to be alone right now or would you like some company?"

When you're with someone who has just received very bad news, who is super emotional, or who is about to have a tough conversation with a third party (like, say, a doctor, lawyer, or detective), it's reasonable to default to doing what you would want a friend to do in that moment. So if you'd hate to be left alone while weeping, you'll probably assume your friend wants you to stay while they cry. And if you can't imagine letting a friend listen in while you receive test results from your doctor, you may bounce the moment their provider appears. This is the right instinct, but if you guess wrong, the other person might feel worse. So just ask what they'd prefer, and then do exactly what they say they want.

Go easy on the fact-finding questions.

In *There Is No Good Card for This,* Kelsey Crowe and Emily McDowell point out that asking too many clarifying questions can actually get in the way of sharing. "Fact-finding questions can divert the conversation away from what a person really wants to talk about to what the asking person wants to know," they say, "and fact-finding conversations create a detached, clinical portrayal of the problem rather than an emotional one. Getting the facts can be important to your helping in the long term, but you don't usually need a lot of specific facts to comfort someone."[38] That last part is key—remember that this conversation is about how they are *feeling,* not the minor details of what happened.

Know that there's no shame in a genuine "I'm so sorry."

"I'm sorry" is such a well-established Thing to Say When Things Are Bad, you might feel like it's lost all meaning or want to come up with something more inspired. But really, there's no need! If you want "I'm so sorry" to have meaning, just make sure you *say it with meaning.* There's a huge difference between offering a robotic "I'm sorry for your loss" before you've even had time to process the news, and a sincere, genuine, "Oh, friend, I'm so sorry."

Clichés to Avoid

"Everything happens for a reason" or "God has a plan."
You may genuinely believe this, but many people don't find comfort in these types of expressions. In fact, people can find them infuriating.

"It's probably for the best."
Is it *for the best* that your friend found out their dirtbag spouse was cheating on them before they had a kid with the person? I mean, yes, *technically*, it is. Is that the thing they want to hear in that moment? It is not!

"I don't know what I'd do if this happened to me."
People say this in an attempt to empathize and communicate, "This is bad but you're dealing with it pretty gracefully." But it comes across as out-of-touch—especially if the person feels like they aren't handling it too well or has no choice but to keep it together.

"You're strong . . . I know you'll get through this."
This is often said with the best of intentions, but when someone feels utterly broken, being told they're strong isn't necessarily helpful and can actually leave them feeling less seen and understood. So instead, give them the space to be soft. "Friend, I have so much faith in you, but this is really terrible/sad/overwhelming, and you're allowed to feel terrible/sad/overwhelmed for a while."

Let people be "frivolous."

In her excellent memoir *We're Going to Need More Wine,* Gabrielle Union describes the heartbreaking process of losing her best friend Sookie to cancer. Union shares an anecdote from when Sookie was on her deathbed, surrounded by family and friends, that has stuck with me:

> What I loved most was when she said out of nowhere, "Will *somebody* go and get me some hair removal cream?" A side effect

of one of her meds was hair growth, and she was getting a mustache. Her sisters were trying to make her feel as pretty as possible. I was ready to have deep conversations about life and death, but she wanted nothing to do with that. So I gave up control and allowed Sook to lead me. "I want to talk about the Kardashians," she said. That was Sook, a girls' girl to the end.

When people are going through a tough time, they often just want to feel *normal* and like *themselves*. And if illness or tragedy has altered their appearance or dealt a blow to their self-confidence, they might just really want a manicure, or a blowout, or someone to pencil in their eyebrows for them. So follow their lead, and don't force them to be "serious" if what they really need is a friend to make them feel like their old self.

Remember that "good" times can also be bad times.

While most of us are aware that we need to show up for people during a well-established bad time (like after a big loss), we often overlook the "good" times that might present unexpected challenges for the folks in our lives. But feeling like you can't talk to anyone when you're struggling with good news or a seemingly happy event is incredibly isolating; as friends, we can easily help remedy this. Here are some situations in which you may want to probe a little to see how a friend is feeling about their "good" news.

- Getting accepted to college
- Getting a promotion or landing a dream job
- Getting engaged or married
- Having their partner or family member experience a big success moment
- Having a child
- Buying a home
- Having their health improve in a significant way
- Getting a financial windfall

In these moments, "How are you feeling about everything?" is a simple but powerful question; it gives your friend permission to name and share negative feelings during a seemingly happy time. And even if they are feeling great about the event, being asked is still affirming.

Embrace ring theory.

Ring theory is the brainchild of clinical psychologist Susan Silk and arbitrator and author Barry Goldman. Here's how they describe it.

> Draw a circle. This is the center ring. In it, put the name of the person at the center of the current trauma. For Katie's aneurysm, that's Katie. Now draw a larger circle around the first one. In that ring put the name of the person next closest to the trauma. In the case of Katie's aneurysm, that was Katie's husband, Pat. Repeat the process as many times as you need to. In each larger ring put the next closest people. Parents and children before more distant relatives. Intimate friends in smaller rings, less intimate friends in larger ones. When you are done you have a Kvetching Order.
>
> Here are the rules. The person in the center ring can say anything she wants to anyone, anywhere. She can kvetch and complain and whine and moan and curse the heavens and say, "Life is unfair" and "Why me?" That's the one payoff for being in the center ring. Everyone else can say those things too, but only to people in larger rings.[39]

The TL;DR? Comfort *in,* dump *out.* When your friend is dealing with something difficult, they shouldn't ever feel like *they* need to make *you* feel better about their situation.

I'm a big fan of ring theory but would be remiss if I didn't add this caveat: Only dump out what you have *permission* to dump out. More than once, I've had a close friend get so emotional about a terrible situation I was experiencing that they felt like they had to talk about it with some of their other friends. While this was the right *idea,* it was a huge violation of trust because I hadn't given them permission to share that information with anyone, let alone the people in the bigger circles. It taught me that we should always get permission before sharing our feelings about someone else's trauma with others—because even if I believe I'm just processing my own feelings and reactions to the situation, and even if I'm doing it with the best intentions, the person whose story I'm sharing might feel very, very different. So before you dump out, double check that talking to someone in an outer circle is OK with your friend.

Try not to foist or fret.

In *There Is No Good Card for This,* Kelsey Crowe and Emily McDowell write about "chronic helpers," aka folks who "might be looking to use someone else's needy situation to improve their self-worth."[40] Chronic helpers tend to do one of two things: *foist* or *fret.*

Foisters push themselves onto the person who is struggling, offering a lot of advice and unappreciated overtures; they are more concerned about their own opinions and agendas than the person who is hurting. Fretters anxiously react with extreme neediness to someone going through a difficult time; they are likely to ask a *lot* of questions about what they should be doing to help and need a ton of reassurance that they're doing a good job.

If you have either of these tendencies or have done this in the past, don't panic! Both are really common, especially if you are a good person who cares about supporting your friends (hello, everyone reading this book). It's just good to be aware of these behaviors, so if you do catch yourself foisting or fretting, you can take a step back.

Don't judge.

When someone is vulnerable with you, responding with contempt, disapproval, or judgment can affect their willingness to open up to people (not just you!) for *years.* It's especially important to keep judgment in check if the person is sharing something particularly private, or that is a source of shame for a lot of people. (Think: sex, adultery, money/debt, being caught cheating or lying, getting fired, committing a crime/getting in trouble with the law.) Regardless of the topic, you can usually tell if someone is feeling shame or guilt by their tone, facial expressions, and body language. As soon as you notice it, that's your cue to shift into neutral.

Non-judgmental listening is, in part, about your *face;* if you side-eye or grimace in response to what the person is sharing, they are going to notice and feel bad. But it's really about your *heart*. The simplest way to not come across as judgmental when people are opening up to you is to *not judge them*. If you're prone to judginess, consider spending more time engaging with people, places, traditions, cultures, and ideas that are outside your current set of experiences. The more you hear or read about new-to-you experiences firsthand, the less shocking human behavior becomes, and the easier it is to react calmly and offer compassion to the people in a particular situation. (It might sound silly, but reading advice columns and the r/relationships subreddit is a *great* way to start doing this.)

That said, if you do mess up and react badly in the moment, it doesn't have to be the end of the world! Just own your mistake and offer a genuine and heartfelt apology.

Try not to police their coping mechanisms.

Since you're now in the habit of noticing, you might observe that your friend seems to be acting out of character following a big loss. But . . . of course they aren't acting "normal!" Their life *isn't* normal right now!! Yes, you should probably intervene if they are about to do something *really* dangerous, and you can gently mention it if the behavior has gone on for an extended period of time (like we covered in the previous chapter). But if they are just kind of wilding out? Resist the urge to judge, and try to remember that some unusual behavior is pretty common following a big loss.

Give the gift of *privacy*.

I process grief like a cat that's about to die; I prefer to quietly drag myself to a private spot and come undone in solitude. I know I'm not the only one who doesn't want to process my feelings in, say, the checkout line at the supermarket, so I think it's best to err on the side of caution when offering support and comfort. This could mean mailing a sympathy card or bouquet to a person's home instead of leaving it on their desk at work, or emailing them to tell them how sorry you are about their loss instead of texting them. It's also about reading their cues and body language; if you ask how they are doing when you run into them at the gym and they look uncomfortable or attempt to change the subject, assume that this isn't the best time/place.

If you're worried about seeming insensitive or out-of-touch, you can say something like, "It's so good to see you—I've been thinking about you a lot in the past few weeks." That communicates, "I'm aware you're going through some shit right now, I care about how you're doing, and I'm here to talk if you'd like to" without pressuring them to open up in that moment.

Remember: Just because something is *common* doesn't mean it's not the worst thing in the world to this person.

In your effort to make your friend feel less alone, you might be tempted to whip out some statistics that demonstrate exactly how *normal* their experience is. This isn't always a bad thing; knowing that, say, a lot of pregnancies end in miscarriage can be really comforting when you're feeling isolated and ashamed about the loss of your pregnancy. But it can also slide into dismissive or unhelpful territory *very* quickly. I promise that your friend who is getting divorced knows the stats about divorce and doesn't need to hear them right now.

Focus on the food.

If your friend is struggling, ask them if they are eating and/or remind them to eat. Tragedy, trauma, and illness can wreak havoc on eating habits, and your friend genuinely may not realize they haven't eaten all day. If they are having trouble nourishing themselves, you can offer to bring them dinner (or just a smoothie); have takeout delivered; drop off some groceries (or arrange delivery); and/or organize a meal train.

Good Gifts That Aren't Flowers

If you want to send a person who is experiencing a loss a little gift, here are some of my favorite options.

A puzzle

The process of literally putting something back together when your life is falling apart is incredibly healing. (Bonus: It's a relatively cheap gift.) And if you're more of a traditionalist when it comes to sympathy gifts, you can select a puzzle that depicts flowers.

An enamel pin or button

I love a good, on-brand pin! It's especially nice if the person needs a consistent pick-me-up or reminder that they're not alone. Every time they put it on (or glance at it in their bedside dish) they'll think of you cheering them on.

Bedding

Linens are comforting, practical, and beautiful. If your friend is going to be spending a lot of time in bed grieving or recovering, a cozy throw blanket, cushy pillow, or even a set of crisp new sheets might be the perfect thing.

Art

A small painting, drawing, or sculpture, or a beautiful object for their garden (like a birdbath) can be a really thoughtful way to honor a loss.

Share the context or inspiration behind your gesture.

If you're going to get creative with your support, consider sharing what inspired it, like so: "After my sister got laid off, she told me that learning to knit helped her feel creative and productive and less bored during those first couple months. So I thought this knitting kit might be comforting to you right now. But if that's not your thing at all, feel free to regift without regret!" That way, if it, *uhhhhhh,* doesn't *quite* land (or it's not totally obvious why you chose this gift) they'll at least understand where you were coming from and have a better sense of your intent. They also might be more likely to engage with it if they know that someone else in a similar circumstance found it helpful.

If you do something nice, don't expect a response or a thank-you message.

I respect the importance of thank-you notes, but all bets are off when a person is in crisis. If you give someone a gift in terrible circumstances, do so with the knowledge that it might go "unnoticed." They might not have the bandwidth to thank you or send a card . . . and then a lot of time might pass and they'll either forget or feel too embarrassed to do so. Don't take it personally. (I actually recommend adding "no need to respond" or "no need to thank me" to the card accompanying the gift to free them of this burden.) And by the way, if you were the receiver of such a gift and are feeling guilty about not acknowledging it at the time, 1) let it go and move on with your life, or 2) just thank them now!

Keep inviting them to social events . . . but always give them an out.

Sure, a person might want to hunker down while they are going through a tough time, but they also might want a little fun and distraction. Rather than assume they are super fragile, go ahead and (gently!) invite them to a game night or house party or brunch. "I know you haven't been in the mood lately, but I still wanted to ask." "I know you might not be up for it, but I wanted to make sure you know you are welcome." As my colleague Anna Borges has written, a *lot* of folks worry that saying no a few times will mean they are never invited again, so try to assuage that fear. And if they are continuously saying no to your invites, you can always ask them—in an open, relaxed way—if there's something that would make it easier for them to hang out. See if they'd like some company while they do chores or run errands, or if they just want to talk about their situation.

Don't put a moratorium on all good news.

In past few years, I noticed something curious among my friends: A handful of people mentioned to me that a respective friend was really struggling, so they decided to share some positive personal news—because it seemed like their friend really needed to hear it. I didn't understand it (or, frankly, believe it) until a few months later when I had coffee with a friend who was feeling really bummed out about work. She was so down, and it was just so evident that she was hoping I had something fun or exciting to talk about. I could tell she didn't want commiseration, or even to talk about her own problems at length; she wanted to hear something genuinely positive from me. Suddenly, the feeling my friends had been describing made perfect sense.

Of course, telling a friend in a bad spot about your win requires a delicate touch and should be done very thoughtfully, especially if it's in the same realm as their bad news. But! It's worth remembering that good news is, well, *good,* and your happy story can provide a genuine flicker of hope, joy, and positivity during a friend's season of darkness and despair.

Keep an eye on whether or not they are spending time with other people.

Social isolation is a very real problem and isn't always obvious if you aren't looking for it. So be on the lookout for mentions of socializing, and find occasions to gently ask: "Have you seen your parents much lately?" "How's [sibling] doing these days?" "Have you been able to visit with [best friend] lately?" "Are you still going to trivia these days?" "What did you get up to this weekend?" And, if things are pretty dire: "Have you left the house today?"

After a big crisis or just a big life change, set reminders to check in with the person periodically.

Those follow-ups mean a lot, and even if the friend doesn't need any support the first four times you ask, they'll know exactly who to call when they do. And don't assume you're off the hook just because someone seems to be doing better. According to therapist Andrea Bonior, there can actually be a *higher* at risk when they appear to be bouncing back.[41]

Reaching Out to an Old Friend During a Crisis

If you and a friend have fallen out of touch, you might feel conflicted about what to do if you learn through the grapevine (or social media) that they are going through a tough time. My advice: Unless there is a *lot* of bad blood, or they told you never to speak to them again, you should do something. I think it's best to reach out in a way that is low-key or that gives them a little more space, particularly if you had some kind of falling out. Receiving a card or an email with a kind, thoughtful message—written by someone who once knew them well—can be incredibly meaningful for someone going through a rough time, and they'll likely recognize and appreciate the risk you took in reaching out.

When a Friend Seems . . . Off

Sometimes, the red flags we covered in Chapter 8 will start to pile up and might be a sign of a bigger problem. Whether you should say anything *really* depends on your relationship. At a basic level, it requires you to genuinely care about the person and their well-being (see also: radical candor, on page 248).

When approaching these conversations, curiosity is key. For me, that means 1) asking gentle questions, and 2) not diagnosing anything. Like, I don't know their life!!! And even if I'm correct in my suspicion that something is amiss, I know how terrible it feels to be on the other end of that conversation. None of us wants to believe that other people know more about us than we know about ourselves, especially if/when it relates to a taboo or something we're trying to hide. If you're not sure how to have that conversation, here are some ideas.

What to say

"Are you doing OK [buddy/pal/friend]? I've noticed you're [sleeping a ton/drinking a lot/acting really paranoid/joking about hating your life] and you've mentioned [trouble sleeping/how exhausted you are/ how hopeless you feel] quite a few times recently. I just wanted to check in."

If you have a relevant personal experience to share, you can mention that, too.

"I know that when I was [doing/experiencing similar things], I actually [was really depressed/needed to find a new job/was in an unhealthy relationship] so I just wanted to gently flag and ask you how you're doing."

From there, just see what they say! Plan to listen with an open heart and mind, and be prepared to drop the issue if they get defensive or aren't willing to engage. Here are some potential responses you might want to have at the ready.

If they agree that there does seem to be a pattern that indicates something is wrong:

"Have you ever experienced anything like this in the past, or is this new?"

"Do you feel like you have a support system in place for dealing with this stuff?"

"It might be a good idea to talk to your [doctor/therapist] about it." (I don't feel comfortable diagnosing another person or insisting I know what the issue is, so I like this option a lot.)

If they don't think the behavior you're describing happens that often:

"It might be a good idea to start tracking [behavior] in [an app/your calendar/your journal]. Then you can see how often it's actually happening, and if you do eventually want to talk to a [doctor/ therapist] about it, it'll be helpful to have that info."

If they get super defensive or insist there isn't a problem:

"OK! You know yourself better than I do, so I'm not going to push it. But maybe keep an eye on it in the next few weeks to see if it [gets worse/keeps happening] and be sure you're making enough time for [yourself/sleep/hobbies/self-care/things that feel good]."

In my experience, there isn't much to be gained by pushing it when a person is defensive; backing off immediately can go a long way toward diffusing the situation. And in many instances, letting it go warmly and sincerely will give them the space necessary to think about what you're saying, and perhaps to really consider it.

When They Can't Stop Venting

When a friend is going through a hard time, several things can be true at once: You can deeply love your friend, you can deeply *care* about your friend, and you can also be extremely tired of listening to your friend talk about their problems. It feels sacrilegious to even say this, but it's still true. We *all* have limits on how much venting and negativity we can tolerate, and even the person you love most in the world can test that limit from time to time.

If a friend's venting is draining your time and energy, or if you're ignoring your own emotions and needs in the process of supporting them, that's a problem. It can be difficult to tell when you're "allowed" to be fed up with a friend's venting, or to know what to say if you need a break, so I spoke to therapist Ryan Howes to get his advice about how to handle these delicate moments. Here are some tips and scripts he shared.

Recognize the difference between people feeling their feelings and merely ruminating.

I often struggle with responding to friends who are over-venting because I don't want to cut them off or discourage them from sharing their feelings, but I also know that sometimes, I—like everyone!—feel exhausted by it. Howes says that if you're not sure whether it's officially Too Much, look out for *repetition*. If the person is just rehashing the same events over and over again, and you're starting to feel helpless or bored, the friend is likely ruminating. And yes, you're *allowed* to ask them to stop venting. "You don't need any excuse beyond 'I don't have energy for this right now,'" says Howes. Not sure how to commnuciate this? Howes gave me some specific language that might be helpful.

💬 What to say

"Hey, I gotta tell you, I feel a little helpless here. You've gone through this story a couple of times and I've already told you what I think. You're still going over it, and it's feeling kind of frustrating for me."

"I don't know that there's much more I can tell you. I'm getting kind of activated here, and I'm afraid if I listen any longer, I'll get frustrated, and I don't want to get mad at *you*."

"We need to either talk about this in a different way or switch topics, because I'm finding my thoughts are drifting."

Remember the forty-five-minute rule.

We covered this in Chapter 5, but I think it's worth mentioning again here: During an intense conversation, forty-five to fifty minutes is likely the listener's limit. If you've passed that point, you could suggest taking a break from the discussion by saying something like, "Friend, I could use a moment to stretch and make tea and process some of what you've been saying for the past hour. Can we take thirty and then continue?" Or, if you just need to be done—which Howes says is totally reasonable—"Can we table this conversation for tonight?"

Modeling good boundaries for people *is* helping them.

"So many times, people's complaints have to do with the fact that they are feeling taken advantage of," Howes says. "If you can help them by showing them how to set a good boundary, that's even more important than the words that you say." When you communicate genuine caring and love while modeling good boundaries, you give them permission to do the same—and that is a true gift.

When It Comes to Showing Up in a Crisis, Do What Comes Naturally

In *There Is No Good Card for This,* the authors write, "If you care, doing something is important. But doing something you *like* to do, and not something you would normally *resist* doing, is invaluable. That's because doing something we naturally like to do means we're more likely do it." They offer a full "empathy menu" of ideas for the roles you can play in a crisis moment. A sampling: the Chef (drops off food); the Entertainer (invites the person to drinks, or joins them for a reality TV marathon); the Listener (asks good questions and is attentive to the answers); the PR guru (is the point of contact for sharing all updates); and the Project Manager (coordinates other people's help). Take a look back at all the values, personality traits, tastes, and priorities you identified in Chapter 1, and think about what role (or roles) you're best suited for when things get bad.

Showing Up for Friends Who Are Dealing with Big Life Events

Not all loss is felt the same way, and situations that are similarly devastating often call for *entirely* different responses. That's why it's worthwhile to familiarize yourself with the ways in which certain losses are unique, and be prepared to respond accordingly. All of the tips from the first half of this chapter still apply in these situations (and you can and should do those, too!). But if you want to go above and beyond when it comes to showing up, here are some not-always-obvious tips to keep in mind about some of the most common difficult situations that can happen to the people you care about.

BREAKUP

Do:

- Honor the relationship and the loss. Just because a relationship didn't end in marriage doesn't mean it wasn't legitimate.

- Offer to be their +1 at upcoming events or to just tag along for outings or errands their ex would have been present for; having company can really help when you're suddenly alone.

- Ask if they need you to retrieve their belongings from their ex's apartment, take their phone and unfriend/block the ex on social media, or sell all of their ex's shit on Craigslist (or if they just want you to hang out with them while they do these things).

Don't:

- Try to convince them to "make it work" because the other person is "so nice."

- Shit-talk their ex; it can be really dismissive and make them feel worse about being upset. (Also, you never know when people are going to suddenly get back together.)

- Offer unsolicited updates about their ex. If they want to talk about the person's new job or hear about their new partner, they'll say so.

- Try to set them up with all of your single friends.

DIVORCE

Do:

- Include the person in social events. A lot of people worry about losing their friends and community after a divorce, so keep the invitations coming.

- Know that they might not be interested in dating for a while. Everyone moves at their own pace, and giving them time to heal is a way to honor and validate their loss.

- Be gentle with your language. Words like "divorce" and "ex-husband/wife" can be painful at first; if they seem to be avoiding these terms, follow their lead.

- Text them on or a few days before what would have been their next wedding anniversary to let them know you are thinking of them.

Don't:

- Trash their ex. If someone is heartbroken and misses their partner, hearing "You're better off without that deadbeat" isn't helpful and can make them feel really judged.

- Gossip about what happened. If other people ask you or attempt to get you to talk about it, shut it down.

- Tell them how shocked you are, because "You two seemed so happy!"

- Assume they'll be sad or that they won't be able to handle seeing happy couples, talking about weddings, etc. If they aren't treating it like some big tragedy, you shouldn't either.

CHRONIC ILLNESS OR CHRONIC PAIN

Do:

- Believe them. People with illnesses and pain often spend years trying to get doctors to take them seriously or to diagnose them properly.

- Educate yourself on their condition so they don't have to teach you. And don't just read the scientific info—read articles or posts created by people living with it. Sometimes, a good Tumblr meme can tell you a lot more than the Mayo Clinic website.

- Familiarize yourself with Spoon Theory, a helpful framework for understanding what it's like to live with a chronic medical condition.

- Ask them what kinds of accommodations are helpful/necessary and remember what they say.

Don't:

- Suggest ~alternative~ healing or treatment options or ask them if they've considered yoga.

- Say "But you don't *look* sick."

- Try to force them to be positive or optimistic.

- Lionize them. Not everyone wants to be an "inspiration" or a "warrior." Just let them be a person.

CANCER, SERIOUS ILLNESS, INJURY, AND/OR HOSPITALIZATION

Do:

- Look up the rules for visitors, gifts, and outside food before you show up at the hospital. And respect those guidelines once you're there.

- Ask if they need entertainment. So often, being ill is just *boring*. Consider showing up for a visit armed with the latest news on the royals, a book you can read out loud to them, work gossip, or stories about Facebook group drama.

- Focus on making them *comfortable*. Think about bringing them cozy socks, a decent pillow, a water bottle that's easy to sip from, or pajama pants to wear under a hospital gown.

- Check in before showing up with food. A lot of medications can cause a loss of appetite or nausea, so it's good to ask what they can handle right now. (If you *must* bring food, maybe offer it to their family/caregivers instead.)

- Establish another point of contact so you aren't always bugging your friend. If you're not the main caregiver, get the info for the person who is (a parent, a sibling, a partner, etc.) and reach out to them.

- Offer to paint their nails, style their hair, or research colorful, comfy caftans. Remember Gabrielle Union's story about her friend Sookie and the hair removal cream (see page 208), and let them indulge their "frivolous" side.

Don't:

- Blather on about how doctors and modern medicine aren't to be trusted. "Big Pharma" might actually be what's keeping them alive right now.

- Question their treatment plans. This isn't the time for "Have you considered . . . ?"

- Show up unannounced. Allowing people to see you when you're ill is *incredibly* intimate; even if they've said they'd love to see you, they may want a chance to put on pants or a bra first.

- Talk to their health care team without their permission or act rude, aggressive, or demanding to the hospital staff. Unless your friend is specifically asking you to advocate for them, plan to just chill.

- Set up a GoFundMe campaign for them or their family without running the idea by them first.

- Assume they are comfortable with your being present for certain types of treatment or conversations with their doctor. People often feel very vulnerable in those moments, and they may want some privacy. Instead of waiting for them to ask you to leave, get in the habit of offering to excuse yourself (e.g., "Oh, let me give you some privacy" or "I'll just wait in the hallway until the nurse is finished")—and actually make a move to leave, so they know you really mean it.

- Share horror stories, articles, or studies about their illness or medical condition. The last thing they need is an anxiety attack.

MAJOR ILLNESS IN THE FAMILY (A PARENT, SPOUSE, A BABY, ETC.)

Do:

- Offer to keep them company while they sit at the hospital or to take their place on bedside duty from time to time so they can sleep, shower, get a haircut, catch up on emails, or just be alone for a little while. Or ask if you can be more useful *elsewhere*—taking care of their pet, picking their kids up from school, etc.

- Bring them anything they might need—a change of clothes, a six-foot phone charger, a travel pillow, snacks, dry shampoo—that would make them more comfortable or that would make life a little easier as they sit with their ill family member.

- Ask them if there is anything they need you to research, or any phone calls they need you to make.

- Take care of them so they can focus on taking care of their loved one.

Don't:

- Show up at the hospital without getting your friend's permission first.

- Be rude, aggressive, or demanding to the hospital staff.

- Set up a GoFundMe campaign for the family without clearing it with your friend first.

- Pester them for updates on the ill person's condition. (But if you're close to the person, you might want to offer to be the point of contact for other friends, and/or to put together something like a daily/weekly email with updates.)

- Ask if they know when the person will be coming home. If they have that info, they'll tell you.

- Abandon them once their loved one has been discharged from the hospital. Caregiving at home can be even more exhausting because there are no longer trained professionals around, so keep on showing up for them.

DEPRESSION, ANXIETY, AND/OR OTHER MENTAL ILLNESSES

Do:

- Listen. They may need to vent or cry and just be *heard*.

- Remind them that you love them and care about them, and that you aren't judging them.

- Familiarize yourself with the different ways their particular issue can manifest. (For example, depression isn't just feeling sad; it can also look like an inability to concentrate, impulsiveness, irritability, and guilt.) Maybe even ask what it typically looks like for them.

- If they are feeling overwhelmed, offer to do (or simply be present for) an errand or task they are struggling with. For example, if they mention that laundry is a huge source of stress lately, offer to do a few loads for them, or make a plan to go to the laundromat together.

- Celebrate the small wins. It really helps to have someone cheering you on, someone who is proud of you for overcoming what felt like an insurmountable hurdle.

- Encourage them to seek treatment from a professional and to follow their treatment plan.

- Be patient. It can take people a while to figure out what meds (if any) work for them or to find a good therapist—and that process can be exhausting.

Don't:

- Take their mental illness personally. It's really, really not about you.

- Shame them or guilt them. Everything from personal hygiene and chores to socializing can take a backseat when someone is going through it, but rest assured that they are *extremely* aware of everything that is slipping right now.

- Tell them to think positive, remind them of all the reasons they shouldn't feel depressed or anxious, or expect them to "just snap out of it." If it were that simple not to feel this way, they . . . wouldn't.

- Forget to honor your own boundaries and show up for yourself. You don't have to provide 24/7 support, let them vent endlessly, discuss topics you find personally triggering, allow them to treat you badly, or act as a stand-in for a therapist. (In fact, please do *not* act as a stand-in for a therapist.)

FAMILY DRAMA OR ESTRANGEMENT

Do:

- Trust that they have made the right choice in separating from their family. Cutting off family is typically not easy, and if your friend has made that decision, there's probably a very good reason (or *years* of good reasons) that you aren't privy to.

- Offer to run interference at events if they are anxious about a family member acting up. Maybe you can distract Gramps with pleasant small talk at the barbecue, or ask Mom for help with something "urgent" so your friend can get a few minutes of peace on their wedding day.

- Reach out to them in advance of holidays (even small ones!), their birthday, and other big occasions (like a grad school graduation) to see how they are feeling and/or whether they'd like to make plans or join your celebration.

- Take them at their word if they decline your invitation or tell you they're good, or say that this holiday really isn't a big deal to them. Not everyone thinks being alone on Christmas or their birthday is the worst fate in the world—truly! Let them know the offer stands if they change their mind at the last minute, and then drop it.

- Let them know you are thinking of them on Mother's Day or Father's Day if they have a bad relationship with their parent. When everyone is posting photos of themselves with their mom at their wedding, or describing their dad as their hero, it can be very painful and isolating.

- Get comfortable with the fact that families sometimes let each other down in serious ways that can't be repaired or forgiven (or that will simply require a *lot* of time and distance before healing is possible). We live in the real world, where abuse, rejection, cruelty, manipulation, addiction, and violence exist and can happen to the people we love and care about.

Don't:

- Pry. If they say they have a bad relationship with their parents, avoid asking nosy questions about what happened. If they give you a few vague details, assume that's all you need to know for now.

- Pressure your friend to "forgive and forget" or "just move on." Again, not all violations are fixable or forgivable, and even if that might change someday, today is not that day.

- Guilt-trip your friend or insist that they'll always regret, say, not having their abusive sibling at their wedding, or missing their horrible grandparent's funeral. There's a very good chance they *won't* actually regret this. But also: Maybe they will! It happens! Regardless, it's their call, and if one day they do regret it, trust that they can own that decision.

- Push them to reconcile ASAP, because the family member might die someday. No need to take it to that level, y'all! Also: Sometimes our lives don't have tidy, happy endings, and it just . . . is! Let it go.

- Get way more emotional about the situation than your friend is. If you can't let it go or you're feeling very strongly about, say, the fact that your friend's father won't be at their wedding, it might be more of a You Problem than a Them Problem.

COMING OUT AS LGBTQ+

Do:

- Say something like "Thank you for trusting me" or "This doesn't change how I see you."

- Respect their right to come out on their own terms. If they don't want anyone else to know right now or they want to be the one to tell people, that's OK. And if you weren't the first to know, don't give them a hard time about it.

- Allow them to self-identify, and use their labels and/or pronouns. If they say they are queer, say queer; if they say they are bi, say bi; if they say they have a partner instead of a girlfriend, say partner instead of girlfriend. (If you're not sure what labels they use or don't use, just ask!) If they will be using a different pronoun or going by a different name, start using that pronoun or name.

- Apologize for any past behavior or comments that you now regret. If you made some "jokes" that you're now feeling embarrassed by, offer a genuine apology. (More on how to do that on page 274.) And if you don't have the guts or the wherewithal to do it in the moment, you can definitely follow up with it later.
- Make Google your friend. If you, like most of us, didn't get a queer sex education in school, this is a *great* time to learn some new vocabulary words.

Don't:

- Say "I always knew" (cool???) or "It doesn't matter to me" (which is well intended, but actually trivializes what they've just told you).
- Take it personally if they want to spend more time with their queer friends or if you aren't invited to queer events or spaces.
- Be super nosy. If they want you to know the details of their sex life or their bits, they'll tell you.
- Try to set them up with your one other queer friend (whom they actually have nothing in common with).
- Think you now have license to use slurs that they have reclaimed, make jokes about their sexuality (or about other LGBTQ+ people), or tease them for exhibiting stereotypical "gay" behavior.
- Expect a cookie for not rejecting them.

JOB LOSS

Do:

- Remember that "loss" is the key word here. Being fired or laid off can also mean losing friends, your daily doses of human contact, your routine/schedule, access to technology or other resources (like a printer or a computer), your trusted health care providers, and the ability to plan for the future in a practical way.
- Affirm their talents, skills, and worth. Losing your job can be a real

blow to the ego, especially if their work/success and their identity are intertwined.

- Be conscious of the fact that they might be *really* worried about money.

- Respect their time. Just because someone is unemployed doesn't mean they are down for long afternoon phone calls or weekday playdates.

- Ask how much career/job talk they are comfortable hearing right now. They may not be the best audience when you need to complain about your petty cubemate or talk about your new title/promotion in great detail.

- Be patient and realistic. Getting a new job typically takes *way* more time than most of us think it does.

- Continue to check in after a couple of months have passed, or after their other laid-off colleagues have gone back to work. Being unemployed can be an incredibly *lonely* time, and it doesn't feel good to be the only person you know without a job. If you can occasionally carve out a little time to see or talk to them during the day when they are alone and bored, it could mean a lot to them.

Don't:

- Game out every possible worst-case scenario, or push them to answer a bunch of hypothetical questions about how they'll handle not finding a job on a certain timeline.

- Bombard them with job listings that you think they might be interested in or should apply for (unless they tell you that this is OK).

- Give them unsolicited advice on what they should be doing differently with regard to their job search, cover letters, résumé, or during interviews (*especially* if you're in a different industry than they are).

- Make them feel guilty for watching reality TV, going to a museum during the day, or taking a nap. Unemployed people typically feel like they have to work (i.e., search and apply for jobs) all the time, and can feel guilty about taking necessary breaks or doing errands like laundry or grocery shopping.

- Expect (or ask for) frequent updates on the jobs they've applied for, or on the job search in general. They might not be sharing much because they don't want to get their hopes up, or because they don't want to have to tell everyone they didn't get the job they really wanted.

EATING DISORDERS

Do:

- Know that recovery isn't as simple as "just eating." People with eating disorders view food, eating, and their own body very differently than people who don't have eating disorders do.

- Let your friend eat or not eat in a given moment as they see fit. If you are really concerned about their not eating and if you have a relationship where it's appropriate for you to mention this (a major IF!!!), at least wait for a good time to bring it up—that is, not at dinner.

- Invite them to hang out. Isolation can trigger feelings of worthlessness or the sense that no one likes them.

- Plan activities that aren't related to food. (If they are further along in their treatment or trying to get back to "normal," you can ask them if they'd like to join you for a meal.)

- Check your own biases. If you're constantly talking shit about your appearance, or you judge others for their size or for not eating "healthily" (as you define it), you may be part of the problem. You can also ask if there's anything you've done or said that they find triggering.

Don't:

- Talk about their body, even in a "nice" way. Saying "You look great" or "You're not fat" isn't helpful and, in fact, can enable disordered thinking.

- Take their eating disorder personally. It's really, really not about you.

- Blame or shame them via "you" statements. Watch out for questions that begin: "Why can't you?," "Why aren't you?," and "Why don't you?"

PREGNANCY, CHILDBIRTH, AND HAVING A NEWBORN

Do:

- Let their schedule dictate your plans to hang out. Babies go to bed *very* early, and your friend can't just blow off naptime.

- Offer to come to them when making plans. They'll appreciate not having to travel far with a little one or pay a babysitter for extra time spent in transit.

- Know that using a breast pump is a whole other thing they might be dealing with. If they say they need to pump at a certain time, they do.

- Reassure them that they don't have to tidy up, do their hair, or be in "host" mode when you come to their place for a visit.

- Plan to wash/sanitize your hands when you enter their home, and *definitely* before you hold their baby.

- Respect any and all boundaries they set for posting pictures/videos of their child on social media.

- Consider choosing a little gift for *them* instead of a gift for their baby. It's a nice way to tell them you still think of them as a person, not just a parent. Also, their kid is likely getting a *lot* of attention right now; it's not a bad idea to communicate, "You still matter too."

- Remind them that they are doing a great job and are a good parent.

Don't:

- Ask if this was planned, a surprise, if they were "trying," etc. When in doubt, go with, "Oh! How are you feeling?"

- Ask personal questions about their child's other biological parent, if, say, the pregnant person is unmarried or queer. It's *truly* none of your business.

- Say "You'd better sleep now!" when they are expecting. It's silly (that's not how sleep works) and weirdly negative.

- Visit them when you're sick. Babies have fragile immune systems!

- Overstay your welcome. Your friend is probably tired, and their child likely has a firm schedule they need to stick to. That said, your friend might be bored and really excited to have some company. So when planning your get-together, you can say something like, "What are you finding is a good length of time for a visit with friends? Obviously, I'm very excited to see you and catch up with you, but I don't want to crash naptime or feeding time, or wear you out with socializing."

ADOPTING A CHILD

Do:

- Know that adoption isn't "easier" than pregnancy. It's expensive, emotionally draining, and time-consuming, and it comes with no guarantees.

- Keep in mind that their life might be very uncertain as they wait to be matched; they might not be able to make plans too far in advance during this process.

- Educate yourself on the latest vocabulary. Small language tweaks (like saying "placed for adoption" instead of "given up for adoption" or "was adopted" versus "is adopted") matter.

- Ask them if they'd like to have a baby shower, the same way you'd ask any of your friends who are expecting.

- Treat their child as *their child.* Use the terms son, daughter, mother, father, parent, family, and so on to refer to the relationships; there's really no need to add "adopted" or "adoptive" as a descriptor.

Don't:

- Use the term "real" (e.g., *real* children, *real* mother, *real* family) to denote biological relationships.

- Expect your friend to tell why they chose to adopt. People adopt for a range of reasons, some or all of which they may choose to keep private.

- Assume you have a right to know details about their child's background or birth parents.

- Ask them how much money their child "cost" (YIKES) or how much they spent on the entire process.

- Say "You gave them a better life," "They are so lucky," or anything that implies that your friend rescued their child or has done something particularly *charitable*.

- Forget that taking care of a newborn and being a parent is hard, regardless of whether you birthed said newborn or not. Show up for them with all the love and empathy that you'd offer any new parent.

MISCARRIAGE

Do:

- Follow their lead if they are using their baby's name. It's a powerful way to acknowledge that their child existed and will be remembered, and that their loss and grief is real.

- Remember that the other parent is experiencing a loss, too; even though someone wasn't physically carrying the child, they are still grieving and need your love and support.

- Offer to help with any unexpected and difficult tasks they mention. For example, if they say that they are dreading taking down the crib or returning it to the store, offer to be there when they do, or ask if they'd like you to do it for them.

Don't:

- Try to play detective and determine the cause of the miscarriage.

- Trivialize the loss based on how early in the pregnancy it happened. This isn't the time to debate the definition of a "real baby."

- Make "at least" statements—like, "At least you know you can get pregnant" or "At least you don't have to deal with stretch marks now!" or "At least you already have one healthy child!"

- Ask when they are going to start trying again or say, "You'll be able to get pregnant again."

- Talk about the time your pet died.

INFERTILITY

Do:

- Make a mental note of anything your friend mentions in conversation that you should research later. They might not be up for explaining what Clomid or intracytoplasmic sperm injection is, or defining all of the acronyms and abbreviations that pop up on infertility message boards. If your friend uses "TTC," "2WW," or "BBT," just Google it later!

- Recognize that trying to conceive can mean existing in a sort of limbo, where the future is unknown; they may not want or be able to make plans for a year from now.

- Know that they might not be up for traveling anytime soon because they may need to be home to receive injections and also because infertility treatment can be *expensive*. Even if they haven't mentioned their finances, err on the side of suggesting budget-friendly activities.

- Be mindful of how you talk about pregnancy and parenting in general in front of them. This isn't the time to share your thoughts on how "having a baby isn't impressive, anyone can do it." They literally can't!!! And be thoughtful when sharing your own baby news with them. Ask them what kind of updates they are comfortable hearing (and what they can't deal with), and always give them permission to opt out of baby/pregnancy talk.

Don't:

- Offer medical advice or suggestions. If they've decided to try (or forgo) a particular treatment option, assume that they have their reasons and move on.

- Bring up adoption. It's not actually an easy alternative (or even an option for everyone). Also, it's not like adoption hasn't occurred to them.

- Share stories about people who successfully had children after years of trying (unless they tell you they want to hear them).

- Say, "You just need to relax!" or "It'll happen when you stop trying!" or offer up anecdotes about your coworker who finally got pregnant after quitting IVF treatments and taking a vacation.

- Expect them to share all the details of their journey with you. It can be easy to forget that talking about conception means talking about their sex life, a topic this person might not really want to discuss with you.

SEXUAL ASSAULT OR RAPE

Do:

- Familiarize yourself with the facts: Sexual assault includes way more than just P in V penetration, and coercion doesn't necessarily involve a weapon.

- Believe your friend. False accusations about rape and assault are incredibly rare.

- Remind them that this isn't their fault.

- Offer to go with them to the hospital or a clinic for a medical exam. (If they have injuries or want a rape kit done, they should do this ASAP.)

- Ask before initiating physical contact (like hugs or touches).

- Pay attention to if/how they identify themselves; "victim" and "survivor" mean different things to different people, so follow their lead.

- Be patient. Healing from trauma takes time.

Don't:

- Ask questions that place responsibility on them (e.g., "Why did you go home with them?").

- Pressure them to go to the police or report their assault if they don't want to or if they don't feel safe doing so.

- Make extreme/aggressive statements like, "I'd like to murder the bastard who did this to you."

- Treat rape or sexual assault as the worst crime in the world; while it is traumatic, going hard on the "It's life-ruining!!!" rhetoric can reinforce the (false!) idea that people who are sexually assaulted are dirty or broken.

INTIMATE PARTNER VIOLENCE

Do:

- Know that it can be extremely hard for people—even highly intelligent, shit-together people—to recognize abuse when it's happening to them, and to actually leave the situation once they've realized it.

- Believe your friend if they say they are being abused. Even if the abuser has never been abusive in front of you, even if they "seem so nice," even if the abuse isn't physically violent, even if your friend doesn't match your idea of how an abuse victim looks or behaves.

- Remind them it's not their fault.

- Be patient and gentle. Do your best to make sure they feel seen, supported, and encouraged.

- Allow them to be the expert on their own safety. Come up with a plan together for how you'll respond in certain escalating or full-on crisis situations. Establish a neutral code word or emoji that they can use if they are in danger and/or need you to take a specific action, or to simply let you know it's safe to talk.

- Be *extremely* thoughtful in how you communicate with them. Their phone, laptop, and DMs might be monitored, and/or they may be trackable via GPS at all times. Don't text them about the situation without receiving some kind of signal that it's safe to do so, and ask permission before you post photos/videos of them, tag them, and/or add a location to a social media post.

- Stay in regular contact with the friend; it might be wise to set up a recurring time to hang out (ideally someplace safe/private). Encourage them to remain involved in their favorite hobbies, activities, and social groups; those connections *really* matter.

- Do what you can to make it easier for them to stay in touch, and to get help. That might mean allowing them to set the specifics of when/where/how you meet up, letting them use your phone or laptop to do research or make calls, or offering to pay for dinner if they are concerned the abusive person is monitoring their bank account.

- Take threats, stalking, abuse, and violence seriously, particularly if the abusive person owns or has access to weapons, and *especially* if your friend is taking the situation seriously.

Don't:

- Blame or shame them. There's a good chance their partner is regularly putting them down. Be the person who affirms them and reminds them of their worth.

- Give up on them. Abusers succeed, in part, by isolating people from their friends and family. So don't give them a big "It's me or your abusive partner" ultimatum.

- Tell them what to do. Your friend is already dealing with one person who shows "love" via control; they don't need another. If you push your own beliefs or shame them for staying in contact with the abusive person, they may stop being honest with you. You can (and should!) communicate that you are scared for their safety, but ultimately, you have to trust them to make their own decisions.

- Accuse them of being "irrational" if they won't leave the abuser. What seems illogical to you can actually be incredibly rational, the result of dozens of tiny invisible calculations based on your friend's intimate knowledge of the abuser's past behavior.

- Forget to think about your *own* safety. Don't confront the abuser, assume the abuser doesn't realize that you're onto their behavior, or be careless about posting on social media and/or sharing your location.

ADDICTION

Do:

- Remember that addiction isn't a choice or something people can "just stop" doing. Quitting is really, really hard, even when a person wants to.

- Offer to help them find treatment, if that's something they want. You can also show up for them by sitting with them when they tell their loved ones, driving them to appointments, or taking care of their home/pets/kids while they get treatment.

- Encourage them. Getting help is scary, and recovery is *work*. Remind them that you're proud of them and that you are rooting for them.

- Focus on safety—yours and theirs. Instead of waiting for a crisis moment to occur, make a plan with them (and other friends/loved ones) for what you'll do if the person becomes abusive or violent, tries to drive while drunk or high, or appears to have overdosed.

- Set and enforce boundaries. You are allowed to refuse to be around them while they are using, not get in a car with them when they are high, or deny them access to your children, your other friends, your home, and your belongings.

Don't:

- Take their addiction personally.

- Believe you can manage or end their addiction on your own. If there were ever an instance to call upon professional help, this is it.

- Attempt to control them. They get to decide what (if any) treatment is right for them, and ultimately take responsibility for their own health and healing.

- Try to protect them from the negative consequences of their behavior and choices. You can't, and you'll lose yourself trying to.

- Overlook the value of support groups, online communities, or other resources for families and loved ones. You have to keep showing up for yourself when dealing with this, buddy.

INCARCERATION OF A FRIEND OR THEIR LOVED ONE

Do:

- Stay in touch with an incarcerated friend. If you can't call regularly, send letters or cards, or emails, if they're permissible.

- Entertain them. Being in prison is often incredibly boring, so get creative. Print and mail a bunch of funny memes or tweets, talk about what you're reading or what's in the news, or just keep them updated on all the "boring" drama in your everyday life.

- Research what you can mail, bring, and wear to the prison they are in; it would be a bummer for them to not receive your card because, for example, it had glitter on it.

- *If your friend's loved one is incarcerated:* Treat it like the loss that it is. Offer to drop off meals, help out around the house, babysit their kids, and lend a sympathetic ear. And do your research; read up on the criminal justice system and what life in prison is like.

Don't:

- Feel obligated to tell everyone you meet why your loved one is in prison. It's perfectly OK to keep that private.

- Tell yourself that you have to "be strong" or think that you don't have the right to share your everyday struggles and disappointments with the person who is incarcerated.

- Do this alone. Join a support group or otherwise connect with people whose loved ones are incarcerated.

- *If your friend's loved one is incarcerated*: Don't be nosy or judgmental. Keep an open mind and heart, and let your friend direct the conversations about their loved one.

DEATH OF A PET

Do:

- Take the loss seriously. The death of a pet is heartbreaking, and your friend is probably going to be sad for a while. If you catch them invalidating their own grief (e.g., "I know it's silly to be so upset but . . ."), remind them that it's not silly to be sad or to cry.

- Share your favorite memories of their pet with them.

- Participate in any sort of funeral ritual or memorial they organize. It's a really simple way to honor their loss and validate their pain.

- Keep an eye on whether they are getting out of the house regularly and/or engaging with other people, particularly if they live alone and/or are a senior citizen.

Don't:

- Ask them if/when they are planning to get a new pet.

- Forget that pets are special and meaningful for a lot of people, even if you don't feel that way about animals.

DEATH OF A LOVED ONE

Do:

- Validate their loss. If they are clearly communicating that they are upset, or telling you that the deceased was deeply important to them, it doesn't really matter if, say, the person was "technically" a close relative or not. On the other hand, if it's not immediately obvious what the relationship was like, you might want to say something to the effect of "Were you two close?" before making any assumptions. That gives them the space to say, "Actually, my parent and I had a very complicated relationship and haven't spoken in some time."

- Invite them to tell you about the life of the person who died. You can say, "What was your grandma like?" or "If you're comfortable sharing, I'd love to read the obituary/your eulogy later" or "I'd love to see photos of them." And then *listen* when they tell you. (Note: Use your best judgment on when to do this; the days between the death and the funeral are typically a good time. That said, if you're not sure what exactly to say to your coworker who just told you their dead grandfather was their best friend, try something like, "He sounds really special, and I'd love to hear more about him if you'd like to share more with me at some point.")

- Send a card. This isn't to say you should *only* send a card; sometimes, you should also send flowers, or food, or go to the funeral. But if you're wondering if it's OK to send a card, the answer is yes, it is. My dad died more than twenty years ago, and I can still tell you the names of the classmates who sent me a sympathy card after his death. I was genuinely touched by their gesture, and it taught me to do the same if given the opportunity.

- Familiarize yourself with the funeral rituals of other religions or cultures if you think/know the deceased's traditions are different from yours.

- Always go to the funeral. This tip comes from Deirdre Sullivan in a lovely NPR piece of the same name. "Sounds simple—when someone dies, get in your car and go to calling hours or the funeral," she writes. "'Always go to the funeral' means that I have to do the right thing when I really, really don't feel like it."[42]

Don't:

- Go to the funeral if you're explicitly asked not to go to the funeral. Showing up for people means taking them at their word.

- Say, "How did they die?" This is especially important to remember for less recent losses that happen to come up in everyday conversation. Some causes of death are *really* upsetting, private, or taboo, or just Not Good Brunch Talk. Instead, try, "I'm so sorry to hear that; I had no idea."

- Talk about the time your dog died.

If ever you're not sure what to say or what not to say, ask yourself: Is this necessary? Is this kind?

How to Be a Good Ally

An ally is a person who stands with or advocates for individuals and groups that they are not personally a part of. You might have heard the term in the context of race, gender, and/or sexuality, but it applies to a lot of other circumstances as well. Showing up is about showing up for *everyone*, especially people who have less privilege and power than you do. Here are some tips to help you get started.

Actually see people's full identity.

Believing everyone is equal and deserving of love, support, and happiness is a good thing, but saying "I didn't even realize you were [identity]" or "I don't see color" communicates that these differences don't matter. What you probably mean is it *shouldn't* matter. But here in reality, it does, and it's important to acknowledge that.

Instead of expecting others to educate you, educate yourself.

We are so blessed to live in a time when Google exists!

Listen.

When a person from a marginalized group is talking, it's a good time to STFU. But also: Listen to people from different groups or backgrounds *regularly*. Look at the authors you're reading, the influencers you follow, the podcasts you listen to the most; do they all look/sound/seem alike in key ways? And seek out a broad range of voices within these groups (because all of the people of a certain background don't necessarily share the same views).

Shut down shitty jokes and comments.

My two favorite responses for these moments come from Alison Green of *Ask a Manager*: "I hope you aren't saying that because you think I/we agree with you" and "I hope you don't mean that like it sounds." Elegant, direct, effective.

Hand over the mic.

Sometimes speaking up on behalf of someone *is* the work; other times, you should seek to amplify the voices of people whose lived experiences are being discussed. If you're not sure, ask what they'd prefer. You can also apply ring theory here—dump your thoughts and feelings *out* to the people who are not marginalized versus *in* to the people at the center of the ring in a given situation (see page 210).

Let people label themselves, reclaim slurs or insults related to their identity, and/or make jokes about their identity.

Not all words are ours to use, not all jokes are ours to make, and the "But [someone else] said it!!!" argument is intellectually dishonest. The appropriateness of certain words, nicknames, and jokes is dependent on the identity of the speaker and their relationship to the subject matter. This isn't complicated or confusing; if you called your teachers Mr. or Mrs. instead of using their first names or calling them "Mom" and "Dad," then you already understand this.

Avoid bombarding people with upsetting articles/news that relate to their identity.

Here's what I mean: I, a woman, read and share articles about sexism and violence against women fairly frequently. Sometimes my male friends will come across an article about a really horrible incident of sexism or violence against women and think, "I should send that to Rachel!" Which I get! It seems like the sort of thing I'd be interested in. But sometimes it's really jarring or triggering or I need a break from the terrible news cycle. So it's wise to be gentle and thoughtful when sharing this kind of content.

When you need help or support, lean on other allies.

There will be times when you as an ally might feel overwhelmed, confused, or even defensive, and you'll need to work through or process those feelings with someone. A person in the marginalized group affected isn't the right audience for this. That's when it's helpful to turn to Google or talk to your fellow allies.

Why Venmo Is My Favorite Sympathy Card

When something awful happens to a friend, our first instinct, as decent people, is to do one of two things: send flowers or bring food. These are the classic "Sorry everything is terrible" options that have stood the test of time. Except they . . . kind of haven't. If you're in Maryland and your friend is in a suburb in Michigan, it's not like you can just leave a casserole on their front porch, and sending not-shitty flowers long-distance can be surprisingly difficult. Even if you live nearby, these options aren't for everyone—some people don't like flowers, or you may be a terrible cook. Enter Venmo, the dark-horse third when it comes to expressing sympathy.

Yes, Venmo, the app that lets you seamlessly send and receive money from friends without ever paying any fees. Since I've entered my thirties—a time when shit starts getting REAL real, turns out—I've discovered that the PayPal's sexier younger sibling is also a fantastic way to be there for someone when they are in crisis, in whatever way they need you to be there.

After a friend's miscarriage a few years ago, our friend group discussed sending her flowers. But in the end, I just collected money from everyone via Venmo, and then Venmo'd the sum to the friend privately with a note to use it for cabs to and from doctor's appointments, takeout, wine, and snacks— anything that might make one of the worst days of her life a tiny bit less bad. Another time, when I was having a very shitty week, a friend Venmo'd me fifteen dollars with the bouquet emoji. "I couldn't get flowers delivered to you that quickly," she said. "So pick some up for yourself on your way home." I don't think I ever bought the flowers, and instead spent the money to have a burrito delivered that night. Who cares? Not my friend; it was important to her that I get some kind of nice thing for myself, not that I get the exact nice thing she believed I needed. We both understood that the cash was meant to be a choose-your-own-solace-adventure care package.

Venmo also comes in handy when the thing your friend needs most is . . . money. In that moment of unexpected awfulness, your friend may not have it. And that is where you can, on occasion, step in. Of course, this assumes that you have the money to spend in the first place, but if you were going to send flowers, then that's a safe assumption.

Now, to be able to get on board with this, you may have to set aside some deeply held cultural beliefs about money and etiquette and the "right" way to respond to tragedy. And I get that delivering a sympathy gift to a grieving friend in Venmo's pizza emoji–laden interface might sound a little . . . newfangled. But not everyone mourns the same way or wants a lot of attention when they are grieving. There's something to be said for offering support from a distance—especially if your friend is dealing with the sort of loss that tends to be stigmatized. Beaming a sympathy gift directly to someone's phone lets them receive it and react to it privately.

The key to making this not seem weird lies in what you say when you Venmo the money. What you're not going to do is send fifty dollars with "sry bout yr cancer" followed by the "see no evil" monkey emoji. Instead, reference the established expression of sympathy that the money is standing in for. "This is for flowers" tells them "This is for you to buy something lovely." "Snacks/wine/bourbon" is code for "Something comforting to consume." "Seamless" or "Dinners this week" clearly means "Foodstuffs of any sort." And "Ubers/Lyfts" translates to "Something to make your life slightly more convenient." When in doubt, you can always add a "Because I can't do this for you IRL" to it, as in, "Because I can't be there to do X for you, use this to pay for Y."

When it comes to responding to grief, trauma, and tragedy, the thought is very much what counts. So whenever you don't know what to do to support someone who is struggling, maybe just Venmo them. Remember to set the visibility to "participants only." Be sure to say "I love you and I'm here for you." Select your finest emoji. Then tap "pay," and be grateful that we have modern technology to make the age-old tradition of comforting the sick, the sad, and the grieving a tiny bit easier.

Chapter 10

So, Somebody Fucked Up

Fuck-ups *will* happen—we're humans, after all—but you can still choose to show up in those moments. And that doesn't mean swallowing your hurt or letting people walk all over you. Far from it, in fact. Showing up in this context means approaching failures (your own and other people's) with true compassion, generosity, vulnerability, and confidence. It means having difficult conversations, addressing boundary violations and jerk behavior, owning your mistakes, offering genuine apologies, and—yes, sometimes—ending friendships.

If somebody fucked up and you aren't sure how to proceed (Reach out? Ignore it? Run away and change your name???), you can always return to the four basic steps: noticing, processing, naming, and responding. Whenever you're feeling lost in a friendship, showing up—for them, for yourself, for both of you—is a compass that will guide you on your way.

Radical Candor in Friendships

So often when a friend hurts or disappoints us, we convince ourselves that it's better for everyone if we just swallow our feelings and say nothing—and then either slowly pull away from the person who hurt us, or harbor bitterness for years. But both of those options can seriously corrode a relationship; being honest is often the kindest course of action for both you and the other person.

Think of an instance in which someone you care about confronted you about something you did that upset them, or told you honestly that they believed you were making a bad decision. Did it suck to hear that? Probably. Did you live? Probably!!!! Because you know what's worse than someone you like and respect telling you that you messed up? Finding out that someone you like and respect secretly thought you were making a mess but was too chickenshit to tell you. Or having someone blow up at you—or ghost you—because of years of simmering resentment over grievances they didn't have the nerve to tell you. Or feeling—rightfully!—like you can't *really* trust your so-called people. That hurts way more than hearing kind, thoughtful, honest feedback from people who genuinely want the best for you and who want to maintain a close relationship with you.

This is why I aim to practice radical candor with my people. Radical candor, the brainchild of Kim Scott (who worked at Google and has consulted for several other big tech companies), is direct communication that is rooted in caring personally. It's mostly used as a framework for management/leadership, but I've found it even more useful in my personal relationships.

Scott explains radical candor via a matrix. At the top is "care personally." On the right side is "challenge directly." In the four quadrants, moving clockwise from the far-left corner, you'll find *ruinous empathy, radical candor, obnoxious aggression,* and *manipulative insincerity.*

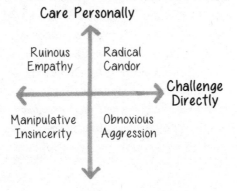

Ruinous empathy occurs when you care personally but refuse to challenge directly. It's an unwillingness to be honest with people about what you think because you believe that your directness would hurt or embarrass them. In the context of friendships, it might look like responding to a friend's "Do you think I was too drunk last night at Ari's party?" text with "Definitely not! No one thought that!" . . . when in reality, *everyone* thought that, Ari is rightfully furious, and your friend is no longer going to be invited to the group's hangouts.

Obnoxious aggression happens when you challenge directly without caring personally. Using the same example, it might look like approaching the drunk pal—who you never really liked to begin with—during the party, and calling them out for their behavior in front of everyone in the meanest and most humiliating terms you can think of. Yes, there's honesty, but it's rooted in shame and blame instead of a genuine desire to see the person grow or change.

Manipulative insincerity occurs when you neither care personally, nor challenge directly. Like ruinous empathy, it begins with an unwillingness to be honest with people about how you perceive a situation . . . but in this case, it's rooted in a desire to be liked or to gain some kind of social advantage. In the context of friendships, it might be telling the person who was definitely too drunk at the party that it was perfectly fine—not because you don't want to embarrass them, but because you're *really* hoping to stay on their good side so they'll invite you to their amazing beach house this summer. It might also look like telling them it was fine, but then talking shit about them to everyone else in the friend group for the next month.

Radical candor happens when you are willing to speak honestly about how you perceive a situation because you care about the person and genuinely want the best for them. It's saying, "Honestly, yeah—I think you had a few too many last night. I know Ari was pretty upset about your behavior, and to be honest, I don't think they are wrong. You might want to think about apologizing to them, and also to Sasha, who you were pretty nasty to, and Quinn, who called you a cab because you couldn't find your phone."

Radical candor might also look like adding, "Are you doing OK? I've noticed you've been drinking a lot since your breakup, and I'm worried about you." It also could have been pulling your friend aside during the party and saying, "Hey, buddy, this behavior isn't cool and I think you should call it a night. Let's talk more about it tomorrow; here—I'll call you a car home."

I love radical candor because it aligns so well with two of my core values: sincerity and compassion. It's important to me that the people in my life know they can trust me—that my word is good, that I mean what I say. When I think about radical candor in relationships, the word that comes to mind is *gentle*. It's not about being harsh or aggro to get through to people, or doing a big performative takedown. You don't have to say, "Yeah, buddy, we've all watched you slide down this booze-filled slope since your breakup and it's not cute." You can simply say, "Honestly, I think you had too much to drink." Radical candor is firm, but it's quiet.

It's also possible to not care personally and not be candid and not *necessarily* be insincere or manipulative. Sometimes you've just gotta say "Yep" or "Mmhmm" for your own safety or sanity or because you're dealing with a person who is what we might call "a handful" and you *don't* care about them enough to be the one who tells them. In that case, try to disengage overall—because if *they* think you care a lot about them, they might view your silence as approval of their behavior.

Radical candor can be difficult and feel incredibly uncomfortable, especially if you've been socialized to believe that your worth is dependent on your being likable. It also means you have to welcome radical candor when it's directed at you—so, receiving feedback with grace, letting go of your defensiveness, swallowing your pride, and saying, "Thank you for being honest with me. I'm sure it wasn't easy." (A friend once said this to me after I was direct with her, and it made my heart swell up because I felt so seen and appreciated after having just done something rather stressful.)

Practicing radical candor is one of the ways that showing up for others can really feel like work. It requires confidence and trust and genuine empathy. You have to set aside your own need to be comfortable and risk your likability for the benefit of someone else.

How to Have a Difficult
Conversation with a Friend

One of my favorite bits of wisdom is "The only way out is through the door."
I think of it whenever I or someone I know is spending a lot of time and
energy trying to think of a creative solution to handle a problem that can
really only be solved one way: by having a straightforward conversation. I
used to do this *all* the time, particularly with crushes. I actively avoided any
conversations where I had to be vulnerable and share my true feelings and
needs. I was so afraid of being rejected and feeling bad that I spent a ton
of energy trying to find an alternative exit. I tried every option and made
every excuse for why I couldn't possibly just walk through the damn door.
And, unsurprisingly, this never worked out too well. It never got me what I
wanted. More important: This behavior didn't *protect* me. I still got hurt; all
I was really doing was delaying the inevitable, and/or making things worse.
Over time, I started facing difficult conversations with more courage, and I
learned that it often sucked but was also *fine*.

I'd be lying if I said that I now *enjoy* having conversations about my
needs, or that I like being vulnerable. I'm still not a fan of conflict or con-
frontations. But now at least I know I won't *die*. And I also know that these
interactions—like everything else—get easier with practice. Sometimes, the
only way to deal with a situation is to have an honest conversation. Sometimes, the only way out is through the door.

DO YOU REALLY HAVE TO HAVE THIS CONVERSATION?

If you're conflict averse, you may be tempted to cut and run the second anyone does something that bothers you. Perhaps you'll tell yourself that the
person isn't going to change their ways, or that this friendship isn't *that* important to you anyway. "Friends: who needs 'em?!" you say. And the answer
is: you! You need friends! We all do! You don't need to be friends with *everyone,* and yes, it's good to recognize when people are toxic and aren't going
to change, but so often, we use this as an excuse to get out of doing the hard
work of showing up.

If you're never willing to have difficult conversations with people, you're never going to be able to have authentic, meaningful relationships. Most of us recognize that vulnerability is necessary for true intimacy, but for some reason we don't view *being honest* as a way of being vulnerable. But of *course* admitting you have a need is a form of vulnerability.

A difficult conversation makes space for *trust*—trust that you can be honest with each other about how you're feeling, trust that you can survive a tough talk and remain friends, trust that you both genuinely want the relationship to work and continue.

Some Common Scenarios That Might Call for a Conversation

The person . . .

- borrowed something of yours and still hasn't returned it.
- owes you money and you'd like your money back.
- keeps flaking on you.
- said something kind of mean/nasty about you (to your face or to someone else).
- is making a mess in your space or in a shared space.
- violated (or is attempting to violate) a boundary of yours.
- said something hurtful and offensive about a particular group of people.

You . . .

- think you hurt or upset someone
- know you hurt or upset someone.

RESPONDING IN THE MOMENT

In many instances, the best option is just to respond to a shitty or hurtful comment when it happens. But so often, we don't know what to say. Here are a few responses to keep in your back pocket for those moments.

"What do you mean by that?"

I like this as a response to snide, snarky, or sarcastic comments that could be construed as a joke. It's not a bad idea to get clarity—because there is a real chance you misheard them or misunderstood their tone, and that is good to know.

"Wow, that's a really [rude/unkind/mean/thoughtless/hurtful] thing to say to me."
Straightforward and sans equivocation.

"Oh, actually, I don't think Casey would be OK with [you sharing this/us talking about this]."
You can interject with this if people are gossiping or sharing someone else's personal business and you aren't comfortable with it. And if they are attempting to get you to shit-talk a mutual friend, you could say something like, "Oh, I really like Casey," and even add "so let's change the subject."

"Ouch."
I like this response because it's *really* unambiguous. It's also *short,* which comes in handy when you're too hurt or shocked to articulate yourself well. "Ouch" is the conversational equivalent of a referee blowing a whistle; it's a little blast to indicate that everyone needs to pause for a second to address what just happened.

"Ouch" is also great if the person didn't say something nasty about you but to or about another person who is present. In that instance, "ouch" communicates "You crossed a line and I'm not OK with it"—which the person the comment was directed at will likely appreciate.

"Uhhhhh, YES offense???!!!"
Use this one when someone tacks "no offense!" onto the end of an extremely offensive statement.

"I don't think that's funny" or *"I don't like those kinds of jokes."*
I have very little patience for people who say shitty things and then claim they were kidding, or insist that you need to lighten up. That sort of behavior can be really hard to call out; the person is counting on the fact that you'd rather let them act like an ass than be seen as "crazy" or "uptight." But . . . whatever!

If people think I'm uptight or sensitive because I expect my so-called friends to be respectful and kind toward others, that's actually fine with me.

And remember: Body language *really* matters! Sometimes the best way to communicate hurt or offense is to furrow your brows and let your mouth and tone go flat. There's nothing like a visible frown to say, "Wow, dick move."

TALKING TO SOMEONE AFTER THE FACT

Most difficult conversations don't happen the second someone messes up; they happen later, once the aggrieved or hurt person has had time to process what they're upset about and plan what they want to say. And this isn't necessarily a bad thing! (As therapist Ryan Howes said to me, "Strike when the iron is cold"—i.e., sometimes, it's best to deal with something when it's not actually happening.) If you've found yourself in a situation where you realize later, *Oh, that was deeply not OK and I need to say something,* here are two tips to keep in mind.

1. **Before you confront them, reflect on what you could have done differently.** Should you have spoken up sooner? Communicated your needs better? While the list might be short, going through this exercise can dampen any self-righteousness and help you approach them from a more open and curious place.

2. **Figure out what you need from this person to right the situation.** Do you just want to be heard? Do you want an apology? Do you hope they'll take some kind of action (e.g., pay for the cost of your movie ticket after they bailed at the last minute)? Celeste Headlee says that this step is "the equivalent of walking into a grocery store with a list instead of browsing through the aisles; you're much more likely to get what you want and leave feeling satisfied."

ADDRESSING THE PROBLEM

In some instances, the way you broach the subject can be very straightforward. For example, "Hey, friend, I just realized it's been three months since I loaned you my red top; could I get it back from you tonight? I'd like to wear it this weekend." Or even, "Hey, after you returned my red top last night, I realized it had a huge stain on it that wasn't there before. The dry cleaner said it's not possible to get the stain out, so could you cover the cost of replacing it?"

If you're tempted to overthink this sort of low-stakes "confrontational" message, I get it, but it's just not that deep! There's no need to add, "I think you're a really good person so please don't take this the wrong way; I wasn't sure if I should even bring this up." Just focus on remedying the immediate problem. Keep it matter-of-fact and neutral, and they'll likely respond similarly. (And if they don't, that's a Them Problem.)

When you're communicating more serious behavior to a friend, you'll probably want to give it extra care. In that case, here are a few tips to keep in mind.

Separate what they *did* from who they are.

Harriet Lerner, a therapist and the author of *Why Won't You Apologize?*, says if you're genuinely seeking an apology or a reconciliation, it's worth remembering that people will shut down if they feel their entire sense of self is on the line. (And the greater the offense, the likelier that is the case.) If you can avoid labeling and shaming them *as a person* and instead focus on their *behavior,* you create more space for them to reflect and apologize.[43]

Believe me: I *know* how frustrating it is to have to think about the offender's feelings when you're hurt or angry. But this doesn't mean you can't express your pain, anger, or exasperation. It just means that if you want the person to truly hear you and to apologize or change their ways, you should try to avoid name-calling or going in hard on their very *being.*

Name the behavior.

There is power and practicality in clearly stating what, specifically, you're upset about. So, say "When you said 'all cat owners are slobs'" or "When you groped me" instead of "Your comments . . ." or "Your actions . . ." Even though using euphemisms might feel more "polite" or make you feel less vulnerable in the moment, directness matters in the long run, particularly if the behavior was really egregious. This can mean moving away from the oft-recommended "I" statements—but sometimes it's appropriate to say "That comment was mean and uncalled for" instead of "I just really felt like that comment was mean and uncalled for."

State the consequences of the behavior.

This could be something like "Your comment made me, a cat owner, feel terrible" or "What should have been a fun day was ruined." I recommend doing this because it can be very easy to assume that their action was so *obviously* bad, they'll immediately understand how you're feeling or why it was a problem as soon as you name it. But that's not always the case! So tell them in plain terms what resulted.

Consider sharing the consequences of their not apologizing/changing/remedying the behavior.

Again, that outcome may feel fairly obvious to you, but it might not be to them! So you might add something like, "I have to be honest: This is making me not want to hang out as much." The goal is to communicate "This is a serious problem, so please treat it as such."

Whatever you say, keep it *short*.

Harriet Lerner says that when we're seeking an apology, most of us tend to go into great detail about the reasons we're angry and upset. This feels satisfying, but it doesn't help us resolve the situation or get through to the other person. "People take in very little information when they don't want to hear what you're saying," Lerner says. "If your intention is to be heard and to make room for a sincere apology and behavioral change, opt for brevity. This is especially challenging if your automatic tendency is to say too much." Do everyone a favor and keep it brief.

Stay curious.

Even if you're 99 percent sure this person definitely fucked up, there's a pretty good chance *they* didn't think they were fucking up. So instead of bulldozing them with declarations about their intentions or character, say your piece and then let them speak. Listen to their explanations with an open mind, and be willing to admit it if you're a little less right than you thought you were. It's not always easy to do, but I've found that keeping "Stay curious" in mind during difficult conversations makes me softer, gentler, and kinder and really doesn't detract from my ability to communicate that I'm upset or unhappy.

"You Fucked Up" Mad Libs®

So often, we don't say anything when someone is acting up—or we talk about it in vague terms—because we simply don't know what to *say*. But naming bad behavior is really important, so it's helpful to develop a vocabulary for it.

While I believe in being as specific as possible, occasionally you'll need general shorthand for "that thing you did," particularly if you've already repeated "When you said 'all cat owners are slobs'" several times in a row and you're kind of short on time. So, here's how to name these moments.

- Action
- Comment
- Insult
- Message
- Negativity
- Outburst
- Rant
- Reaction
- Response
- Tirade
- Words

Here are some words to describe said behavior.

- Aggressive
- Bizarre
- Concerning
- Deeply concerning
- Creepy
- Cruel
- Embarrassing
- False
- Fucked-up
- Gross
- Harsh
- Heartless
- Hurtful
- Illegal
- Insulting
- Judgmental
- Mean
- Misogynistic
- Negative
- Not cool
- Not funny
- Offensive
- Predatory
- Racist
- Really not OK
- Rude
- Scary
- Shitty
- Snarky
- Snide
- Snotty
- Thoughtless
- Unacceptable
- Uncalled for
- Unkind
- Upsetting
- Violent
- Wild
- Wrong

Here are some ways to describe the consequences of the behavior: "I/we/folks . . ."

- feel uncomfortable
- feel unsafe
- are constantly apologizing for your behavior
- are constantly walking on eggshells around you
- feel embarrassed by your behavior
- are questioning your character
- don't trust you.

"The behavior . . ."

- is exhausting
- is stressing me out
- really crossed a line
- is sucking the joy out of what used to be a fun space
- is making it difficult to get [thing] done
- has caused other people to stop participating.

Here are some ways to communicate "This ends now."

- Cut it out.
- Knock it off.
- Cool it.
- Fucking cool it.
- I'd rather you didn't.
- Can you please stop?
- This is unacceptable.
- This has to stop.
- This cannot happen again.
- I'm really over it.
- I need to know it won't happen anymore.
- I'm done acting like this is OK.

I know that at a glance, this list can look scary and harsh and make you think I expect you to burn down your house to kill a spider. But! When you skip the words/phrases that aren't right for your situation, pick a few that suit you, and add your own tone, feelings, and lived experiences, this list can cover a whole host of situations that range from "This behavior is kind of annoying" to "You ruined my wedding."

Here's what your confrontation or difficult conversation might sound like in practice.

💬 What to say

> "Hey, Parker, I'm not really here for all these snarky comments you're making about my DIY hamster hotel plans. The 'jokes' aren't funny to me, and are actually making me feel pretty shitty. Can you please knock it off?"

> "Hey, Riley, I think I'm reaching my limit on listening to you make mean comments about everyone we work with. Jordan is a good manager who really deserves this promotion, and I'd really like you to stop talking shit about them to me."

> "Taylor, you know I love hanging out with you, but I've been feeling lately like we're focusing a lot on your dating drama and I'm not getting a chance to share what's going on in my life. Can you try to shift the balance a little so I'm able to talk about my stuff, too?"

> "Hey, Skye, I've noticed recently that you've been nitpicking everything I say and shouting me down in group hangouts. I'm not sure if you even realize you're doing it, but I end up feeling pretty terrible every time we get together. This is a space that used to feel really joyful and inclusive, and now it's feeling very negative and toxic. I'd really appreciate it if you could try to be more conscious of it and make more of an effort to let me speak without interrupting me."

When Your Friend Is Wilding Out

Sometimes, the people we love dearly can get so caught up in their own narratives that they lose all self-awareness and just start . . . wilding out. Maybe they are getting themselves in hot water at work, treating their dates badly, pissing off their other friends, and exhausting all good will—all while complaining about how all this conflict is so unfair and is everyone's fault but their own. Their behavior might not be fully *dangerous,* but it's still destructive. It can be incredibly tough to be their audience when all you want to do is say, "Actually, maybe it's *you.*" Here are some tips for handling those moments.

Yes, you should say something.

If you're telling yourself it's not your responsibility to speak up or be honest, reconsider that stance. Therapist Ryan Howes says, "As a friend, it's important to step in because people can be so unaware of what they're doing. A big part of our job as friends or in any relationship is to hold a mirror up sometimes, and say, 'Here's what I'm seeing right now. I could be wrong, but it seems like this might be going on.'" Sometimes showing up means reflecting our friends' behavior back to them.

If you can't say anything, just be boring.

When people complain, they are seeking validation. They don't want to solve the problem; they want to hear that they have every right to be pissed. If you don't offer much in the way of an emotional reaction, you'll be far less "fun" to talk to. So when they launch into the same story for the fourth time, you can offer very boring responses (e.g., "Hmmmm," "That sounds rough," "Yeah, ugh"). I'm not a huge fan of this approach because it's so indirect, but it's a good option when you can't be honest with someone for some bigger reason. It may not *entirely* solve the problem, but it's an OK place to start.

If they refuse your help or tell you you're wrong, you don't have to keep intervening.

There is only so much we can do in these moments; sometimes, you have to let people make their own mistakes. Howes says that once you've said your piece, you're free to let them deal with the consequences of their actions. You also don't have to convince them that you're correct in your view of the situation; they don't have to agree with you in order for you to be able to draw a boundary. You can just say something like, "I've already told you how I feel about this; I don't think I'm the best person to vent to about it anymore." Or "I feel uncomfortable being around [behavior]. I don't want to be in that position anymore."

When Envy Invades Your Friendship

Envy (wanting what someone else has) is normal, but it can sometimes be a malignant force in friendships. If you're feeling envious of, say, your friend's relationship or promotion, and acting out as a result, it can make your friend feel awful, and ultimately pull away. And if your friend is treating you differently because they are envious of you, you might feel angry, annoyed, hurt, or disappointed. Here are some quick tips for handling envy, regardless of which side of the equation you're on.

If you're the one who is envious . . .

- Remember that this is mostly a You Problem, and has nothing (or very little) to do with your friend.

- Try to be kind to them as you work through your own feelings, and remember to be excited for their accomplishments. While dealing with the root of your envy, do your best not to lash out or treat them differently.

- See your friend's humanity. When we're envious of someone, it's easy to erase their struggles from the narrative, or to assume there aren't any. But of *course* your friend's life isn't perfect. Try not to create a glossy narrative of their life that erases all the hard parts.

- Own up to it. If envy is affecting how you treat your friend or making you pull away, it's probably time to be vulnerable. You might say something like, "I want to be honest with you; I'm having a hard time being excited for you right now and it has nothing to do with you. I know it's not OK and I'm working on it. I'm doing my best not to let it affect our friendship, but I know it has started to and I'm so sorry."

If you suspect your friend is envious of you . . .

- Remember that this is a Them Problem. It might feel super personal, but it's likely about what you (or your win) *represent*.

- Talk to your friend about their behavior. If your friend is making snide comments about something you're excited about, it's perfectly reasonable to say something! (The tips for difficult conversations in this chapter should be a good place to start. See page 252.)

- Don't accuse your friend of being jealous or envious. Saying "Why are you so jealous of me?" can lead to shame and defensiveness that will make it impossible to have a productive conversation. Instead, focus on their *behavior* and how it makes you feel. ("I've noticed you've been making a bunch of negative remarks about my new job, and it's not cool. What's going on?")

- Don't treat your friend like they are fragile. They probably know, on some level, that they are envious of you, and aren't very proud of that. But knowing *you* know, and are tiptoeing around them as a result, usually feels even worse. Be kind and thoughtful, but unless they tell you they need something different from you, proceed overall as normal.

- Avoid diminishing yourself to make them feel better. Be real with them about your struggles, but faux-humble complaints about how your life isn't perfect are condescending and insincere, and won't make either of you feel good.

Dealing with the Jerk in Your Friend Group

Building a friend group where everyone vibes is *so* wonderful and special and rare . . . which is why it's *such* a bummer when an individual's behavior suddenly threatens to upend this lovely little community you're assembling. Bad friend group behavior comes in all different flavors, and can range from relatively minor (e.g., someone is obnoxious or kind of a boor) to incredibly serious (e.g., someone is racist or is a serial sexual harasser). As tempting as it might be to ignore the behavior, let things play out, or dismiss it as "drama," there may come a point when it has to be dealt with it more directly. If there's a jerk in your friend group and you aren't sure what to do, here are some tips to keep in mind.

Call out bad behavior in the moment.

While it often makes sense to confront bad behavior after a hangout, this is one situation where I think it's worth doing it in the moment. First, it signals to everyone in the group that you're not OK with some kinds of behavior. Second, it can be an important wakeup call. So often, we operate on autopilot with friends and don't realize that something they are doing is out of line until someone else points it out. It also validates everyone else who has secretly been feeling the same way you are. You may find that others are *relieved* that you spoke up.

Responding in front of others in the moment makes it harder for the person who is misbehaving to blow you off, twist your words, or pretend it didn't happen. And when you speak up, you give other people in the group permission to address the bad behavior, both now and in the future. To speak up is to start establishing a friend group and a culture where inappropriate or unkind behavior isn't tolerated. If you're not sure what to say in those moments, here are some options.

💬 **What to say**

"I hope you're not saying that because you think I/we agree with you."

This is, to me, the gold standard, particularly in scenarios when you need to keep it polite and cordial (like in a work setting, or when you're with in-laws). You can keep your tone mild, but be *confident.*

Other ideas:

"Yiiiiikes."

"Ouch."

"Wait, what?"

"That is . . . not a funny joke."

"Wow, that's a really [rude/unkind/mean/not funny/inappropriate/gross/fucked-up] thing to say."

"Wow. Can we change the subject please?"

And, once again, don't underestimate the power of tone and body language! If someone is making a terrible "joke," dead silence and linemouth from everyone present is a *great* start. (If you're texting, try "........." or "*blinks repeatedly*.")

Sometimes, you gotta be The One.

It will probably not surprise you to learn that I am often the person gently calling out bad behavior. I do this not because I *want* to, but because someone has to in these moments, and no one else is doing it. Which is really frustrating! Confrontation is emotional labor that can cost real social or professional capital, and it's frustrating when my friends and colleagues don't recognize that and offer to share the burden.

The more power/privilege you have in a given situation, the more responsibility you have to speak up. But, all else being equal, if one person in your friend circle is always The One, it's *probably* your turn to speak up. If you're telling yourself it's OK to stay quiet because this other person "is just better at it" or "they like doing it," you may want to reconsider. Over the years, I've noticed which of my friends have been silent time and time and time again, even though they agreed with me, and even though they had more power or privilege. And over time, their silence has eroded our friendship. So if it's been a while since you were the first one to step in and say, "Hey, maybe don't" to a friend who was crossing the line, find your courage, and remember the only way to get good at something is to practice.

If you're the one who is feeling hurt, uncomfortable, angry, etc., decide what you want/need from mutual friends to manage or remedy the situation.

Once you've realized you have an issue with someone else, figure out what you need and expect from others going forward. Here are some questions to ask yourself, plus what to say in each scenario.

Do you need a *gut-check* to get a sense of whether others feel this way?

> "Every time I hang out with Remy, I leave feeling really drained—they talk over everyone, constantly interrupt, make really mean 'jokes' about me, and never bother to ask me how I'm doing. Have you been getting that vibe, too?"

Do you just need mutual friends to *know* about the problem for the time being?

> "Remy has been making mean 'jokes' about me lately and I really don't like it. I'm not confronting them about it right now for Reasons, but I'm also not inviting them to my birthday party. I'm not asking you to take sides or take action; I just wanted you to know why they aren't on the invite list."

(That second sentence might also look something like "I've already had a conversation with them about it, but I also don't really want them at my birthday party" if you have, in fact, confronted Remy.)

Do you need mutual friends to *take action* or *do something different?*

> "Remy has been making a bunch of mean 'jokes' about me lately and it's been really draining. Can you please let me know if you are planning to invite them to future hangouts so I can emotionally prepare and plan to avoid them?"

Variations on this one:

> "Can you please intervene in the moment if you notice it happening?"

> "Can you please let me know if you're planning on bringing them along? I might want to opt out in that case."

> "Can you please tell them to cut it out since [you're the host/they're your close friend/you're the reason we keep inviting them/I already have and they aren't listening]?"

> "Can you please stop inviting them to our hangouts?"

And if a friend comes to *you* and says "Hey, Mutual Friend is pissing me off" but doesn't tell you what they need from you, ask: "How can I help?" "Do you want me to say something?" "Would you prefer if I stopped inviting them?"

Remember: Friend groups are governed by their own rules.

"Innocent until proven guilty" and "beyond a reasonable doubt" may be the legal default in the US, but friend groups are different—as my friend Jennifer Peepas, aka Captain Awkward, has said, you aren't required to cite a dozen examples of iron-clad evidence before deciding a mutual sucks. The law of a friend group can be, "If several people are getting icky vibes from someone, that's reason enough to stop inviting them!" It might also be, "We don't give racists/misogynists another chance because that *increases the chances that more friends will be harmed.*" Some folks in your group may attempt to litigate invite lists or push back on ostracization, whining about due process and the presumption of innocence, but you don't have to accept these debates. (And, I'd argue, you *shouldn't* accept these debates or spend much time/energy on them—because doing so legitimatizes them.)

If a friend says, "This person makes me uncomfortable and I don't want to hang out with them," *believe your friend.*

Don't interrogate them, try to convince them their feelings are wrong, or default to a "Well they've never done anything to ME" defense. If your friend is taking it seriously, assume it's a pretty serious matter. It *is* OK to ask for information if you're genuinely not understanding the issue, but those questions should come from a place of curiosity and thoughtfulness, which you can communicate through your phrasing and tone.

Then again, if you don't believe your friend, just own that.

Siding with the alleged jerk is a choice that you're allowed to make—a choice that may cost you this other friendship, yes, but a choice that you might feel is best in this moment. In those instances, it's better just to say, "I think you're overreacting/being unfair/wrong and I'm going to continue to invite this person, but I don't expect you to attend" to the aggrieved person, and then deal with whatever consequences that choice spurs. Pick a side (and know that not making a decision *is* making a decision), be confident in it, and accept the fallout.

It's really, really OK if we aren't all best friends.

Sometimes, you have to accept the fact that two people you really like just don't like each other all that much. If neither is doing anything egregious, and they aren't asking you to intervene, it's probably not your problem to solve. Trying to force a friendship for the sake of group harmony rarely ends well.

If you're going to start excluding someone from the group, you may need to say something.

You may be able to get away with not saying anything if you're choosing not to include them in a fairly intimate, private hangout. They might find out—and will likely be hurt—and it's up to you to decide if you're OK with that. (More on this in a moment.) But if you're disinviting them from an established weekly gathering, then . . . yeah, you can't just pretend the group disbanded.

If you decide to give them a head's-up, you can approach that the same way you'd approach any difficult conversation with a friend and utilize the tips from earlier in this chapter. But you may need to turn your confidence up a notch. Be prepared to hold firm if they insist it's not fair, say their bad behavior was just a joke or "no big deal," or try to plead their case to the other people in the group. And if you're telling them to stop hitting on all your female friends because it's making everyone uncomfortable, or telling them to knock off the racist jokes, know that they are probably going to protest. That doesn't mean you shouldn't do it. (Please, I'm begging you, tell them to stop hitting on everyone!!!) But feelings of shame tend to skyrocket in group situations, which can result in heightened defensiveness and emotional reactions.

Use your best judgment when deciding how blunt to be. If the friend is being obnoxious but not super harmful, or their behavior is rooted in a lack of self-awareness or a more delicate Them Problem, be gentle and kind but still direct. But if they are being actively harmful, ignoring clear boundaries, and/or have disregarded all previous attempts to get them to knock it off, you might need to make it clear that this is a serious problem. Here's what this conversation might sound like.

"Hey, I wanted to talk to you about all the 'jokes' you've been making about Quinn the past few times we've hung out. These comments are incredibly cruel and not funny, and I'm not comfortable having you at my birthday party or around much in general right now. I hope you'll take this to heart and apologize to Quinn, and work on earning back everyone's trust again."

Alternatives for other scenarios:

"All of this negativity is sucking the joy out of what used to be a really fun space."

"These comments aren't funny and are, in fact, incredibly concerning."

"This behavior is creepy and really, really not OK."

"These comments are so cruel they make me question your character, and I'm not comfortable being around you right now."

And if the person isn't making you *personally* uncomfortable, definitely talk to the person who raised the issue and find out what exactly they're OK with you sharing. They may be fine with your saying, "You've been really nasty to Quinn lately and it's not cool" ... but they may prefer you go with a more vague option like, "You've made a *lot* of really mean comments during our past few hangouts, and folks were getting fed up with it." That said, try not to pass the buck too much here; it might be wise to add "and I can see why" or otherwise communicate that you agree that the behavior is a problem.

If you decide not to tell them why you're blowing them off, be ready to give them a non-bullshit answer if they confront you about it.
A lot of people will ask you why they weren't included or invited when they expected to be, so it's worth thinking about that when you decide to not invite them.

"The truth is, I've been pretty upset about all the mean 'jokes' and nasty comments you've been making about me recently, and I didn't really want you at my birthday party."

"The truth is, your 'jokes' have been making people uncomfortable lately, and I can see why, quite honestly."

"It's important to me that all my friends feel comfortable in my home, and your mean 'jokes' and nasty comments are standing in the way of that."

"Honestly? You've been *really* negative lately and it's a problem."

When a Friend Confronts You

There are few things worse than having someone you care about tell you that you hurt them or did them wrong. When it happens, most of us tend to react quickly; before you can even process your red-hot shame, it's been flushed away by a huge wave of self-preservation and defensiveness. The next thing you know, you're in fight-or-flight mode, pouring gasoline all over an already fiery situation. Not ideal! Here are some tips to try to keep in mind instead.

Breathe.
This is classic advice for a reason. When your signals are jamming, breathing helps you stay grounded so you can respond more thoughtfully.

Listen to *understand.*
So often, in moments of conflict, we listen to *disagree.* Instead, aim to understand. If you need to ask questions, go ahead—but come from a place of curiosity, not defensiveness. (As usual, your tone will do most of the work here.)

Curiosity: "I'm surprised to hear you say that you don't think I care about the success of the Popcorn Gala, because I'm really enthusiastic about it and its mission and have been putting a ton of effort into the decorations. Can you tell me what I'm missing here?"

Defensiveness: "So when I offered to make ALL of the decorations, that didn't COUNT?!?!?!"

Try to identify something you agree with.

It won't always be possible, but saying something like, "You're right—I totally forgot to prepare the Popcorn Gala Committee meeting agenda for today, and I looked like an ass" can diffuse a lot of tension and be a small step toward a resolution.

Know that it's OK to request a minute to take it all in.

Most of us need time to process criticism—to cool down enough to truly hear it and respond to it thoughtfully, or to offer a meaningful apology. If you feel yourself getting defensive or angry, ask for a moment to collect yourself.

💬 What to say

"I can feel myself getting emotionally flooded right now, which is making it harder for me to process what you're saying and respond appropriately. Could I have a second to collect my thoughts?"

"I am feeling a little defensive hearing this and I know that's going to stand in the way of our being able to have a productive conversation right now. Would you be willing to give me a minute to [take a lap/get my bearings/process what you're saying] before I respond? I know that's a lot to ask, but I care about you and I don't want to respond when I'm feeling so emotional."

They may not be willing to acquiesce, but it's still a completely reasonable request!

If you can, thank them for being honest with you.

I know this might be difficult if they are really pissed at you, or if you disagree with what they are saying. But ultimately, they are doing you a favor by telling you how they feel, and expressing gratitude legitimizes their need and honors their vulnerability in this moment.

If you _didn't_ respond well, own up to that ASAP.

So, you blew up. It happens! You can still say something like: "Hey, I just wanted to apologize for how I reacted earlier when you mentioned that I've flaked on the Popcorn Gala Committee a few times recently. I [got defensive/snapped at you/was super argumentative/told you I hadn't been blowing you off when I knew I had], and that wasn't cool of me. You didn't deserve that, and I'm sorry." (And yes, you should still do this even if you've already apologized for the core issue they were upset about.)

"ARE YOU MAD AT ME?"

When a friend suddenly starts blowing you off, making snide comments about you, or otherwise treating you differently, it feels bad—especially if you have no idea what has caused this change in their behavior. In that case, you might be tempted to confront them to ask what's up. Great! I'm all for that! So, let's talk about how to make that conversation better, regardless of which friend you are in this scenario.

If you're the one doing the asking

First, know that "Are you mad at me?" is a _fine_ way to ask them about this, but if you want to spark an honest answer or productive conversation, you can tweak the question a bit. Instead, try this: observation + curiosity + space.

1. State your observation: "Hey, I've noticed you [have been blowing me off/are making a lot snide comments/are way less talkative/didn't invite me to your birthday party]."

2. Come from a place of curiosity and genuine humility: "Of course, it could be my imagination, but I'm getting the sense you're upset or unhappy with me, and I am not sure what I did or said to cause that. If I did do something wrong, I definitely want to know so I can stop doing it, apologize properly, and make things right."

3. Offer space (because they are likely shitting their pants at this point): "I don't want to put you on the spot, but maybe we can talk about it [later/tomorrow over coffee/after the Popcorn Gala]."

Your tone matters a *lot* here; you want to communicate genuine openness and contrition. If you can't have this conversation without guilt-tripping them, you may not be in the right headspace to have it at all. Also, don't apologize preemptively ("If I did something wrong, I'm sorry"). You can't apologize if you don't know what you're apologizing for!

Once you've said your part, *be prepared to hear them out.* Try not to get defensive; instead, stay in that place of humility and contrition.

If you're the one who is being asked, "Are you mad at me?"—and you are, in fact, mad at them

Being confronted in this way can lead to a panic moment where all you want to do is make it stop—so you lie and say that nothing is wrong, that you're just really busy; or you say you *haven't* been making snide comments (when you know damn well you have). And I get it, I really do. But unless you're opting to be less than truthful for reasons like personal safety or super extreme circumstances (like you're actually about to testify against them before a grand jury), the right thing to do is be honest.

Look: they aren't wrong to ask you if something has changed in the relationship—because something *has* changed, and they're picking up on that. They worked up the courage to ask you about it, which isn't easy. Telling them everything is fine when it's not is cruel; it's going to make them feel *crazy.* Fight the urge to panic-lie, and try something to this effect instead:

💬 **What to say**

> "You're right. I have been [doing that thing], and that was [unkind/immature/uncool/shitty] of me. The truth is, I've been pretty upset about [thing you're upset about]."

Then—non-defensively!!!—offer an honest explanation for your behavior. This isn't about justification; it's about helping them understand how you got here. So, that might be something like . . .

> "I didn't have the guts to talk to you directly about it."

"I was hoping these feelings would go away once I had a little time/space to process them."

"I've been trying to figure out the best way to handle it."

"I was planning to say something to you this weekend over coffee."

"I didn't realize it was affecting how I treat you."

"I was afraid to talk to you about it because the last time we had a similar conversation, you screamed at me."

If the reason you're upset is too big or nebulous to get into in that exact moment, or if responding with total honesty is out of the question (e.g., you've been blowing them off because you've been secretly helping their spouse prepare to leave them), you can still get in the *neighborhood* of honesty! Try something vague like, "I've honestly been pretty frustrated about a couple of things that have happened recently. I'd been planning to talk to you about it soon but now isn't the right time; I'd like to gather my thoughts a bit. But maybe we can make some time to discuss at [a soonish date/time/planned hangout]?"

How to Properly Apologize

It's never fun to admit you've made a mistake or to face the hurt you've caused, especially if you consider yourself a good person (as most of us do). But if you want to have meaningful, authentic relationships, you *have* to be willing to apologize, and learn to do it well. A mediocre "apology" can undermine trust for *years* or fully kill a friendship. Showing up means admitting you fucked up when you did, indeed, fuck up.

I feel very lucky to have been on the receiving end of a few incredibly thoughtful apologies in my life. These apologies saved important, valuable relationships that might have simple withered on the vine had my friends not had the grace and maturity to say, "I'm sorry," and really mean it. Yes, my friends upset me, but their apologies were meaningful enough for me to forgive them and to think even more highly of them than I had before. That's the power of a good apology.

First, know that much of a good apology comes from what you *don't* say.

If you can't offer an apology without qualifiers like "I'm sorry if I . . . ," "I'm sorry, but . . . ," and "I'm sorry you feel that way," you might not be ready to apologize yet. Also skip "Do you forgive me?" and "Please forgive me," which puts your friend on the spot and pushes them accept your apology before they've fully processed their anger or pain.[44]

Make sure you really hear the person out before you say, "I'm sorry."

People who are upset want to be heard; don't cut them off in your rush to apologize. "Words of apology, no matter how sincere, will not heal a broken connection if you haven't listened well to the hurt party's anger and pain," Harriet Lerner says. This probably won't be fun for you, but it will make a big difference to them.

Try not to center your own feelings about messing up.

Excessive use of phrases like "I feel awful" or "I'm so distraught about this" or "I'm a miserable piece of shit and I hate myself" can come across as insincere and leave the other person feeling like *they* need to comfort *you*. The person you hurt is not the appropriate audience for your tears or distress. Be sure to process your feelings with someone else before you attempt to apologize, and check yourself if you start sliding into this territory.

Embarrassed is a magic(ish) word when you're apologizing.

"I'm so embarrassed" is a phrase we rarely hear, probably because it's one we all hate saying out loud. But it's so often *exactly* how we feel after realizing we've let someone down. We're embarrassed we didn't know better or that we were so thoughtless. We're embarrassed that this other person had to spend time thinking about our bad behavior and that they may have even *told* other people about it.

In my experience, saying "I'm embarrassed" or "I'm mortified"—when you are, in fact, embarrassed or mortified—goes a *long* way in diffusing a tense situation. It tends to disarm people (myself included!) and helps us connect as human beings instead of opponents. If you're struggling to communicate what it is you're feeling when you've been confronted by a friend, "embarrassed" might be the exact word you're looking for.

Don't overdo it.

Yes, you should make it clear you're taking this seriously, but the tone of your apology should match the seriousness of the offense. If you write a three-page apology letter for spilling coffee on a friend's rug, it's not going to land (and is probably just going annoy them).

Know that you have no control over what happens next.

Your apology may be accepted, but it may not. Or it may take them a little time to truly forgive you. If you enter the conversation thinking that the apology guarantees you a happy ending or means you'll both move on and pretend this never happened, you may be disappointed. Try to come from a place of humility and open-heartedness; if you do, it will come through. Regardless of the outcome, you should be proud of yourself for apologizing.

Here's a sample apology you can dial up or down as you see fit.

💬 **What to say**

> "Friend, this wasn't easy to hear, but I'm really glad you were honest with me—I know that was probably a hard thing to do, and I'm grateful you did it. You're completely right that I [said something cruel/dropped the ball/let you down/have been acting like a brat lately]. I'm really sorry I hurt you. My behavior was so thoughtless, and you didn't deserve it. I'm incredibly embarrassed but I want you to know that I'm doing [XYZ] to make sure this never happens again."

Friend Breakups

Sometimes, despite our best efforts, a friendship will need to end. You may already know this on some level, but I think acknowledging that friend breakups are real and necessary is really important.

When we tell ourselves it's OK to settle for toxic friendships, we aren't giving friendships nearly enough credit. Of *course* our friends have the power to hurt us so deeply that we need to walk away; to say otherwise disregards the significance of these relationships. I didn't realize until after my first friend breakup that the fact that this person was indeed so important and influential in my life was exactly why it was OK—and necessary—to end our friendship.

IS THIS FRIENDSHIP OVER?

If you're not sure it would be "right" to end a friendship, here are some signs it might be time.

- There's a mismatch in terms of effort, investment, interest, or fondness.
- There was a serious betrayal or boundary violation.
- You feel like you no longer have *anything* in common or anything to talk about.
- You don't *like* your friend, or they don't seem to like you all that much.
- You don't like who you are when you're with them, or you feel like you need to change to make them happy.
- You feel like the only way it could work is if the person changed in significant ways.
- You dread hanging out with them.
- The friendship is negative or toxic (i.e., there's a lot of jealousy, criticism, fighting, meanness, pressure, shaming, dismissiveness, negging, accusatory behavior, anger, dishonesty, passive-aggression, straight-up aggression, manipulation, controlling behavior, and/or drama).
- One or both of you has already tried to fix the friendship, but it's still not working.
- You just know in your heart you want to break up with this friend.

There are a few different ways a friendship might end (or that you can end it): a fizzle, an adjustment, breadcrumbing, ghosting, or a formal breakup.

The Fizzle

Sometimes, it makes the most sense to let a relationship come to its slow, inglorious end. In practice, it might look something like this: You tried to make plans, one of you bailed, the other was supposed to check their calendar to find a new time and never got around to it, no one followed up, and now it's suddenly three months later and both of you feel pretty *shrug* about it.

The fizzle is typically *mutual*—both parties just sort of know they've grown apart or no longer have much in common, and neither feels a strong need to talk about it or fix it. And while it *can* be the result of a conflict, it doesn't have to be.

The Adjustment

An adjustment happens when you reduce the amount of contact you have or the level of intimacy present in the friendship—without calling it quits. It answers the question, "What if two friends break up . . . but remain friends?" If our friendships exist on a scale of 1 to 10 (with 10 being our very best friends), an adjustment might mean going from an 8 to a 3 or a 4. (It can also be a precursor to the fizzle—because once you're at a 3, a 1 or a 0 might naturally follow.)

You *could* do an adjustment quietly, without any sort of conversation about it; that might make sense if you both know what happened or if you can't be totally honest for social/professional/practical/safety reasons. But this is risky! It drags the process out, and a lot of people—particularly closer friends—will call you out for pulling away, or ask you what they did wrong. So if you're hoping to avoid any sort of confrontation or conflict, it might not be possible this way.

The other option is to be open about it. You can tell the person what you need instead of hoping they'll figure it out on their own. This might be the right option if you want (or have) to remain in each other's lives but need to reset a few boundaries, do some work on yourself, rebuild trust, have less frequent contact, or reduce the level of intimacy . . . and you think they'll be open/responsive to the idea. It won't always make sense to be up front about it, but it can definitely work in some friendships and is worth trying if you and your friend genuinely care about each other but need a little space. (And if it doesn't work, well . . . it'll still "work," you know what I mean?)

Breadcrumbing

When you think you're doing an adjustment but the other person really doesn't understand what's happening (so they keep asking you to hang out and you keep claiming you're too busy even though you're not), you might actually be breadcrumbing. That looks like staying in contact but always dodging real plans, disappearing for days at a time but continuing to like their Instagram posts, insisting that everything is fine when it's not fine, giving them *very* plausible excuses for why you can't show up for them right now, and effectively leading them on. It's easy to tell yourself that they know what they did or that you're being obvious about the fact that you don't want to be friends, but they might not know! It might not actually be obvious! Breadcrumbing is kind of a bummer for all parties, so I don't really recommend it.

A Formal Breakup

Sometimes, it makes the most sense to officially end the relationship with a Serious Conversation. A formal breakup can be something you do for yourself or for the other person or for both of your sakes. I don't think all relationships call for such a formal ending, and, in fact, it might be a little odd if you "break up" with a friend you aren't all that close with! But before you breadcrumb because you think it's the "nice" option, it's worth asking yourself whether you're *really* being kind in avoiding them, or if you're actually doing it for selfish and kind of shitty reasons. Sometimes, the purest way to honor what a friend meant to you and taught you is with a clean break.

So, You're Thinking of Ghosting

Ghosting is ending the friendship without any sort of communication or explanation and ignoring all contact going forward. It's going from an 8 to negative 20 without so much as a hint. If someone is abusive, manipulative, or has ignored multiple "Hey, no, really, this behavior isn't cool" warnings already, it might make the most sense to GTFO and pretend the relationship never happened. That said, it *really* hurts to be on the other side of this, especially in a close friendship; I don't recommend doing it unless the circumstances are fairly extreme.

HOW TO OFFICIALLY BREAK UP WITH A FRIEND

If you've decided a clean break makes the most sense, you might be wondering *how* to break up with a friend. And the answer is . . . just like you'd break up with anyone else! But let's get into some of the specifics of officially ending a friendship, including *exactly* what to say.

Decide how you'll have the conversation.

Maybe it's because I'm a phone call–hating millennial, but I'm actually not opposed to a text or email friend breakup. I think it's more important that the medium make sense for **this relationship.** So if you two never, ever speak on the phone but exchange lengthy, well-written texts all day every day, calling them to dump them might actually feel weird or be harder. On the other hand, if they are a die-hard "I'll call you" person who uses emojis *all* wrong, it might be easier on both of you if you just do it in person. You don't have to have a difficult conversation via a medium you're not fluent in just because it's the "right" thing according to an etiquette guide written by someone who never had to compose an AIM away message that communicated *everything* in a single sentence.

Plan what you're going to say in advance.
You don't need to go in with a stack of handwritten index cards, but you also shouldn't wing it. So scribble down some notes and memorize the broad strokes of what you come up with. (This shouldn't be hard; as you'll see in a moment, it's going to be a pretty short conversation!) If you're really stressed or anxious, it's not a bad idea to practice your breakup speech on someone else.

Be very clear about what is happening, and say the most important words right away.
This isn't the time for a long-winded *clears throat* "Merriam-Webster defines friendship as . . ." introduction. Just spit it out! Be very direct about what, exactly, you need; actually use the words "break up with this friendship" or "end our friendship" or "I don't want to be friends anymore." This is a good move in *any* breakup, but it's even more important during a friend breakup, which not everyone is going to recognize in the moment is even a *possibility*. Muttering a lot of "I think we've both just changed" without saying what you want or need can be incredibly confusing.

Keep it *short*.
Listen: I *feel* you on wanting to present an itemized list of twenty years of disagreements here. But as satisfying as it may feel to air all your grievances on your way out the door, it's not *really* productive or helpful in most cases. That said, it's a kindness to give them *some* sort of explanation (assuming the reason isn't *wildly* obvious). And if you don't tell them why, they will likely ask you anyway! So come up with an honest, brief, and relatively tidy explanation for why you're calling it quits, and try to use "I" statements.

⚬ What to say

If they let you down or betrayed you: "I don't feel like I can trust you."

If they are nasty to you: "I don't like how you talk to me and treat me."

If they are incredibly negative, or their unhappiness is affecting you: "I don't like how I feel when we're together."

If it's a boundary thing: "We clearly have different needs and expectations with regard to [time/energy/openness/intimacy/availability] in our friendship, and I don't actually think it's something either of us can or should change."

If it's a You Problem and/or you just no longer like them as a person: "This friendship is bringing out the worst side of me." If it's definitely a You Problem, you may also want to add something like, "I know that I need to do some work on myself to figure out/fix what's going on with me. But I know I need to step away to be able to really do that."

If they are wilding out: "You've been [acting really possessive and jealous/making a lot of racist comments/doing an astonishing amount of coke/making a lot of really inappropriate 'jokes'] and it honestly makes me pretty uncomfortable. I can't ignore it anymore or pretend it's OK with me."

If your core values or personalities are incompatible: "I think we are different in some pretty significant ways, and I actually don't think either of us is wrong or should be expected to change. But I am realizing it's difficult for me to be friends with someone who [doesn't share any of my interests/has certain political beliefs/feels so different about their career than I do]."

If you need a good catch-all:

"Our friendship has become really toxic."

"In the past few months, I've realized we are just incompatible in a bunch of ways that have started to add up." (Note: They may want specific examples; be prepared and tread lightly.)

"This friendship doesn't feel right to me anymore."

"I don't think this friendship is serving either of us anymore."

Communicate how you want to handle any obvious social or logistical conundrums.

Before you have the talk, think about what you want to happen next, and come to the conversation with a plan in mind. That might sound something like . . .

"FYI, I'm going to unfriend you and unfollow you on social media."

"I'm planning to stay at my parents' until I find a new place to live, but I'll continue to pay my portion of the rent in the meantime."

"I know I'll still see you in class until the semester is over; I hope we can keep things civil."

"I'd like to come by this weekend to collect all of the books I've loaned to you over the years; if you want, you can box them up and leave them on the porch. If you prefer to go that route, I'll send you a list ahead of time so we can make a clean break."

"Given this, I've decided not to attend your wedding in May; I will, of course, pay for the cost of my dinner since I'm canceling so late."

"Obviously we still have to work together, but I'm prepared to be polite and professional, and I have no intention of sharing what happened between us with anyone else if they ask."

Put It All Together, and What Do You Have?

Here's what your actual friend breakup might sound like, using the tips and scripts above.

"Hey, Harper, I am writing to say that I need to break up with our friendship. Ever since you told Casey and Ali the private details of my sex life without my permission, I haven't felt like I could trust you. I've always considered you one of my best friends, but this was a huge violation, and I can't be friends with you anymore. I know I'll still see you at Jordan's wedding next month, and I hope we can keep things civil. But beyond that, I am planning to stop all contact."

"Harper, I think it's time to end this friendship. We're bringing out the worst in each other, and it's become exhausting. I know my behavior played a role in this, and I'll own that; I really crossed the line at Jordan's party and I am sorry for how shitty I was to you that day. But I've given it a lot of thought and realized that I need to step away from this friendship. I genuinely wish you the best and am sad that everything is ending like this."

"Hey, Harper, I know you've probably noticed I've been pretty quiet lately, and I want to be honest with you about what's going on. The truth is, I don't want to be friends anymore. You've made a lot of comments about Sam that have made me super uncomfortable, and I'm not OK with it. I had hoped things would get better with time, but it's been three months, and I've realized I'm done with this friendship. I'm sad to lose you, but I think it's for the best."

Be prepared for them to react negatively or to be painfully honest. You don't have to listen while someone berates you, but you can give them a few minutes to say their piece before you bounce. That said, remember that a breakup isn't a *negotiation*. You're making this decision for a reason, and it's important to hold firm, even if they cry or blame you or promise to change. If they try to talk you out of it or guilt-trip you, you can communicate that it's not up for debate by saying something like, "I hear you, but I feel pretty strongly about this and know that's not going to change." If you want to own up to your shortcomings, you can add, "You're right, I did really let you down last month and that wasn't cool."

Give yourself time and space to grieve.
My first friend breakup was made harder by the fact that I didn't know how to express my hurt in terms that other people would understand. Had I broken up with a romantic partner, I would have had no problem reaching for the ice cream/French fries/tequila. But I spent the night after my friend breakup feeling embarrassed about how sad I was. It was actually a feeling I knew well, back from my dating days, when I struggled with the fact that we only seem to give credit to Officially Defined Relationships. I had done a lot of "Is this dating?" I "had a whole thing" on multiple occasions. In many cases, both parties were really emotionally invested, and there was genuine disappointment and sadness all around when things ended. But they were still hard to talk about once they were over. I couldn't say, "I'm sad that I broke up with my boyfriend," because, well, he wasn't my boyfriend, so what right did I have to be sad?

Whenever a relationship like this ended, I'd think, *This went on for a while! This was something! I want credit for what we had and sympathy for this pain I'm feeling!* I'd feel sad, but also ashamed of being so upset over someone who wasn't officially anything to me. I never really knew how sad I was "supposed" to be or "allowed" to be, so I was too embarrassed to talk about how I felt, or to admit that getting over it was going to take time and effort. Grieving, like breakups, was for people in real relationships.

But with my friend breakup, it hit me: A "real" relationship is any relationship that involves relating, labels be damned. So I put on my comfy clothes, snuggled on the couch with my dogs, and the next day I told my other friends that I was sad because I was going through a breakup. They responded with the same kind of love and support that they would have if I had broken up with a partner. Despite the fact that this isn't something a lot of people talk about, I've realized it's something that most people inherently understand as soon as you give it a name.

Final Thoughts

A few days before I turned in a final draft of this book, I had a series of physical sensations that were . . . odd. First, I had a bad reaction to environmental allergies, which isn't that unusual for me. Then my chest started to feel tight and constricted, and I couldn't breathe easily or get comfortable. I just felt *off*. My girlfriend made me promise that if I didn't feel better the next day, I'd go to urgent care, and I agreed.

The next day, I didn't exactly feel better, but I could breathe, which was good enough for me. I got to work on the book—revising Chapter 8, specifically, which includes signs something may be physically wrong with a person—and was so absorbed in getting that done that I didn't check in with my body in a meaningful way. I *noticed* that I felt off, but I didn't really *process* it. Afternoon rolled around and I realized I wasn't hungry for lunch (weird for me), so I finally stopped and did a mental body scan. I was still feeling pressure in my upper back; my left shoulder, neck, and jaw were hurting a lot and my fingers were tingling; and I was experiencing something like indigestion. Every Google search turned up basically the same result: *These are textbook "woman having a heart attack" symptoms. It happens more than you might think to young, healthy women who don't see it coming. Go to the doctor, you dummy.*

And yet . . . I hesitated. I genuinely can't explain why. I didn't have a "good" reason; I just . . . didn't want to? I had work to do and didn't feel like stopping. I was worried about looking silly (what if it was just heartburn?), and also worried it was something serious. (If it was serious, I—rather inexplicably—did not want to know that???) I was worried about the cost. (If this had happened just two weeks earlier, when I still had barebones freelancer health insurance, I don't think I would have gone.) If I'm being honest, the main reason I finally decided to see a doctor is because I'd promised my girlfriend the night before that I would.

After I made the short walk to the nearby clinic, I was asked a million questions and given an EKG. The doctor—who blessedly took me very seriously—ultimately said everything was normal, and that my symptoms were likely a "cascade of reactions" related to my allergy attack the night before. But, he said, if I had *any* shortness of breath or chest pain, any dizziness or nausea or sweating, I was to go to the ER immediately and take my EKG with me.

On my way home, I felt embarrassed—not because I wasn't actually dying, but because I have written an entire book about showing up and yet I still, occasionally, have to be convinced not to ignore the *literal pain in my literal heart.*

The whole experience was, to me, exactly what showing up looks like in practice. It's doing mundane tasks, like going to the doctor, even when you don't want to. It's saying, "You need to get help," to someone you love. It's listening to your people when they tell you it's time to talk to a professional. It's not pretending to be chill when you're actually quite worried. It isn't easy or sexy or fun; it's often inconvenient and potentially very expensive and incredibly vulnerable. It doesn't usually happen in ways that end with a dramatic "and that *changed my life.*" Sometimes, it's just going to a boring-ass doctor's office and answering some questions and getting some tests run and then going home. But not everything has to be super high-stakes or avert a tragedy to be worthwhile.

Each time we show up for ourselves or for someone else, it's like we're turning on a single bulb in a strand of Christmas lights. A bulb can be anything: a text, a hug, a pair of pajamas, a puzzle. Occasionally, we'll get to make a grand gesture that illuminates several bulbs at once, but for the most part, showing up is done one small, quiet act by small, quiet act.

Every single day is a new opportunity to show up—to be curious, connected, soft, brave; to create a kinder, healthier, lovelier world. My wish for you is that you'll take each chance you're given, no matter how small. Because when more of us show up for ourselves and each other regularly, the more lights we collectively turn on, and over time, we'll create a connected line that glows brightly, lighting the way when life gets dark.

*

Notes

1. Kristen Bialik, "Americans Unhappy with Family, Social or Financial Life Are More Likely to Say They Feel Lonely," Pew Research Center, December 3, 2018, pewresearch.org/fact-tank/2018/12/03/americans-unhappy-with-family-social-or-financial-life-are-more-likely-to-say-they-feel-lonely.

2. Juliana Menasce Horowitz and Nikki Graf, "Most U.S. Teens See Anxiety and Depression as a Major Problem Among Their Peers," Pew Research Center Social and Demographic Trends (February 2019), pewsocialtrends.org/2019/02/20/most-u-s-teens-see-anxiety-and-depression-as-a-major-problem-among-their-peers.

3. Kelsey Crowe, PhD, and Emily McDowell, *There Is No Good Card for This: What to Say and Do When Life Is Scary, Awful, and Unfair to People You Love* (San Francisco: HarperOne/HarperCollins, 2017).

4. Louis Menand, "What Personality Tests Really Deliver," *The New Yorker,* September 3, 2018, newyorker.com/magazine/2018/09/10/what-personality-tests-really-deliver.

5. Olivia B. Waxman, "Where Do Zodiac Signs Come From? Here's the True History Behind Your Horoscope," *Time,* June 21, 2018, time.com/5315377/are-zodiac-signs-real-astrology-history.

6. David Walton, *Emotional Intelligence: A Practical Guide,* London, UK: Icon Books, 2012.

7. "Needs Inventory," The Center for Nonviolent Communication, 2005, cnvc.org/training/resource/needs-inventory.

8. Andrea Bonior, PhD, "10 Important Boundaries Everyone Should Set in 2019," BuzzFeed, January 2, 2019, buzzfeed.com/andreabonior/a-definitive-guide-to-setting-boundaries.

9. Cal Newport, *Digital Minimalism: Choosing a Focused Life in a Noisy World* (New York: Portfolio, 2019).

10. Teddy Wayne, "Are My Friends Really My Friends," *The New York Times,* May 12, 2018, nytimes.com/2018/05/12/style/who-are-my-real-friends.html.

11. Andrea Bonior, *The Friendship Fix: The Complete Guide to Choosing, Losing, and Keeping Up with Your Friends* (New York: Thomas Dunne Books, 2011).

12. Rasmus Hougaard and Jacqueline Carter, *The Mind of the Leader: How to Lead Yourself, Your People, and Your Organization for Extraordinary Results* (Boston: Harvard Business Review Press, 2018).

13. Anna Borges, "Everything You Could Possibly Want to Know About Therapy," BuzzFeed, October 23, 2018, buzzfeed.com/annaborges/how-to-start-therapy.

14. Rachel W. Miller, "How Often You Really Need to Shower (According to Science)," BuzzFeed, January 12, 2015, buzzfeed.com/rachelwmiller/how-often-you-really-need-to-shower.

15. Rachel W. Miller and Anna Borges, "Here's How to Use a Bullet Journal for Better Mental Health," BuzzFeed, August 19, 2016, buzzfeed.com/rachelwmiller/mental-health-bullet-journal.

16. Rachel W. Miller, "10 Life-Changing Things to Try In 2016," BuzzFeed, January 4, 2016; and Rachel W. Miller, "15 Tips From Marie Kondo That Have Genuinely Changed My Life," BuzzFeed, January 14, 2019.

17. "Why We Need to Create a Home," The School of Life, theschooloflife.com/thebookoflife/why-we-need-to-create-a-home.

18. Florence Williams, *The Nature Fix: Why Nature Makes Us Happier, Healthier, and More Creative* (New York: Norton, 2017).

19. Online Etymology Dictionary, "habit," etymonline.com/word/habit.

20. Tonya Dalton, *The Joy of Missing Out: Live More by Doing Less* (Nashville: Thomas Nelson, 2019). Copyright Kotori Designs, LLC.

21. Meg Keene, *A Practical Wedding* (Boston: Da Capo Lifelong Books, 2012).

22. Shasta Nelson, *Frientimacy: How to Deepen Friendships for lifelong Health and Happiness* (Berkeley, CA: Seal Press, 2016).

23. Rachel W. Miller, "Not Great, Bob! The Case for Actually Being Honest When People Ask How You Are," SELF, June 19, 2019, self.com/story/not-great-bob.

24. Bonior, *The Friendship Fix,* op. cit.

25. Wayne, "Are My Friends Really My Friends," op. cit.

26. Diane Weston, *Small Talk: How to Start a Conversation, Truly Connect with Others and Make a Killer First Impression* (Hamburg, Germany: Monkey Publishing, 2019).

27. "How to Cope with Snobbery," The School of Life, theschooloflife.com/thebookoflife/how-to-cope-with-snobbery.

28. Jeffrey A. Hall, "How Many Hours Does It Take to Make a Friend?" *Journal of Social and Personal Relationships* 36, no. 4 (2019): doi: 10.1177/0265407518761225.

29. Allie Volpe, "Why You Need a Network of Low-Stakes, Casual Friendships," *The New York Times,* May 6, 2019, nytimes.com/2019/05/06/smarter-living/why-you-need-a-network-of-low-stakes-casual-friendships.html.

30. Ibid.

31. Nelson, *Frientimacy,* op. cit.

32. Bonior, *The Friendship Fix,* op. cit.

33. Gyan Yankovich, "11 Tiny Ways to Keep Your Long-Distance Friendship Strong as Ever," BuzzFeed, March 7, 2018, buzzfeed.com/gyanyankovich/long-distance-friendship-tips-advice.

34. Nelson, *Frientimacy,* op. cit.

35. Susan David, Emotional Agility: *Get Unstuck, Embrace Change, and Thrive in Work and Life* (New York: Avery/Penguin Random House, 2016).

36. Joshua Foer, "Feats of Memory Anyone Can Do," TED, February 2012, ted.com/talks/joshua_foer_feats_of_memory_anyone_can_do/transcript.

37. Celeste Headlee, *We Need to Talk: How to Have Conversations that Matter* (New York: Harper Wave/HarperCollins, 2017).

38. Crowe and McDowell, *There Is No Good Card for This*, op. cit.

39. Susan Silk and Barry Goldman, "How Not to Say the Wrong Thing," *Los Angeles Times,* April 7, 2013, latimes.com/opinion/op-ed/la-xpm-2013-apr-07-la-oe-0407-silk-ring-theory-20130407-story.html.

40. Crowe and McDowell, *There Is No Good Card for This,* op. cit.

41. Andrea Bonior, *The Friendship Fix,* op. cit.

42. Deirdre Sullivan, "Always Go to the Funeral," *All Things Considered,* NPR, April 8, 2005, npr.org/2005/08/08/4785079/always-go-to-the-funeral.

43. Harriet Lerner, *Why Won't You Apologize?: Healing Big Betrayals and Everyday Hurts* (New York: Gallery Books/Simon & Schuster, 2017).

44. Ibid.

Further Reading

***The Art of Gathering: How We Meet and Why It Matters* by Priya Parker**
I've been raving about this book to anyone who will listen since it was first published in 2018. It is absolutely worth your time, especially if you care about having better, more meaningful hangouts with your people.

***There Is No Good Card for This: What To Say and Do When Life Is Scary, Awful, and Unfair to People You Love* by Kelsey Crowe, PhD, and Emily McDowell**
I love this book, which offers a thoughtful, practical, and relatable foundation for showing up for other people in bad times.

***The Friendship Fix: The Complete Guide to Choosing, Losing, and Keeping Up with Your Friends* by Andrea Bonior, PhD**
Dr. Andrea Bonior is a therapist and writer who always gives realistic, thoughtful, and genuinely useful advice. This book is all about complicated friendship dynamics, and it takes a deeper look into some of the topics I've touched on in this book.

***Frientimacy: How to Deepen Friendships for Lifelong Health and Happiness* by Shasta Nelson**
This book is a great read for anyone who wants to dive deeper into making and keeping friends; it includes a *lot* of frameworks and tips that I've personally found helpful.

*Unf*ck Your Habitat* by Rachel Hoffman

If you are living on your own for the first time and/or tend to struggle to care of your space, this book—and the blog of the same name—is for you. Hoffman covers the basics and offers practical tips (some of which you might remember from Chapter 3 and Chapter 5) in a truly kind, non-judgmental way.

We Need to Talk: How to Have Conversations That Matter by Celeste Headlee

I highly recommend this book to anyone who is interested in making the most of their conversations with friends, or who is worried about not being the best conversationalist.

Captain Awkward blog, written by Jennifer Peepas

The Captain gives truly excellent advice on pretty much everything, including Showing Up–adjacent topics like dealing with difficult family members, supporting a friend who is depressed, and advocating for yourself when someone is making you uncomfortable. Jennifer is so thoughtful and smart, and reading her blog for years has made me a better person.
captainawkward.com

"The Missing Stair" by Cliff Pervocracy

This essay, which I first discovered via Captain Awkward, offers a highly useful metaphor for a common social group dynamic, and is really helpful if you're dealing with a jerk (or an abusive person) in a group setting.
pervocracy.blogspot.com/2012/06/missing-stair.html

Ask a Manager blog, written by Alison Green

Yes, this is a workplace blog, but our workplaces are home to many important relationships (that are complicated by things like money, ego, office politics, power imbalances, and the need to keep it professional) and present a lot of opportunities to show up. Alison writes with so much empathy and humor, and her blog has made me so much more confident in dealing with tricky situations.
askamanager.com

Recipe: Deb Perelman's Quick Pasta and Chickpeas

This recipe is my go-to weeknight recipe; it's filling, nourishing, vaguely healthy, very inexpensive, and extremely delicious. (It's also meat-free and dairy-free and warms up well the next day.) I've sung its praises to many, many people, and they are all believers now.

smittenkitchen.com/2017/10/quick-pasta-and-chickpeas-pasta-e-ceci

Recipe: Sue Kreitzman's Lemon Butter Angel Hair Pasta

As I mentioned in Chapter 5, this recipe is one I turn to when I need to feed myself but am kind of struggling. (I also make it when I'm not struggling—I just like it a lot!) Though literally nothing about it is French, I sort of think of it as the "French girl" version of boxed mac and cheese. It comes together in less than twenty minutes, tastes great, and feels elevated and special.

food52.com/recipes/75234-sue-kreitzman-s-lemon-butter-angel-hair-pasta

Permissions Acknowledgments

"How to Say No to an Invite When Your Reason Is 'I Just Don't Want To'" on page 45 was first published in slightly different form as "The Art of Saying No to Invites When You Really Don't Want to Do Something" by SELF.

"Canceling Plans" on page 54 was first published in slightly different form as "How to Cancel Plans Without Losing Friends and Feeling Like a Jerk" by SELF.

The introduction to Chapter 5, on pages 112–114, is adapted from the essay "The best $16 I ever spent: Old Navy pajamas after my husband left," originally published by Vox.

"How to Tell People You're Going Through a Tough Time" on page 124 was first published in slightly different form as "Not Great, Bob! The Case for Actually Being Honest When People Ask How You Are" by SELF.

"Getting Dressed" on page 107 contains language from the article "Giving Myself A Dress Code Changed My Dang Life," originally published by BuzzFeed.

"Why Venmo Is My Favorite Sympathy Card" on page 245 was originally published by BuzzFeed.

Acknowledgments

The Art of Showing Up wouldn't exist without Terri Pous, Gyan Yankovich, and Anna Borges, who were my coauthors of the BuzzFeed post "A More Or Less Definitive Guide To Showing Up For Friends," which inspired this book. Thank you for your insights and your generosity. It also wouldn't exist without my excellent editor, Batya Rosenblum, who didn't flinch when I turned in a first draft that was approximately twice as long as the book you just read.

I'd like to thank two of my best friends and best editors, Sally Tamarkin and Alanna Okun. Sally was the first editor of "How to Tell People You're Going Through a Tough Time," "Canceling Plans," and "How to Say No to an Invite when Your Reason Is 'I Just Don't Want To,'" which first appeared in my column at SELF, and was generous enough to read my manuscript in progress and give her feedback. Alanna edited the longer version of the Old Navy pajama story on page 113 that was originally published as part of Vox's "The Best Money I Ever Spent" series. There are few moments more vulnerable for writers than letting someone else read the first draft of something you've written that you care deeply about, and I feel so grateful that these two, along with Batya, were the ones in my Google Docs.

I'm so grateful for my dear friends/colleagues Tom, Mackenzie, Anjali, Kayla, Devin, Julia L., Julia F., Rachel C., Augusta, Lauren, Cara, Jordan, Terri, Gyan, Alanna, and Sally, who have showed up for me in ways big and small over the years, and who cheered me on as I worked on this book. Thank you to my mom, the most generous person I know, and the person who taught me to show up at a very young age. And my whole heart to my girlfriend, my favorite person in the world. I could not have done this without you.

About the Author

RACHEL WILKERSON MILLER is the editor-in-chief of SELF and author of *The Art of Showing Up* and *Dot Journaling—A Practical Guide*. Previously, she was a senior editor at BuzzFeed and Vox and a deputy editor at VICE. Her writing has also appeared in *The New York Times* and *Huffington Post*, and she's been a guest on NPR, the *Today* show, and *Good Morning America*. She lives in Brooklyn with her girlfriend.

rachelwmiller.com | @the_rewm